Digging the Dirt

Digging the Dirt

THE ARCHAEOLOGICAL IMAGINATION

Jennifer Wallace

Duckworth

First published in 2004 by
Gerald Duckworth & Co. Ltd.
90-93 Cowcross Street
London EC1M 6BF
Tel: 020 7490 7300
Fax: 020 7490 0080
inquiries@duckworth-publishers.co.uk
www.ducknet.co.uk

A catalogue record for this book is available
from the British Library

ISBN 0 7156 3278 7

The author and publisher are grateful to the following for
permission to quote: Faber & Faber Ltd for quotations from
the works of Ezra Pound; Faber & Faber Ltd and
Farrar, Strauss & Giroux for quotations from the works of
Seamus Heaney; A.P. Watt Ltd on behalf of Michael B. Yeats
for quotations from the works of W.B. Yeats. 'Canto LXXXIV'
(excerpt) by Ezra Pound, from *The Cantos of Ezra Pound*,
copyright © 1934, 1937, 1940, 1948, 1956, 1959, 1962, 1963,
1966, and 1968 by Ezra Pound. Reprinted by permission of
New Directions Publishing Corporation.

Picture sources and credits

Plates 1, 2 & 6: British Library;
Plate 3: British Museum;
Plates 4, 8 & 10: Cambridge University Library;
Plate 7: FreeStockPhotos.com;
Plates 9, 12, 13, 14 & 15: the author;
Plate 11: Society of Antiquaries, London.

Typeset by Ray Davies
Printed and bound in Great Britain by
CPI Bath

Contents

To Gillian Wallace

Plates

(between pp. 96 and 97)

1. 'A Scenographic View of the Druid Temple of Abury in north Wiltshire as in its original', from William Stukeley, *Abury, A Temple of the British Druids* (1743).

2. 'Silbury Hill, July 11th 1723', from William Stukeley, *Abury, A Temple of the British Druids* (1743).

3. Lindow Man.

4. 'Excavation of Herculaneum', from Richard de Saint-Non, *Voyage Pittoresque de Naples et Sicile* (1782).

5. 'Pan and the Goat'. (a) Original, from The Secret Room, Archaeological Museum of Naples. (b) Fantasy, from Baron Denon, *L'Oeuvre Priapique de Dominique Vivant* (1850).

6. 'Spinthria, Danseurs de Corde', from César Le Famin, *Musée Royal de Naples* (1836). British Library Cup.366.e.2. Reproduced by permission of the British Library

7. Some of Fiorelli's casts from Pompeii.

8. 'View of the Tombs of Achilles and Patroclus on the shores of Troy', from J.B.S. Morritt, *A Vindication of Homer* (1798).

9. Testing the tomb of Achilles on the plain of Troy with Sehmas.

10. Trojan idol with swastika on her genitals, from Heinrich Schliemann, *Ilios* (1881).

11. Rev. James Douglas excavating a barrow.

12. Ground Zero, New York.

13. Digging at El Ahwat, Israel.

14. Mayan sacrifice in the darkness of Actun Tunichil Muknal, Belize.

15. The Garbage Museum, Stratford, Connecticut.

1

The Poetics of Depth

I begin with two stories about waking, or attempting to wake, the dead. When, in 1876, Heinrich Schliemann was excavating Mycenae in Greece, he found a body in one of the massive graves outside the city, with its head covered by a golden mask. This man, he thought, must be a Bronze Age chief who lived in the heroic years of the Trojan War. It must almost certainly be Agamemnon, king of Mycenae, the leader of the Greek task force to Troy. He lifted the mask carefully away and discovered underneath the face of a man preserved for three thousand years. Excited, Schliemann bent down and kissed it. But after a few minutes of exposure to the nineteenth-century air, it crumbled away. 'I have gazed on the face of Agamemnon', he wrote ecstatically in a telegram to the king of Greece. 'Agamemnon' had slipped away like a ghost, and Schliemann was left with only the gold mask, his dead shell.

One day during the long summer vacation of 1985, which I spent travelling around Greece, I tried to find the lost city of Gortyn in Crete. Together with my friend, a fellow classics student, I ploughed tirelessly through brushwood and olive trees in the south of the island, searching for a suitable set of ruins. Finally we came across a crumbling stone wall. This had to be it. I began to read from a historical account of the city, and as each feature was mentioned in the book, we looked up and located it in the stones in front of us. Finally, the account I was reading referred to the text of the old city law code, etched on the wall. We looked up again. I felt that I could see a few carved letters, but my friend was uncertain. Suddenly she spotted another heap of old stones, a bit further on under the trees. We ran over to it. This, we decided, was in fact what we were looking for. The other wall, which we must have spent some twenty minutes or more studying, had simply been a wall, the remnants of a modern shepherd's house.

I mention these two stories, one magical and the other absurd, because they illustrate what is fascinating, ambivalent and ultimately important about archaeology. In both cases, dead mundane matter – a corpse, a broken wall – is momentarily transfigured by the imagination into something more significant, a story from the past. In the case of Schliemann, of course, the face of the man actually does miraculously stare back at him for a few minutes before it disintegrates into dust. The discovery at Mycenae brings 'Agamemnon' back to life temporarily before it paradoxically kills him off irrevocably. Schliemann's kiss – the crowning moment of myth-making, imaginative transformation – is one of both greeting and farewell. He is left afterwards holding the mask, the trace Agamemnon left behind, the one proof that he was temporarily in the presence of a Homeric hero. Some archaeological writing could be said to be the loving recovery of just such a trace, whose origin has slipped away and will be always out of reach.

My experience in Crete, on the other hand, is a salutary reminder of the difficulties of successful archaeological writing and thinking. If Schliemann's story illustrates the perfect union of imagination and material culture, my story shows their ridiculous mismatch. Excessive fantasy could apparently conjure up a city out of nothing. It could make a few rocks erroneously significant. But it could then be brought down to earth by being reminded of the intransigence of the material with which it had to deal, and the discrepancy between stone and story. By focusing my imagination upon the wrong wall, I had succeeded in exposing the problems of any act of archaeological interpretation. Unless one has a trained eye, one pile of rocks looks much like another; the historical or narrative significance is hard to extract from the raw materials with which one is presented.

This is a book about the power of the imagination, about how it can turn stones into words and the barest bones of our existence into something meaningful and lasting. But it is a book also about the fragility of the imagination, which is threatened by the modern sceptical reduction of everything to a few concrete facts. The imagination is at its most powerful and most fragile in writing that could be said to be archaeological, that digs down in the dirt to bring other worlds back to life.

One of the major differences between Schliemann's discovery in Mycenae and my disappointment in Crete is that he was an actual excavator and I was merely a tourist. He extracted objects from their original context in the earth; I viewed them on the surface from the outside, once they had been unearthed. This difference goes to the heart of what we actually mean by the term archaeology. Is it simply a matter of studying ancient remains? Or does it, by definition, include excavation? Look up the word in the *Oxford English Dictionary* and one finds that the earlier meaning given, dating from the seventeenth and eighteenth centuries, is the simple 'description of antiquities'. Only by the nineteenth century had the notion arisen of it as 'the scientific study of the remains and monuments of the prehistoric period'. Only in the nineteenth century, according to the example quotations given in the dictionary, did archaeology come to involve looking at remains still located *under* the ground: 'Archaeology displays old structures and buried relics of the remote past.'

Yet in the eighteenth century, although the actual term 'archaeology' was not used in this specialised sense of the systematic exploration of ancient remains through excavation, the ideas were clearly developing. While there was little distinction made, for example, between the words 'antiquarian' and 'archaeological', there was a definite separation of thought. 'Antiquarian' study involved the collection and examination of objects in isolation; 'archaeological' study meant the investigation of ancient remains in their context in the earth in order to reach a greater understanding of the past. This distinction was carefully drawn, for instance, by Thomas Pownell in his address to the Society of Antiquaries in June 1770, later published in the society's magazine, *Archaeologia*:

> Curiosity or avarice has excited many persons at different periods to examine into the interior parts of [the] repositories of the dead; the former in hopes of recovering from the oblivion of the grave something at least which might give an insight into the manners and customs of former times, which might become a leading mark to the reviviscence of those times; the other, instigated only by the sordid hope of plunder.

This distinction between archaeologists who are driven by the desire for 'insight' through careful excavation and antiquarians who wish to 'plunder' the past for treasure was also highlighted by Sir Walter Scott in his novel, *The Antiquary*. The source of the disagreement between the novel's two main characters, Jonathan Oldbuck and Sir Arthur Wardour, is over the appropriate attitude to the past. Wardour's desperate desire for buried antiquities which might rescue him from debt leads him to ridiculous credulity. In contrast, Oldbuck's organic sense of the historical nature of the land around him, in which events that shaped the nation are inscribed upon the ground itself, makes him 'much more scrupulous in receiving legends as current and authentic coin'.

By the twentieth century, the definition of archaeology appeared to have stabilised. Archaeological research involved three processes: the careful excavation of ancient objects and structures from the earth, their classification into types, and their subsequent interpretation. 'Archaeology', David Clarke wrote, 'is the discipline concerned with the recovery, systematic description and study of antiquities.' Collecting the data was scientific and objectively precise and, as such, did not require much theoretical analysis. Only the methods for deducing general theories required some reflection, which was arrived at through continual comparison with the data: 'By the continuous feedback cycle of observation, hypothesis, experiment and idealised model, the models and hypotheses gradually become more accurately adapted to the pattern of the observed data.' Central to this kind of archaeology was the idea that there were certain principles of interpretation which were always correct given a particular set of data. Piles of animal bones, for example, might indicate particular farming methods or food preparation, at whichever site they were found. The interpretation of material culture was universally applicable and scientifically verifiable.

In recent years, however, a group of archaeologists have thrown this distinction between material culture and its interpretation, which seemed to be the hallmark of archaeology, into doubt. According to them, the meaning or interpretation which is given to a particular discovery is dictated by the beliefs and culture of the archaeologist and not by objective scientific criteria obtained from excavation as was previously believed. Indeed, they argue that the objects which are unearthed by archaeologists are not unequivocal and self-evident in meaning but are part of a symbolic system of a past culture. They are, in fact, 'metaphorical': 'Artefacts may thus "grow" layers of metaphorical meaning like the rings of an onion', writes the archaeologist Christopher Tilley. 'Like the onion, as we strip layer from layer, we do not reach an inner core or kernel of metaphorical meaning. Rather, what we have is a wider outward growth and a series of transformations.' Drawing upon ideas and techniques current in literary criticism, the new post-processual archaeologists – as they are commonly known – 'translate' the objects they find into a narrative which seems to hold together coherently for each particular site, without making scientific claims about its universal applicability elsewhere. They are happy to inhabit a state of speculation and uncertainty. Even the collection of the data – in other words, the excavation itself – becomes part of the interpretation process, since subjective decisions are made about how or where to dig. As Ian Hodder, the leading post-processual writer, has strikingly put it, interpretation begins 'at the trowel's edge'. 'As the hand and trowel move over the ground, decisions are being made about which bumps, changes in texture, colours to ignore and which to follow.'

If, by implication, excavation is considered to be a creative act involving artistic decisions of style and technique, then the process of digging and the archaeological site itself can be interpreted as well as the objects uncovered there. Somebody visiting an excavation could learn about the archaeologist's interests and priorities simply by looking at the trenches and pits in the ground. At a dig I worked on in Israel, we operated in large units of five square metres at a time in order to get a general impression of the site swiftly. Anyone coming to watch us as we hacked into the soil with pickaxes and threw rocks into a pile at the side would have been able to sense the urgency which governs life in Israel and the unstable political situation which allows nothing to be taken for granted or depended upon.

1. The Poetics of Depth

On an American-led excavation I attended, on the other hand, we began by painstakingly measuring out our much smaller, two-metre square digging units, as if we had all the time in the world. It seemed to me, as I sieved every bucketful of earth, searching the ground for clues with forensic care in line with the expedition's policy, that the thoroughness of the dig matched the precision of the American judicial system and the knowledge that peace there is guarded in a carefully drafted legal constitution. National and political concerns influence excavation methods. Consciously or unconsciously, they impinge upon the archaeologist's decisions: where to dig, how deep to dig, which strata to concentrate upon, which objects to study and which to discard.

The twentieth-century philosopher Walter Benjamin, one of the most archaeological of thinkers, ponders the question of who is digging and how that affects our interpretation of what is dug in his essay 'Excavation and Memory'. The essay depends upon the analogy between digging the earth and the act of remembering:

> Language has unmistakably made plain that memory is not an instrument for exploring the past, but rather a medium. It is the medium of that which is experienced, just as the earth is the medium in which ancient cities lie buried .... Genuine memory must therefore yield an image of the person who remembers, in the same way a good archaeological report not only informs us about the strata from which its findings originate but also gives an account of the strata which first had to be broken through.

According to Benjamin, memory intervenes in the preservation of a particular experience, shaping and reshaping the event, until it reveals as much about itself, about 'the person who remembers' as it does about the original experience. So too the earth intervenes in the conservation of ancient buried remains, shaping and reshaping the ruins, so that – according to the analogy – it becomes more and more difficult to distinguish between the stones of the ground and the stones of the ancient cities. Eventually the intervening 'strata which first had to be broken through' become as significant and meaningful as the archaeological objects or the stratum at the bottom where the objects were originally found. But even independently of the excavator's own trail over a site, the earth itself contains a history of its past and can be read. Each period of time lays down another layer of earth, rather as a tree adds another ring each year. So if a shaft is dug down into the earth, an archaeologist can see the different layers, or strata, and deduce from that visual record a narrative of what happened in that particular place over the centuries. He or she can read the earth and its contents, stratified in layers like the chapters of a novel, in order to get a sense of the past. The stratigraphy of the ground, its division into strata deposited one above another, constitutes the earth's language. The Victorian poet Elizabeth Barrett Browning referred to the grammar of the earth, its different layers like tenses: present, imperfect, perfect, pluperfect. 'O land of all men's past! for me alone/ It would not mix its tenses', she wrote of Italy, comparing implicitly difficult Latin verbs with the hard soil of classical lands, difficult for the weaker female trowel to excavate.

With this language of the earth in mind, what I propose in this book is a poetics of depth, a reawakened understanding of how we imagine our sense of history and of place within the landscape and the earth. The philosopher Gaston Bachelard argued forty years ago for what he called a 'poetics of space'. Bachelard's ultimate aim was to found a 'metaphysics of the imagination', a satisfactory account of the way in which the mind responds to a poetic image. Poetry works, he believed, by awakening in the reader a corresponding excitement or 'reverberation', as what might have seemed new or alien turns out to be familiar. 'The image offered us by reading the poem now becomes really our own. It takes root in us. It has been given us by another, but we begin to have the impression that we could have created it, that we should have created it.' Bachelard felt this creative sense of familiarity was most obvious in images of what he called 'felicitous space', places like houses and outdoor shelters which we have inhabited and loved. 'Space that has been seized upon by the imagination cannot remain indifferent space subject to the measures and estimates of the surveyor. It has been lived in, not in its positivity, but with all the partiality of the imagination', Bachelard writes. He analyses the particular reverberations in the imagination of spaces like cellars, corners, wardrobes, nests and shells to show how his poetics works.

But Bachelard argues that the poetic image has no depth and no past. He is interested in space and not in time. 'The philosophy of poetry must acknowledge that the poetic act has no past ... in which its preparation and appearance could have been followed', he writes, and 'memory does not record concrete duration'. His imagination of space lies all on the surface, flattening everything in time. A poetics of depth, on the other hand, brings a sense of history into the picture, marks the moments when the imagination, the earth and human history are united and 'reverberate'. The grammatical language of the earth, which operates vertically as deep strata, replicates our language. And if our language is mirrored by the language of the earth, this confirms the basic reciprocity between our history and the land.

A poetics of depth is needed all the more now when, for various reasons, we are losing a sense of history and inhabit instead a plurality of surfaces. One of the main thinkers of our postmodern condition, Fredric Jameson, has written of the crisis of history under the state of global capitalism.

1. The Poetics of Depth

When central organisations of government and community become dispersed and when one form of ideology prevails absolutely, universal notions of progress which lie behind traditional history lose their currency. What is replacing the linear pattern of past, present and future? Traditional industrial society, in which the public buys the products it is offered (e.g. Ford cars) and has a clear sense of acquiescence or resistance, is now overtaken by 'post-Fordism', a culture in which the product is 'tailored to its consumers' cultural needs and specifications' and where, since 'everything now submits to the perpetual change of fashion and media image, nothing can change any longer'. Jameson thinks about the chimera of resistance and historical change today in graphic terms of demolition. For him, social changes now no longer carry revolutionary possibilities for political progress but rather erase the past, 'sweeping the globe clean for the manipulations of the great corporations'. In this climate, he argues that 'space and psyches can be processed and remade at will', apparently free and self-empowered but actually malleable, denuded of the power of concerted resistance. As a result, literal and metaphorical demolition begins 'to connote the speculations of the developers far more than the older heroic struggles of oppositional intellectuals'.

Jameson's critique seems all the more urgent now when we witness literal acts of deep demolition in our cities. Stand, for example, on the site of what until recently was Spitalfields old market, in London's East End, and you can witness the evacuation of two thousand years of history in the name of 'development' and 'regeneration'. The Spitalfields Development Group are turning the old market area into new offices and shops and plan to build an underground car park, with foundations eight metres deep, to complete the commercial centre. Three years ago they called in the Museum of London's archaeologists to excavate what they could in a summer's season before the bulldozers moved in. According to the chief archaeologist, Chris Thomas, the site is unusual for its remarkable preservation of different periods of history, with strata of continuous habitation dating back to the Roman period, and for its lack of subsequent disturbance. The team unearthed a large hospital, almshouses which yield important information about medieval charity and a large burial ground apparently full of plague victims.

'Normal archaeological practice would mean that we would preserve the site by covering it over again for future archaeologists to excavate and examine,' Thomas told me, as we stood on the wooden walkway placed over the mud and watched one of the team carefully chisel away the earth from around a skeleton. 'But in this case, the developers want to clear out everything, so we are rescuing what we can.'

In fact by the end of the season the archaeologists had convinced the developers that the charnel house they had found was so important that it was worth preserving. The architects of the car park and the Norman Foster tower above it will have to accommodate the remains of the charnel house into the foundations of the building. But the excavated stones at the base of what was the pulpit cross, from where the open-air Spital sermon was delivered back in medieval times, will probably disappear. If the pulpit stones go, so do the last tangible traces of a continuous history of popular gathering and public debate which have traditionally occurred in this place. For all the physical remains of a history held in common will be removed from this piece of land. The statistical information gleaned from the excavation will be stored on computer. But the actual objects – pots and skeletons – which were shielded from the public gaze during the excavation by screens, will mostly be discarded after being catalogued.

The history of Spitalfields might be preserved in virtual form, but its sedimented context, concretely accessible by future interpreters, is being erased. But why does history in its material, stratified form, available to the excavator's trowel, matter? Why do we need to retain a sense of the past tangibly and visibly embedded in the ground beneath our feet? Percy Bysshe Shelley's utopian poem, *Prometheus Unbound*, which overturns old establishment institutions to usher in a new world of liberation, unexpectedly provides an answer. On first impression, the poem seems to set in motion precisely the wholesale demolition which Jameson describes. Jupiter, king of the gods, is toppled from his throne; all organising principles of our present civilisation – religion, government, marriage, clear and logical communication – cease to exist; even distinct, separate individuality dissolves away. The new utopian world seems to be one of weightless, fluid spirits operating communally and outside time. Everything can be seen as 'frangible' or replaceable by something else on a mere whim of the imagination or poetic turn of phrase. But in a crucial passage in the middle of the joyful celebration of this post-revolutionary state of affairs, one of the spirits, Panthea, turns to describe the earth revealed by flashing beams of light at the moment of its destruction. The description amounts to an archaeological section, history at its most solid. I quote the passage at length, as it is some of Shelley's most arresting writing:

> ... the beams flash on
> And make appear the melancholy ruins
> Of cancelled cycles; anchors, beaks of ships,
> Planks turned to marble, quivers, helms and spears
> And gorgon-headed targes, and wheels
> Of scythed chariots, and the emblazonry
> Of trophies, standards and armorial beasts
> Round which Death laughed, sepulchred emblems
> Of dead Destruction, ruin within ruin!
> The wrecks beside of many a city vast,

> Whose population which the Earth grew over
> Was mortal but not human; see, they lie,
> Their monstrous works and uncouth skeletons,
> Their statues, home and fanes; prodigious shapes
> Huddled in grey annihilation, split,
> Jammed in the hard black deep; and over these
> The anatomies of unknown winged things,
> And fishes which were isles of living scale,
> And serpents, bony chains, twisted around
> The iron crags, or within heaps of dust
> To which the tortuous strength of their last pangs
> Had crushed the iron crags; – and over these
> The jagged alligator and the might
> Of earth-convulsing behemoth, which once
> Were monarch beasts, and on the slimy shores
> And weed-overgrown continents of Earth
> Increased and multiplied like summer worms
> On an abandoned corpse, till the blue globe
> Wrapt Deluge round it like a cloak, and they
> Yelled, gaspt and were abolished; or some God
> Whose throne was in a Comet, past, and cried -
> 'Be not!' – and like my words they were no more.

Wrecks of past cities had become heady political stuff since the French radical Count Volney, one of the deputies to the revolutionary National Assembly of 1789, had published his book on *Ruins*. By contemplating ancient remains which illustrated the demise of oppressive civilisations in the past, the political idealist could envisage the future destruction of the present regime. 'History, with all her volumes vast,/ Hath but *one* page – 'tis better written here', comments Byron in *Childe Harold*, while viewing the ruins on the Palatine in Rome, and Shelley, the optimistic radical, gleefully takes this observation of inevitable destruction to heart. In 'Ozymandias', for example, he relishes the fact that the city of Ozymandias, king of kings, has utterly disappeared and that the 'lone and level sands stretch far away', leaving only fragments of Ozymandias' statue. The apparently invincible tyrant, with his 'sneer of cold command', has literally bitten – and turned into – the dust.

But Panthea's vision of the ruined earth is different because history has not disappeared but simply packed down and crammed its 'cancelled cycles' tightly in geological deposits. This earth is dense and weighs down the airy utopian mood with its harsh and awkward historical strata, in 'huddled', 'jammed', 'crushed', 'earth-convulsing' layers. The obstructions within the earth must be negotiated in any revolutionary upheaval; they represent the real and practical difficulties of any historical change. Panthea places great hope on the power of words to change things. It takes only a god in a comet to say 'Be not' and the whole geological and archaeological earth apparently disappears. The globe, in Jameson's words, seems to be 'swept clean' with the careful use of 'glowing new adjectives'. But in fact the Promethean revolution derives its energy precisely from the threat of reversibility, from the latent but pressing possibility of an alternative politics. Freedom, which is not complacent and far from assured, comes at the end of the poem from the paradoxical capacity 'to hope, till Hope creates/ From its own wreck the thing it contemplates'. So the weight of the earth, with its 'sepulchred emblems of dead Destruction', is a vital ballast for the virtual utopian world, a reminder of past difficulties and historical struggles which ensures that the new politics is always contested and remains ever vigilant and self-aware.

Stratified history is necessary for an effective, grounded, radical politics. The image, in fact, of sedimentation, drawn from archaeology but never overtly acknowledged as such, has been extremely fruitful for post-Marxist thinking. Stratified layers visibly mark the moment when historical processes or the passage of time are turned into things, a solid deposit of soil and debris. They depict strikingly the act of transformation or what Marxists might call reification. But because the strata are then preserved by later deposits and kept buried deep in the soil, they also retain a record of the original historical process. The means of production, in Marxist terms, are not erased but saved strikingly visible in the ground. Stratigraphy, one might say, is a healthy Marxist dialectic made concrete.

This is the sentiment which lies behind the philosopher Theodor Adorno's notion of art. 'Art', he writes, 'is the sedimented history of human misery' and 'to analyse artworks means no less than to become conscious of the history immanently sedimented in them'. Rejecting the Kantian idealisation of a transcendent aesthetic, Adorno argues that artworks are the product of their historical context, figured crucially in archaeological terms. The dynamic nature of the work of art stems from its continual negotiation with the world around it, with the course of history. It oscillates between being part of history and being separate from it, and that oscillation, or dialectic, is described as archaeological or geological sedimentation. 'The artwork's autonomy is, indeed, not a priori but the sedimentation of a historical process that constitutes its concept.' According to Adorno, the artwork is a contradiction since it both magically creates new worlds and also prosaically mirrors the existing one, and this unsettling contradiction disturbs the sedimentation which represses or buries the production processes behind the work of art. Indeed, he describes this disturbance in archaeological terms, as 'excavation'. The inherent irreconcilable elements within a work of art 'excavate' it from the layers of historical repression.

1. The Poetics of Depth

Adorno, who strongly disliked popular culture, is using archaeology to think about the 'autonomy' of art – its alien distance from the mass consumer in the present, a distance which can only be traversed with difficulty. Like Michel Foucault, who welcomed the fact that archaeology treated the past as a 'preserved form of exteriority', Adorno considers stratigraphy a useful image for the discontinuity of the present and the past. There are physical layers to dig through to reach back in time between now and then, layers which vividly illustrate the great distance between one time period and another. But sedimentation also graphically evokes the pressure of time upon a work of art, the years immediately after the art was first produced and the subsequent centuries which absorbed and transformed or buried it. Adorno's sedimentation ensures that art is not so distanced that it becomes idealised or fetishised. The metaphorical layers of earth ground it in history.

This pressure of time is what Walter Benjamin was thinking of when he described works of art as being 'embedded in the fabric of tradition'. The generations of people who have viewed a painting or read a book load it with additional meaning. Just as subsequent deposits add extra layers of significance to an archaeological stratum, so the later history of a work of art becomes part of its meaning or value. Benjamin explained: 'The unique existence of a work of art determines the history to which it was the subject throughout the time of its existence. This includes the changes which it may have suffered in physical condition over the years as well as various changes in its ownership.' Benjamin even described elsewhere the accumulation of metaphorical traces which the eyes of many viewers over the centuries have left upon a painting, building up like readable earth upon a pot sherd. What is important is that Benjamin did not think these layers of reception tarnished the work of art or reduced its value. Far from it. The 'fabric of tradition' in which the work of art is 'embedded' actually gives it its unique value, or what Benjamin calls its 'aura'. A work of art is valuable because it was created at a particular moment in time and then affected and was affected by its owners over subsequent historical periods.

Benjamin's notion of 'aura' is extremely useful when thinking about the significance of an archaeological object. The classic archaeologist's joke – 'Why does an archaeologist love his wife more and more?' 'Because she just keeps getting older' – actually conveys a serious point about archaeological value. For while the original object might have held some charm in its own right – an intricately painted vase or finely wrought metalwork for example – yet its value for the archaeologist, its aura, comes from its context in the ground and in time. It gains significance from its position in the soil, its reception within popular myth or history, the subsequent tales told about it, the historical information it can offer about owners long since deceased and disappeared. To go back to my two initial stories. I had

21

wrongly and temporarily invested the wall in Crete with 'aura', through a willingness to be deceived, but the stones themselves had not been built at that time, had not been etched with an epoch-making legal code, had not made a subsequent impact upon civic constitutions across Greece. So once I realised this, the magic of the wall disappeared and it became simply a pile of stones. On the other hand, though the real wall of Gortyn ostensibly looked just the same, it had, in Benjamin's words, 'the delicate veil which centuries of love and reverence on the part of so many admirers have woven about' it, and so it was special. Schliemann's mask of 'Agamemnon', now on display in the National Museum in Athens, also has an 'aura', not just derived from the precious gold with which it is made or even only its age – it is now dated at 1500 BC – but determined too by that story of Schliemann kissing the vanished face beneath it.

Benjamin's 'aura' can easily be destroyed. Benjamin himself believed that the aura of a work of art withers away when the art is copied or reproduced mechanically. Film, photographs, pre-recorded music, all serve to undermine the original imaginative power or authenticity of the painting or music copied and themselves carry no such resonance. They are not unique nor are they created or performed at one particular time, embedding themselves in that moment. The image which Benjamin uses to describe the shattering of aura is drawn from excavation: 'To pry an object from its shell, to destroy its aura, is the mark of a perception whose "sense of the universal equality of things" has increased to such a degree that it extracts it even from a unique object by means of reproduction.' Prying an object from its shell, taking it from what Bachelard would call its home, pulling it up from the depths, is a felicitous image. For archaeological practice destroys the past almost as quickly as it reveals its remains still preserved in the earth.

I saw archaeological objects prised from their metaphorical 'shells' in a cupboard in Paris a couple of years ago. Finding myself in a café with a friend with nothing to do for an afternoon, we wandered over to St Germain to a gallery owned by a friend of his. After showing us the artworks on public display at the front, the gallery owner shut up shop and took us round to the back. He then brought out tray after tray from his store piled up with ancient treasures, with no labels or apparent order, just random dusty heaps. We marvelled at his collection, squeezing pre-Columbian bracelets onto our arms and Egyptian necklaces about our throats and running our fingers over the fragment of an inscription etched on a brick from a Mesopotamian temple. The gallery owner would not tell us where he had acquired these things or which sites they originally came from and we could only admire what we held in our hands, not imagine their original story. For some hours afterwards I was excited by the experience, but in the months since I have been haunted by the guilty memory of participating in an act of violation.

In the last year we have lived through the most disturbing period of archaeological violation in recent times, which has brought the question of the value of antiquities to international attention as never before. After American troops entered Baghdad in April 2003, the city disintegrated into a frenzy of looting. People grabbed anything they could lay their hands on, but one of the chief targets for theft was the National Museum. Some commentators suggested that the violent raids on the glass cases in the museum's galleries were politically motivated. The museum represented the state in the minds of some Iraqi people, so smashing some antiquities was a symbolic substitute for smashing the Saddam Hussein regime. Later, however, it emerged that the looting was more a calculated and professional burglary than an over-exuberant, angry and celebratory party. Some museum items have been recovered, a few even as they crossed the border into Iran, apparently en route to the flourishing black market in antiquities. But many others must already have been the subject of shady cash transactions. Now owned by private individuals and housed, no doubt, in dusty cupboards, they are lost to public study.

The fate of the Iraq museum caught the imagination of BBC news reporters. But the post-war looting of Iraq's archaeological legacy is even more widespread. Poachers have targeted archaeological sites around the country and drilled holes into the earth as well as raiding glass cases in museums in their search for treasure. In the north of the country, at Ninevah, the ancient capital of Assyria, the king's palace has been stripped of its stone carvings depicting the history of old Assyrian wars. And at Dahaila in the south, looters have drilled hundreds of holes and snatched from the ground old Babylonian tablets with cuneiform writing dating back nearly four thousand years. An American archaeologist, Elizabeth Stone, sent out to assess the extent of the damage in Iraq, observed that each illicit hole in Dahaila is 'a small rent in the fabric of history'. 'The aim of history is to humanise the past', she told the reporter for *National Geographic*, which sponsored the expedition. 'But each object ripped from its context loses its connection with its makers and users, loses its voice, and becomes mute, a mere pretty thing.'

But even if the antiquities are not being looted but being carefully unearthed and recorded, the act of excavation can be damaging. Every archaeologist has to make difficult decisions about reconstruction and consolidation as he uncovers ancient structures, often recording and copying the antiquities before they disappear entirely. So, for example, Arthur Evans notoriously rebuilt the great staircase at Knossos before it could subside completely, once the earth which had held it in place for years had been removed. And Mayanists rely almost as much upon Frederick

Catherwood's nineteenth-century drawings of the Mayan friezes discovered at Copan and Palenque in Central America as they do now upon the originals. Now that the protective layers of jungle have been cleared from it, the soft limestone of the Mayan temples is gradually dissolving away in the tropical rainstorms and the distinct lines of the ancient art are disappearing. When, in this case, is the copy more 'valuable' than the original?

The archaeological imagination is faced, I believe, with a dilemma. Excavation is a fundamentally ambivalent activity. Like Schliemann, the excavator destroys his material as he discovers it. Like Schliemann, he is captivated by the magical past, which vanishes. He is left with only the material remains, which become wrongly but understandably invested with the missing magic. Like Chris Thomas at Spitalfields, he digs deep into the earth, reading the language of its strata, only to bring all the fruits of his quarrying up to the surface, laying one period's debris beside another, flattened out on trays to present a simultaneous history. It is the depth, the sedimentation, the embedding soil, which gives the objects their aura, their historical, political significance or, as Elizabeth Stone puts it, their 'voice'. Nevertheless, those objects can only be contemplated once that context has been disturbed. Though the archaeologist might spend much of his day digging, he studies the results of that excavation back at the top, looking only at debris 'projected up upon the surface', in Jameson's words, 'in the anamorphic flatness of a scarcely recognisable afterimage'.

Thus the archaeological imagination responds to what is missing rather than to what is there. It snatches objects from the ground only to try to restore some sense of their original context in the earth so as to understand them properly. It substitutes a story or an interpretation in place of what actually lies before it or in compensation for what has been lost or still lies buried. It attempts to transfigure the bleakness of the material with which it has to deal and to find something of significance in what can only be imagined, in the fancied depths, in what has disappeared.

There is no place where this active imagination is more vitally necessary than at Ground Zero in New York. This is a site haunted by what is missing. The twin mile-high towers of the World Trade Center, which collapsed in the space of two hours on 11 September 2001, make their presence felt, paradoxically, by their vast absence. Go up to the second floor of the Winter Gardens on West Street and you can see, through the viewing window, the huge sixteen-acre gaping hole where the towers once stood, a great swathe cut in the cornfield of skyscrapers which is southern Manhattan. But, much more poignantly, what is also missing is the thousands of people who died there on that day and whose bodies were never recovered. Firefighters excavated the site for eight months after the disaster, looking for any human remains, however small, which they could match with the victims known to have been caught in the collapsing buildings. But even after they had pushed the dust through a sieve, there were over one thousand people whose bodies had utterly disappeared. Not even a piece of them, merely a quarter of an inch in size, could be identified.

The tragic excavation at Ground Zero brought home to me the importance to us of physical, tangible remains. The desperation of the firefighters to find any material evidence of the dead, no matter how tiny, highlighted people's desire to have actual bodies to mourn. Ideally they need to have something which they can touch and hold in order to focus their grief, even if what they hold is little more than dust. But the excavation also revealed the possibilities of the imagination. For in the absence of actual material remains, New Yorkers have compensated by creating memorials to the dead, staging rituals and acts of remembrance at the site, making the gaping hole significant. A piece of land in the heart of the city which might have been a place of despair and emptiness, marked by the futile search for tangible objects, has become a sacred site, a place for pilgrimage, transformed by a collective act of memory. When I was last there, in September 2003, my place at the viewing wall was suddenly crowded out by the mass arrival of the 'Boston, MA to Ground Zero' bikers' rally. Huge numbers of large, beefy men, in jeans and freedom T-shirts, parked their Harley Davidsons along Church Street and came to peer through the grille of the 'wall' at the clean bedrock exposed inside, in quiet contemplation of whatever that chasm meant to them (Plate 12).

Archaeological sites possess a resonance or 'aura' based on what is there now, what used to be there and what happened in between. This book revolves around certain key archaeological sites which have proved particularly resonant for our culture, for good or ill. It addresses the question of what the excavation of these places has meant to us and just why we do or do not want to dig things up. In most cases I have actually found my way to these places, whether that be hunting out the corners of London which were once vast plague pits, or pacing over the Wiltshire downs looking at stones, or walking over the plains of Troy in the footsteps of Alexander the Great, or hacking through the Central American jungle to look at Mayan bones. For only if one actually stands in a place can one compare its present appearance with what is known about its past, both its original history and its excavation. And that comparison brings home the ambivalent relationship between material culture and the imagination, between what we see before us now and what we must imagine. It sets us a challenge in negotiating the contrast between insignificance and significance, between prosaic things and metaphorical remains. The chal-

25

lenge lies in facing up to the stark reality that we spend our lives, in figurative terms, digging in the dirt looking at inscrutable fragments and solid, inexplicable mess while still retaining a commitment to aura, to the rights of desire, to the poetics of depth.

Romancing Stones:
The Archaeological Landscape

A few miles from the village in Wiltshire where my mother grew up, the ancient pilgrims' route to the prehistoric stone circle of Avebury and the massive artificial mound of Silbury Hill cuts through the fields. As the modern walker hikes along it, she will start to notice more and more rocks scattered beside the path. At first, it may be just the odd boulder, standing squat amid the sheep as they nibble the tufty grass. Then perhaps two or three, lying in clusters or at regular intervals. Until finally the walker climbs up to the top of Fyfield Down, a short distance before Avebury, and finds a whole scattering of grey weather stones, visible in every direction. Some stones appear to be arranged in rings. Others, lying on different promontories, act more like pointers, possibly in alignment with some distant feature on the horizon. Still others seem to be entirely random, the natural result of the rock formation of the area with its mixture of chalky soil and underlying sarsen stone.

My mother never mentioned Fyfield Down to me or even Avebury, for that matter. She did not talk about the ancient landscape in which she grew up nor the stones and strange mounds which must have formed the background to her weekend bicycle rides. Barrows and earthworks must have seemed to her too ordinary to be worth noticing, of little more interest than the hills and valleys which formed her unconscious mental map, on a par with the river Kennet which flowed past her village. She died aged only forty-seven and is herself buried in a beautiful graveyard in the Lake District. All her life, she dreamed of visiting the exotic pyramids in Egypt, an ambition she never realised. She hardly noticed Silbury Hill.

So when I stride over the moor to the top of Fyfield Down, I feel a range of complex emotions. The view of the ridgeway path, snaking between the sarsens towards the town of Marlborough, which must have been so familiar to my mother that she barely registered it, is new to me. It is exciting because of its public archaeological significance but also poignant because of the private significance it might once have held for my family and which has now been lost. I sit on one of the grey boulders at the highest point of the ridge and think how many things about my mother I never actually knew. So much of her life is a mystery, a blank which I will now never be able to fill.

And as I sit on the boulder, the cold October wind whipping across the hilltops, I think also about the stones. It is impossible to tell whether the stones lying all over Fyfield Down are natural or whether they have been placed there deliberately. They tantalise me with the suggestion of different patterns. I jump up and run over to one cluster, wondering whether it might be an ancient circle. But when I get there and see the grey slabs lying beached amid the nettles and tufts of grass, it looks equally as if they might just be a random rock fall. Further down, there appears to be a straight line of stones which suggests a prehistoric arrangement. But it might equally well be a natural rocky outcrop or the remains of a much later, medieval wall. I go back to sit on my boulder, baffled by the stones' resistance to my investigations.

Stones are natural. Wiltshire is full of rocks and boulders lying amid grass and trees, much like Fyfield Down. They lie in the earth where nature and geology left them. When placed by man, however, set up deliberately in a special position, these same stones take on a new significance. Indeed, unlike the stones of Stonehenge which were imported from the Preselli Hills of Wales and were therefore exotic, the stones of the Avebury circle are local, shifted only from one field to another and set in a pattern. But at the point when they were consciously erected, they ceased to be merely stones and became part of our history. These carefully arranged stones mark the places in the landscape which have held some importance for us, which have been the setting for momentous events. The stones, it could be said, straddle the boundary between the world of nature and the world of man.

Archaeology reveals how man is deeply integrated into the landscape. Environmentalists, of course, have pointed out for a long time how closely we are connected with the land. It is not just environmental activists who draw attention to this fact by chaining themselves to trees and tunnelling underground. Philosophers too have reflected on our bonds with the natural world and our capacity to be 'at home' in nature. 'Man's relation to locations, and through locations to spaces, inheres in his dwelling', wrote the philosopher Martin Heidegger. But history too can be said to be natural. The landscape guards the natural continuity between the present and the past. According to many eighteenth- and nineteenth-century thinkers, history should be considered a natural process anyway, an ineluctable and steady progression from past to present to future. Gottfried Leibniz, for example, back in 1714, described historical change in suitably natural, organic terms: 'each created being is pregnant with its future state, and it naturally follows a certain course, if nothing hinders it'.

The geological earth, with its sedimented layers deposited year by year, century by century, gives concrete realisation to the kind of natural history Leibniz was imagining. Like a palimpsest of past ages, the soil can be dug to reveal a vertical shaft going back gradually in time. The eighteenth-century early geologist, James Hutton, thought that anyone could deduce the origins of the earth by studying the gradual changes in the earth's surface since 'the present earth' was 'composed from the materials of a former world'. He pondered the possibility of also predicting the future. By 'contemplating the present operations of the globe', he believed, 'we may perceive the actual existence of those productive causes, which are now laying the foundation of land in the unfathomable regions of the sea, and which will, in time, give birth to future continents'. This should not seem surprising: the two exercises – looking back to the past and imagining the future – were 'consecutive', since all historical process was located and visible in the earth, in the same spot.

The archaeological landscape, one in which the earth contains the remains of previous human building and habitation, enshrines the sense of the continuity between man, his past history and the environment even more strikingly than the geological landscape. The shaft of continuous, geological history which Hutton described does not just reveal indifferent rocks and soil when excavated by the archaeologist, but also traces of human intervention, human creativity. Man's relationship with the environment seems all the closer when it is realised that the very hills and ditches he lives beside may once have been dug by his ancestors and are not purely the work of nature.

The sites which the early archaeological writers were most interested in were earthworks which looked almost natural: barrows, burial mounds, cairns and standing stones. For it was in these sorts of places that the distinctions between nature, man and history were most ambivalent and blurred, or, in the words of the contemporary archaeologist Christopher Tilley, who has studied standing stones in Sweden, the 'natural' became 'encultured' and the 'cultural' became 'naturalised'. Burial mounds and standing stones raised the issue of the archaeological imagination because the imagination was needed to transform the stones into something special and to interpret their significance. They provoked the question: do you need a special kind of imagination to distinguish ordinary boulders from symbolic, archaeological ones?

This chapter is about the connection between stones and words, between nature and culture, because it is in contemplating these connections that the archaeological imagination arguably begins. The eighteenth century marked the moment when, with the development of natural history and geology as ideas and practices, men first reflected systematically upon the archaeological landscape. And, while many enthusiasts began to investigate ancient earthworks and write about ruins, no two men were more exercised by the connection between stones and words than the eighteenth-century writers William Stukeley and William Wordsworth. William Stukeley, who lived at the beginning of the century, was a practising excavator; William Wordsworth, who came to prominence at the end of the century, was a poet. The comparison between them is therefore not obvious. But both, it seems to me, were fundamentally interested in the relationship between the imagination and material culture.

There is a close analogy between archaeological stratigraphy and the operation of the imagination. Like the memory, the earth makes meaning and can be read and interpreted. It contains 'cancelled cycles', the concrete record of the local community embedded in its environment, Adorno's 'sedimented history of human misery'. So although Stukeley literally dug up barrows in Wiltshire and only later described them in his books on his discoveries while Wordsworth took an armchair interest in what was then antiquarianism and uncovered graves purely metaphorically in his poetry, both writers were developing what might be termed archaeological poetics, a sensitivity to the ground's elegiac capacity for recording and memorialising vanished histories and personal loss.

*

William Stukeley was born in the flat fenland of Lincolnshire in the east of England in 1687. He spent his life resisting the expectations of his environment. He left school at the age of thirteen to work in his father's legal firm but found his mind wandering onto his studies of science and antiquities and begged his father to send him to university. At Cambridge, where science was not yet part of the curriculum, he was obliged officially to study the conventional subjects of Classics, Philosophy, Divinity and Mathematics, but spent all his spare time conducting scientific experiments, dissecting every animal he could lay his hands on and becoming, as he later recalled, 'master of the fabric of the human body'. Having left the university, he trained as a doctor at St Thomas's hospital in London, but kept up his interest in antiquities, making a series of archaeological expeditions into Wiltshire and neighbouring counties each year from 1710 until 1725. He played a leading role in forming the Society of Antiquaries in London in 1717, becoming the first secretary of the society and drawing up its constitution. But by 1726, he had withdrawn from the society and from London and retreated back to Lincolnshire, where he was ordained and where, twenty years after his excavation, he published his books on Stonehenge and Avebury in the early 1740s.

This unconventional background meant that Stukeley was able to bring together the world of science and the world of the imagination. While he was classically educated at Cambridge and eager, on leaving university, to travel on the Grand Tour and to visit the celebrated ancient sites in Italy and Greece, his finances would not permit this. So he turned his attention to the antiquities that were available to him in his own country, combining the characteristic Grand Tourist's imaginative wonder at the past with the scientific excavation techniques he had developed when conducting dissections. Similarly his ambivalent relationship with the Society of Antiquaries, at once close and detached, reflects his distance from everything that the society came to represent. Antiquarians had a reputation for focusing solely on objects and treasure with unquestioning 'curiosity'. By the 1780s, for example, an antiquary in the popular imagination could be more readily understood as 'a man who is fond of collecting and commenting on antiques than one who aspires to the important task of illustrating history, laws or poetry'. Stukeley, on the other hand, was passionate about history and imaginative speculation.

So in contrast to both the Grand Tourists, who had no scientific training and wrote of the past in awe-struck general terms, and some of the antiquaries, who focused exclusively upon objects without thinking of the wider context of 'history, laws or poetry', William Stukeley was equally interested in the ancient artefacts and in their wider context in the landscape and in history. He was concerned to investigate the physical remains from the prehistoric past and also to speculate upon their implications, to try to develop his discoveries into a more general theory about ancient history. In other words, he was interested both in the literal stones and in their more metaphorical significance.

Critics have not been kind to Stukeley; indeed archaeologists dismiss his writing as excessive fantasy, preferring his early, scientific fieldwork. In later life he became caught up in recreating what he believed was the age of the Druids and encouraged others to restart cults and to discover ancient bards and priests. This obsession has not endeared him to stricter archaeologists. But I wish to reclaim Stukeley as one of the most imaginative and poetic writers in the archaeological tradition, since he bore witness, arguably, to the moments when the physical and non-physical realms of archaeological study become most blurred, to the places where observation and imagination work organically in tandem.

In his investigation of the stone circles of Stonehenge and Avebury and the burial mounds around them, Stukeley attempted to read the landscape in order to see the relationship between one archaeological feature and another and thus to understand its historical significance. When he arrived at Avebury for the first time in 1719, the henge had been sketchily investigated by John Aubrey and a few others, but nobody had conducted systematic fieldwork or mapped the whole area. The village of Avebury and the downs around it appeared to be littered with random standing stones. Stukeley proceeded to show how they were all connected in a significant pattern (Plate 1). He claimed that the series of stone circles which made up the henge or 'Druid temple' of Avebury was originally approached by two grand avenues of stones, one from the south-east, which he termed Kennet Avenue, and one from the south-west, which he termed Bekampton Avenue. At the head of Kennet Avenue was the temple or 'sanctuary' on Overton Hill, while halfway along Bekampton Avenue a small 'sacellum' or chapel, located at the site of what are now known as the Adam and Eve Longstones, served Druids on 'ordinary days of devotion, viz the sabbath-days'.

In order for Stukeley to develop this picture of the Avebury landscape as a coherent prehistoric sacred site, he had to be attentive as much to what was absent as to what was visibly present. Most of the stones in these avenues and temples had been removed or destroyed. The stones of the 'sanctuary' were actually removed by local farmers between the time of Stukeley's field survey and his written account of the site, so that he was able to mourn 'the vacancy of every stone, the hollows still left fresh' and to write of the original organisation of the temple circle with vivid, first-hand knowledge. But the route of the avenues relied upon his imaginative reconstitution of a whole line of stones from just the one or two boulders remaining. The end of Kennet Avenue, for example, as it grew near the sanctuary, only actually retained two visible stones, one by the river Kennet and another by the hedge of the Marlborough road. But from these two apparently isolated boulders, Stukeley extrapolated an original grand avenue.

Bekampton Avenue demanded an even greater leap of the imagination, since there were scarcely any visible remains at all. Stukeley relied upon observing one or two stones between the houses on the edge of Avebury village and also on local memory of stones which had been used as building material. By plotting these apparently random stones, he realised that, to 'a discerning eye', they made 'a great sweep or curve northwards'. Continuing that hypothetical trajectory, supported by what he maintained were 'many stones just buried under the surface of the earth', he came to the Longstones, two large boulders which were still visible above ground. But rather than seeing them as entirely separate from the Avebury henge, as Aubrey had done, he related them to the whole symbolic complex, claiming their significance for the avenue and for the wider context of 'Druid' religious practice.

2. Romancing Stones: The Archaeological Landscape

*

When I arrive at Avebury to look for Stukeley's Bekampton Avenue, I encounter a certain degree of resistance. My attempt to follow my favourite archaeologist's footsteps goes against all expectations.

'Straight up the path and to the right,' the English Heritage warden intercepts me at the car park, as I consult my map and consider turning left. 'You'll find the henge up at the end.'

'But I haven't come to see the henge,' I remonstrate. 'I've come to see the Bekampton Longstones.'

The warden looks nonplussed. 'I think you might find a path by the churchyard,' she says hesitantly. 'But the henge, you know, is really impressive. It's a world heritage site.'

I turn left at the churchyard, walk across a couple of fields, strewn with old mossy boulders, and past a modern terrace of houses. One man is digging in his garden.

'I'm looking for the Longstones,' I shout over the wall to him. 'They're known as Adam and Eve. Know where they are?'

'Haven't a clue. But I'm intrigued now. Let me know when you find them.'

Two or three houses further down, the village ends and I get a view over the countryside. There, a couple of fields away, are two giant boulders, glowing pink in the autumn sunset. Scrambling over a barbed wire fence and walking nearer to them, I see that they are shaped like two huge human faces, turned towards Avebury half a mile away. Cars in the distance race on, oblivious, to the designated sites of Avebury and Stonehenge. But I stand beside 'Eve', hand on the warm rock, and wonder what 'she' might once have 'seen'.

William Stukeley's thesis about Bekampton Avenue and the Longstones chapel was widely criticised. His detractors thought that it was based upon wildly excessive fantasy and was not supported by any clear physical evidence. But an excavation project, started in 1999 at the Bekampton Longstones, is in fact confirming Stukeley's claims. Photographs of the whole area were originally taken from the air. And guided by those photographs, excavations have revealed buried stones, empty sockets where stones once would have stood and huge pits where the stones must have been deliberately broken up and destroyed in the post-medieval period. From noticing these holes and pits and places where stones are missing, the archaeologists have concluded that an avenue did lead from the henge and that there was a circular 'cove' or 'temple' halfway along it. The project to investigate the whole Avebury area will last five years. Archaeologists, it seems, are finally catching up with Stukeley's vision.

*

As well as imaginatively recreating what the whole religious complex of Avebury might once have looked like, William Stukeley was able to gain a sense of its changing history over time simply by studying the landscape and the stones. He was sensitive, in other words, to the temporal relationship of one layer of earth or stones to another. He carefully dated Stonehenge to the time when 'the Druids had some notice from phoenician traders, of the nature of Solomon's temple'. It is now thought to have been substantially built in the period between 2550 and 1600 BC, much earlier than the supposed date of Solomon's temple in the tenth century BC. But, while he got the actual date of Stonehenge wrong, he was accurate in his sense of its date relative to that of Avebury. Through studying the stones of Avebury closely and calculating the 'effect of the weather' on the remains and the rate of corrosion compared to that at Stonehenge, he concluded that Avebury was twice as old as Stonehenge. Since archaeologists now believe that Avebury was constructed between 3000 and 2200 BC, some five or six hundred years before Stonehenge, Stukeley's interpretation of the stones seems remarkably far-sighted.

William Stukeley also attempted to date the ancient features of the landscape around Avebury by studying their relation to one another. The great long dike, the Wansdike, which runs south of Avebury, stretching from Calne in the west to Savernake Forest, near Marlborough, in the east, was built, he believed, before the Roman period. This could be proved by the fact that 'the bank of the dike is thrown in, in order to form the road', or, in other words, that the old Roman road seemed to slice through the dike. And the Roman road itself, which intersected the Wansdike, for example, could be dated by the fact that the earth used for its construction appeared to have been dug from an old pre-Roman burial mound nearby. Stukeley examined the succession of pits which had been dug in one particular barrow to reach this conclusion.

Besides the stone circles of Avebury and Stonehenge, Stukeley was also fascinated by the many burial mounds which were scattered around the fields nearby. 'These barrows are the artificial ornaments of this vast and open plain', he wrote. 'And it is no small entertainment for a curious person, to remark their beauties, their variety in form and magnitude, their situation.' Given confidence by his experience in dissection and scientific experimentation, he proceeded not just to 'remark their beauties' and note 'their situation' but also to excavate them. By opening the barrows and ascertaining the exact position and depth of the contents and the different strata of earth above them, he was able to deduce the dates of the burial and their historical relationship with the surrounding landscape.

One group of barrows which Stukeley spent time excavating lay just a little to the west of the Stonehenge ring. He recorded that there were two large barrows in the group and ten smaller ones crowded together. The logical interpretation was that these were the graves of one family, the two parents in the large mounds, the children in the smaller ones. He cut a nine-foot trench into the centre of one of the smaller barrows and found that 'a child's body (as it seems) had been burnt here, and cover'd up in that hole: but thro' length of time consum'd'. He was also interested, however, in the archaeological traces both above and below the child's remains. 'From three foot deep', he recorded, 'we found much wood ashes soft and black as ink, some little bits of urn, and black and red earth very rotten. Some small lumps of earth red as vermilion: some flints burnt thro'. Toward the bottom a great quantity of ashes and burnt bones.' The varying depths of burial deposits in this barrow and their differing states of decay suggested to Stukeley that this grave had been used and then re-used by the family. A child's body occupied the prime central position in the barrow, but other bodies had been deposited here, apparently, both before and after the main burial. So from studying both the position of the graves and the different layers of deposit within them, William Stukeley was able to develop a sophisticated and imaginative picture of a whole history of a community or family who had lived around this site.

But while Stukeley was alive to the sense of the readability of history inscribed in the sedimented layers in the earth, yet he seriously called into question its naturalness. In his books, he revealed nagging doubts about the seamless organic integration of excavator, history and the Wiltshire downs, even while he celebrated it. His challenge might have been partly provoked by his early alienation from what might be termed his natural landscape. Having been born and brought up in the excessively flat fens of south Lincolnshire, he could remember well his first encounter with hills, since it came at the surprisingly advanced age of ten, when he went to visit an aunt who lived in north Lincolnshire. He was fascinated by the undulating countryside and returned to tell his schoolfriends of 'strange Relations of the high countrys'. Until that time, he later confessed, he knew only about hills from what he had read in books, 'from the words in the Latin Grammar'. But after that visit, his understanding of what was natural and what belonged to the world of fancy or artifice altered dramatically. No longer would hills belong to the pages of school textbooks. Instead, they were now the touchstone of pure nature while the flat ground of his childhood appeared somehow unnatural. 'I conceived so strong an affection for that country that I never could rightly relish my native plains again', he recalled. 'I felt an uncommon pleasure when I was mounting these hills, the primitive face of the Earth, & turnd my back on the low country which I esteemed only as the leavings of the Ocean & artificial Ground.'

The barrows in Wiltshire, unlike the hills encountered initially in the Latin Grammar, were much more obviously artificial. According to Stukeley, they had been deliberately raised by the early Druids. The most dramatic in its blurring of the distinctions between nature and artifice was Silbury Hill. This 'hill', the largest man-made mound in western Europe, which rises thirty-seven metres above the valley floor around it, dominates the landscape (Plate 2). Stukeley depicted it looming over the Avebury henge and the avenues of stones in various pictures. Even today the purpose of Silbury Hill remains shrouded in mystery. There is actually no evidence of burial in the mound nor of any other deposits. You approach it walking along a path that winds from the Avebury car park along a particularly flat stretch of the Kennet valley, turning a corner to see the bizarre, perfect conical shape rising up out of the fields. It is covered with grass, so it does not look like an ancient monument. But it is so symmetrically shaped that it looks like no ordinary hill either.

Certainly Stukeley was intrigued by the enigma. According to him, the general mystery of Silbury Hill was symbolised by its transgression of the normal boundaries separating nature from artifice. Stukeley pointed out that the natural hilly landscape which existed before the Silbury monument had actually been dug away in order to obtain enough earth to form the artificial hill and that a trench had been made so as to 'render this artificial part more detached from the natural', with just two causeways of natural earth left to allow people to cross the trench and reach the giant barrow.

William Stukeley was developing a strange aesthetics of inversion. The artificial pleased more than the natural because it appeared more natural. The way in which he wrote about Stonehenge was all in accordance with this new sensibility. He described the effect of walking into the circle of Stonehenge and looking up at the lintels, the cross-stones, overhead:

> When we advance further, the dark part of the ponderous imposts over our heads, the chasm of the sky between the jambs of the cell, the odd construction of the whole and the greatness of every part, surprises. ... if you look upon the perfect part, you fancy intire quarries mounted up into the air: if upon the rude havock below, you see as it were the bowels of a mountain turn'd inside outwards.

Stukeley's images here, of 'quarries mounted up into the air' and of the 'bowels of a mountain turn'd inside outwards', invert the normal principles of excavation. The stones point up to the sky rather than down into the earth and the interested spectator must crane his neck, turning his head upwards, rather than peering down into the depths of the soil. The appreciation of significant stones demands a conscious exertion of the imagination which tests the boundaries of nature and culture. Turning the imagination, as Stukeley put it, 'inside outwards' is essential to what I call 'archaeological poetics', as I shall explain later. But I want first to move from the poetic archaeologist William Stukeley to the archaeological poet, William Wordsworth.

*

William Wordsworth was born in 1770, some five years after Stukeley died, so the two men never met. But Wordsworth was steeped in the writing of those who had known Stukeley and who were influenced by his archaeological investigations. Sir Walter Scott, for example, with whom Wordsworth stayed in the Scottish borders, got to hear about Stukeley through the antiquarian John Clerk, who lived locally in Penicuik and who, following Stukeley's advice, set up an antiquarian society in Scotland. Scott, accordingly, became fascinated by stones and the stories they could tell. Similarly the poet Thomas Gray, who actually bumped into Stukeley in the new British Library and who published *Elegy Written in a Country Churchyard* in 1751, was by the end of the century widely recognised by everyone, including Wordsworth, as 'at the head' of the main eighteenth-century school of poetry.

The school of poetry which Gray headed became known as the 'graveyard' school because of its favourite subject matter. While the leading graveyard poets – men like Edward Young, James Hervey and Robert Blair – were not actually paid-up members of the Society of Antiquaries, their obsession with the physical aspects of death and the material culture of cemeteries reveals a strong adherence to Stukeley's concerns. Robert Blair, for example, published *The Grave* in 1743, a poem which concentrated provocatively upon the natural processes of decay and decomposition which occur after burial. According to him, the certainty of archaeological sedimentation is as inevitable as death itself. When we die, we simply add one more deposit within the soil, which in future centuries will be available for archaeologists to excavate:

> What is this World?
> What? but a spacious *burial-field* unwalled,
> Strew'd with Death's Spoils, the Spoils of Animals
> Savage and Tame, and full of Dead Men's Bones?

> The very Turf on which we tread once liv'd:
> And we that live must lend our Carcases
> To cover our own Offspring; In their Turns
> They too must cover theirs. 'Tis *here* all meet.

In death, there is no distinction between rich or poor, high or low; everyone is mortal. Everybody disintegrates back into the 'turf on which we tread', as readable in time and as natural as geological deposits. 'Where is the dust that has not been alive?' commented Edward Young comfortingly in his poem, *Night Thoughts*.

It is no doubt in response to writers like Robert Blair and Edward Young, and ultimately indirectly to Stukeley, that Wordsworth became drawn to graveyards. These were his equivalent of Stukeley's barrows on the Wiltshire plain. He actually imagined at one point in his *Essays upon Epitaphs* the sudden excavation of all the graves in the churchyard which would yield a chaotic vision of 'Shipwreck, of the destruction of the Mariner's hopes, the bones of drowned Men heaped together, monsters of the deep, and all the hideous and confused sights which Clarence saw in his Dream!'

But mostly Wordsworth preferred to interpret the significance of each mound not by imaginary excavation but from its relationship with the other graves around it, with the natural landscape and with the existing village community. Rural churchyards offered a picture of the reciprocity between man and nature, birth and death. 'The sensations of pious cheerfulness, which attend the celebration of the sabbath-day in rural places, are profitably chastised by the sight of graves of kindred and friends, gathered together in that general home towards which the thoughtful yet happy spectators themselves are journeying', he observed. There is a natural, organic harmony between the graveyard and the landscape around it, since both are subject to the same forces of history, the same chastening processes of hope, loss, resignation and fond memory: 'Hence a parish-church, in the stillness of the country, is a visible centre of a community of the living and the dead.'

Wordsworth is buried in the same village in the Lake District as my mother. Nobody visits my mother's grave, except the shadow cast by the looming slopes of the local mountain, Helm Crag, nearby. In contrast, tourists flock to the corner of Grasmere's churchyard, between the old Norman church of St Oswald and the sparkling Rothay river, where Wordsworth is buried. Signposts at the cemetery's entrance point the way to his grave and the headstone is clearly marked with an epitaph. So any visitor is left in no doubt about the significance of this stone.

But Wordsworth himself, with an archaeologist's sense of the eloquence of material culture, ideally preferred headstones to be left bare, with no epitaph. He believed that a stone can signify more than words ever can. It was possible to 'read' a country churchyard, because it guarded a 'far more faithful' record of the lives of local people than a written report by a 'rigorous observer'. The gravestones, reliably and substantially, conveyed the history of the community; the words of any witness were necessarily partial and subjective.

But how can gravestones tell stories? How can they be more eloquent than words? Think, for a moment, of Wordworth's poem 'Michael', a new addition to his 1800 collection of *Lyrical Ballads*. This poem is about the relationship between parent and child. The evening before the young man Luke leaves home to improve his family's fortunes in the city, his father Michael, who is a shepherd, takes him up the valley and invites him to lay the corner-stone for a new sheepfold, which he will build after Luke has gone. These are Michael's words to Luke:

> Lay now the corner-stone,
> As I requested, and hereafter, Luke,
> When thou art gone away, should evil men
> Be thy companions, let this Sheepfold be
> Thy anchor and thy shield; amid all fear
> And all temptation let it be to thee
> An emblem of the life thy Fathers liv'd,
> Who, being innocent, did for that cause
> Bestir them in good deeds. Now, fare thee well –
> When thou return'st, thou in this place wilt see
> A work which is not here, a covenant
> 'Twill be between us – but whatever fate
> Befall thee, I shall love thee to the last,
> And bear thy memory to the grave.

According to this character Michael, the stones of the sheepfold are to act as a substitute for Luke's presence on the family farm and for his daily companionship with his father. At the time when Michael is speaking, when he is still enjoying the 'links of love' with his son, it is 'a work which is not here'. But once Luke has left, the walls will be built and they will be supposedly permanent in order to compensate for Luke's impermanent life, surrounded as he will be by evil, fear and temptation.

Michael's conception of the stones as a substitute for the loss of his son turns out to be more prophetic than he thought. Luke is led astray in the sinful city and, ashamed, emigrates abroad, never to return. His father dedicates the remainder of his life to building the sheepfold. Ostensibly he continues to add stones to the sheepfold for pragmatic reasons: 'to that hollow Dell from time to time/ Did he repair, to build the Fold of which/ His flock had need.' But implicitly Michael keeps returning to the sheepfold for complex, commemorative reasons which he cannot quite articulate: ' 'tis believ'd by all/ That many and many a day he thither went,/ And never lifted up a single stone.' When Michael dies seven years later, the farm is sold, the cottage destroyed and the landscape altered: 'great changes have been wrought in all the neighbourhood'. But the sheepfold, to which the idle traveller is directed at the beginning of the poem, remains as a testimony to a vanished history: 'There is a straggling heap of unhewn stones!/ And to that place a story appertains.'

The poem raises precisely this question of how a story can 'appertain' to a 'straggling heap of stones'. According to the New Historicist critic Marjorie Levinson, the absorption of Michael's history into the stones constitutes the most troubling act of depoliticising reification. 'Resorbed by nature (dehistoricised), the sheepfold communicates Michael's experience in the form of a generalised, ideal (plastic and polysemic) experience of human loss.' As such, the poem 'betrays its historical materials' by making the animate inanimate. In other words, Wordsworth ducks out of discussing poverty and exploitation and all the malevolent political forces that drove Luke to the city and Michael to a despairing early death by palming the reader off with a beautiful but irrelevant tale about the walls of a sheepfold.

But Levinson's intepretation is not alive to the archaeological import of this poem and ignores the way in which significant stones are equally subject to the historical forces which shape the landscape and the community. While the stones of Michael's sheepfold are permanent in that they remain available for inspection and contemplation after the family has disappeared, they are by no means outside the processes of history. Initially built up slowly, stone by stone, over a period of seven years and left still unfinished on Michael's death, the sheepfold is subsequently subject to gradual disintegration until it is a 'straggling heap of unhewn stones', the process of 'straggling' reflecting the passage of time. Indeed, Michael himself suggests the analogy between the stones in the memorial sheepfold and human bodies in a grave, when he tells Luke the fold will be 'an emblem of the life thy Fathers liv'd'. The lives of their fathers were chiefly characterised by their dutiful willingness to 'give their bodies to the family mold'. Just as the ancestors are gradually mingling their dust with the farm soil, so Michael and Luke's stones slowly lose their closely-packed formation as walls on the hillside.

There is, in 'Michael', no major division between people and the landscape around them, nor, as Levinson would see it, a negative substitution of inert stones for living history. Reification, which means the process of turning people into things or substituting isolated objects for history, does not run counter to the active life of the community. Stones are not examples of political bad faith on Wordsworth's part. They are not a cowardly substitute for proper political discussion. As any archaeologist knows, and especially one who has walked across the ancient landscape of Wiltshire, they are vital demarcators of a people's history.

But the problem, as I realise sitting on my boulder on Fyfield Down, lies in interpreting their significance. In 1793, Wordsworth hiked across Salisbury Plain, when he almost certainly must have read William Stukeley's account of the remains he would see there. The walk resulted in a distinctly Gothic poem, 'Salisbury Plain', which addressed this question of the degree of fantasy required to understand ancient stones and earthworks. At the beginning of the poem, the protagonist, a traveller, is hailed by a ghostly voice from one of the ancient barrows:

> The Sun unheeded sunk, while on a mound
> He stands beholding with astonished gaze,
> Frequent upon the deep entrenched ground,
> Strange marks of mighty arms of former days,
> Then looking up at distance he surveys
> What seems an antique castle spreading wide.
> Hoary and naked are its walls and raise
> Their brow sublime; while to those walls he hied
> A voice as from a tomb in hollow accents cried.

Here Wordsworth describes the traveller looking at the signs on the ground of 'mighty arms of former days' and later in the poem he talks of the 'warrior spectres of gigantic bones'. He suggests, in other words, that the barrows were the special tombs of ancient great warriors. This was a commonly held belief and one which Stukeley challenged in his book, *Stonehenge*: 'This shews, *they* are but superficial inspectors of things, that fancy from hence, great battels on the plain; and that these are the tumultuary burials of the slain. Quite otherwise; they are assuredly, the single sepulchres of kings, and great personages, buried during a considerable space of time, and that in peace.' Stukeley based his theory on the fact that he had actually excavated the tombs and had found objects – bronze and other precious metal – which suggested the careful and loving burial of a valued person, not the hasty disposal of a corpse in the thick of battle. But the dislocated and attenuated voice which Wordsworth depicts emanating from the tomb in hollow accents is produced by the fanciful subjectivity of the traveller who has not excavated the barrow and who is overinterpreting what he sees.

In this poem, Wordsworth is being deliberately ironic. He is parodying bad archaeological fieldwork, one which is conducted by melodramtic fantasy rather than by the careful work of the imagination which compares one ancient landscape feature with another and which analyses excavations. In his later poem, 'The Thorn', in the 1798 *Lyrical Ballads* collection, he does a similar thing, bringing together the Gothic and the

41

archaeological in the ironic voice of a garrulous narrator. The poem is basically about three landscape features on the edge of a village: a little mound of earth, a pond and a thorn bush. Each day, a distraught woman sits beside the thorn bush and weeps. These are the only facts we are given, but from them the narrator elaborates a big melodramatic story about the woman killing her child. The idea behind the poem is to challenge the possibilities of the imaginative interpretation of material culture through parodying a bad exponent of the art.

Ostensibly, Wordsworth seems to be writing a serious poem about archaeological investigation. Where his original source for the poem, Burger's ballad 'The Lass of Fair Wone', referred to 'a shallow grave' as the resting place of the killed child, Wordsworth transforms this into a burial mound, a visible earthwork sticking up above the ground. The supposed grave is repeatedly described as 'a hill of moss', 'this heap of earth', the 'beauteous hill of moss'. While Burger's version is just a receptacle, a grave, Wordsworth's appears packed with artefacts waiting to be opened. Yet the poem hangs upon the necessity of matching the visible data of mound, pond and thorn with the mystery of the story, the sight of a distraught woman, Martha Ray, crying 'O Misery' beside the thorn. The woman, we deduce from this sighting, murdered her illegitimate child and now grieves beside its grave. The narrator becomes more and more elaborate in his fancies about the woman and the grave, suggesting, for example, that the blood of the murder is actually visible on the ground: 'I've heard the moss is spotted red/ With drops of that poor infant's blood.' But ultimately the poem ends in doubt, for the narrator is forced to concede that, without excavation, the story is long on subjective melodrama and short on material proof. At least Stukeley was able to unearth the contents of the Wiltshire barrows; the Wordsworthian narrator can only speculate:

> And some had sworn an oath that she
> Should be to public justice brought;
> And for the little infant's bones
> With spades they would have sought.
> But instantly the hill of moss
> Before their eyes began to stir!

Superstition impedes the excavation process rather than complementing it. The implication of the poem is that if the villagers had actually opened the grave, they might have been able to substantiate the story and the speculation would be at an end. There is nothing more solid and authenticating than a physical set of bones. What prevents this act of scientific inquiry is the supernatural event of the ground beginning to 'stir', an experience provoked precisely by the superstitions of the villagers. Of course, even if the villagers had plucked up enough courage to face the fears whipped up by the Gothic legacy and had dug up the grave, there is no guarantee that what they found would have clinched the story. They might have found bones but there would still have been questions. Whose bones? And why? What did they mean to the woman? What had happened? It is always problematic to integrate the physical bones and flints and axes of an excavation with the narrative account of the now vanished people who used them, and Gothic speculation only highlights this inherent difficulty in a more extreme way. But at least digging up the remains and studying the relationship between them and the soil in which they were embedded offers some possibility of grounding literally the wilder flights of Gothic fancy.

Wordsworth repeated the Gothic vision of 'Salisbury Plain' in the first part of the Salisbury Plain episode of the 1805 *Prelude*, inspired by what he called the 'monumental hillocks', which thrill with the voices of dead soldiers and sacrificial victims:

> I had a reverie and saw the past,
> Saw multitudes of men, and here and there
> A single Briton in his wolf-skin vest,
> With shield and stone-ax, stride across the wold;
> The voice of spears was heard, the rattling spear
> Shaken by arms of mighty bone, in strength
> Long mouldered, of barbaric majesty.

But immediately after writing this in 1805, he began the process of grounding Gothic 'reverie' in a newly corrected and more organic vision. Now from the barrows or 'monumental hints' he traced, retrospectively, the beginnings of his imaginative conception of the relationship between man and nature. I quote, from the 1850 *Prelude*, the climax of this correcting process, at length:

> At other moments (for through that wide waste
> Three summer days I roamed) wher'er the Plain
> Was figur'd o'er with circles, lines, or mounds,
> That yet survive, a work, as some divine,
> Shaped by the Druids, so to represent
> Their knowledge of the heavens, and image forth
> The constellations; gently was I charmed
> Into a waking dream, a reverie
> That, with believing eyes, wher'er I turned,
> Beheld long-bearded teachers, with white wands
> Uplifted, pointing to the starry sky,
> Alternately, and plain below, while breath

43

Of music swayed their motions, and the waste
Rejoiced with them and me in those sweet sounds.

This for the past, and things that may be viewed
Or fancied in the obscurity of years
From monumental hints: and thou, O Friend!
Pleased with some unpremeditated strains
That served those wanderings to beguile, hast said
That then and there my mind had exercised
Upon the vulgar forms of present things,
The actual world of our familiar days,
Yet higher power; had caught from them a tone,
An image, and a character, by books
Not hitherto reflected. (XIII, ll. 336-60)

In the earlier 'Salisbury Plain' poem, the narrator views the barrows at night when he cannot investigate them properly and when Gothic ghosts are more likely to appear. But in this later version which Wordsworth included in the *Prelude*, he describes viewing all the barrows carefully in the daylight and over the course of three summer days. He is therefore able to examine how the plain is shaped into 'circles, lines and mounds' and to think about the significance of these patterns.

When Wordsworth's archaeological imagination works properly, it operates at the level of 'monumental hints'. Rather than having the significance of the earthworks spelled out, Wordsworth prefers to imagine what they mean from the hints which they offer, from the suggestion of the fullness of their meaning buried literally beneath the covering turf. Just as Stukeley deduced the overall pattern of the avenue of stones from noticing the 'hints' of where boulders might once have stood, so Wordsworth gained a sense of the significance of Salisbury plain just from the suggestion of the history buried beneath the monumental mounds. It is this kind of understatement – apprehending the meaning of something by what is lost or lies hidden or is hinted at – which is fundamental to what I call archaeological poetics, the way of writing and imagining which William Stukeley and William Wordsworth both practised.

*

The French philosopher Michel de Certeau has argued that walking is a metaphor for language. In his essay, 'Walking in the City', he describes viewing a city from a skyscraper as an act of 'reading' it while wandering through its streets is an act of speaking it. 'The act of walking is to the urban system what the speech act is to language or to the statements uttered', he writes. He goes on to elaborate with examples of the 'rhetoric of walking', pointing out the figures of speech which owe their origins to travelling around the earth: the 'turn' of phrase, the 'way' of speech, the 'leap' of thought. The effect is an image of the ground as a medium of meaning, inscribed by the journeys of people criss-crossing it every day. Their routes become established by that daily act of walking, just as strange figures of speech become conventional through customary use in language. Their paths become 'the thicks and thins of an urban "text" ' which walkers 'write without being able to read'.

If this is the case – that paths are well-trodden texts and the earth an accumulation of words and memories – then it seems as if burial must be considered a type of understatement and understatement a metaphorical act of burial. If the ground surface carries clear messages which can be read, then what is buried below the ground, under the fascinating barrow, can only be suggested or hypothesised from previous excavations or from a well-practised archaeological imagination. Archaeological poetics finds meaning in what is buried or unstated and subtly implied. It is sensitive to the density of the earth which covers what is significant. It testifies to the difficulty for anyone of teasing out what is felt most passionately or poignantly.

Wordsworth's poetry suggests its meaning through hinted depths. The most striking use of metaphorical depth in his poetry occurs at the end of the poem, 'Ode: Intimations of Immortality from Recollections of Early Childhood'. The poem charts the loss of Wordsworth's youthful vision and the ways in which he attempts to compensate for that loss in later years. In early days he saw nature as glorious; now he can only remember how once he had that visionary capacity. The poem ends with these lines:

> Thanks to the human heart by which we live
> Thanks to its tenderness, its joys and fears,
> To me the meanest flower that blows can give
> Thoughts that do often lie too deep for tears. (ll. 203-6)

By this stage in the poem, the reader knows the emotional levels which the poet has experienced and reburied with the passage of years, the lines of joy and loss and recovery recorded earlier in the poem. He has been disturbed by Wordsworth's sudden discoveries and excavations, the 'obstinate questionings/ Of sense and outward things,/ Fallings from us, vanishings' and has trembled 'like a guilty Thing surpriz'd' – surprised presumably by some event in the past which resists the natural decay of time, like the ghost of Hamlet's father before which Hamlet is surprised 'like a guilty thing'. The reader has learnt too the archaeologist's art of resignation, being satisfied with the remains of the past rather than yearning for the original. He has learnt to try to guess what once might have existed by reading those metaphorical burial mounds of subsequent earth: 'We will grieve not, rather find/ Strength in what remains behind/ In the primal sympathy/ Which having been must ever be' (ll. 182-5)

So by the time we reach the final line of Wordsworth's poem, full explanation is unnecessary. The understatement, 'too deep for tears', is more powerful because it assimilates and implicates all the previous thoughts with a conciseness which is poignantly telling in its density. The poem is a sorrowful and solid heap of memories. The poet's explicit meaning lies 'too deep' for clearcut analysis, just as the barrow's contents can only be understood in the context of the burial mound as a whole, in the context of the 'heap of turf' above it.

William Stukeley implicitly likened the writing of his book on Stonehenge with archaeological fieldwork. Stones and earth were the type of metaphorical language he worked in and therefore, in preparing the book, he was effectively, in the archaeologist Christopher Tilley's words, 'converting material or solid metaphor into linguistic metaphor'. He covered the bare bones and facts with a layer of imaginative interpretation and selective presentation, like the layers of earth covering the missing stones in Bekhampton Avenue. 'The method of writing which I have chosen is a diffusive one, not pretending to a formal and stiff scholastic proof of everything I say', he warned in the preface to *Stonehenge*. It was up to the reader to use his or her imagination to interpret the observations which Stukeley made in the book and to develop an appreciation of the hidden and mysterious history of the Druids from the hints which Stukeley gave in the text. 'The knowledge I have acquired in these matters, was from examining and studying their works; the proofs are deriv'd from distant and different topicks, and it would be inconvenient to marshall them syllogistically', Stukeley explained. 'In all matters of so great antiquity it must be found out by the reader; and to one that has proper sagacity and judgement, conviction will steal upon him insensibly.'

But there lies the rub. To interpret stones correctly, one needs to be possessed of the 'proper sagacity and judgement'. One needs to have the right kind of imagination. What looks highly significant to a particular person might just look like a pile of rocks to another. So is the archaeological imagination elitist and exclusive?

William Stukeley tried to make the imaginative power of stones available to everyone but came up against some resistance. He criticised the workmen, for example, for not appreciating the significance of stones, for treating them simply as stones. The farmers around Avebury kept removing the boulders to clear their fields for easier ploughing and the villagers often used the stones as building material. In fact the villagers had to go to great efforts to break up the sacred stones and make them less significant. At first they would dig great pits and bury the stones and later they developed a method of burning the stones to destroy them. Stukeley described the process with utter bewilderment, noting how they would 'dig a pit by the side of the stone, burn many loads of straw under it, draw lines of water along it when heated and then, with smart strokes of a great sledge hammer, divide it into many lesser parts'. This process cost often more than thirty shillings. So while he was doing his utmost to transfigure the landscape by his imagination and to tease out the hidden significance of the isolated boulders on Salisbury Plain or the Marlborough downs, the local people were making equally strenuous efforts to transform the place back again into somewhere ordinary and workable. They were trying to turn symbolic stones back into natural ones which they could cut up and cart away.

As William Stukeley developed his poetics more seriously, then, a growing gulf seemed to open between him and the local inhabitants. There was a gulf between his capacity to appreciate the symbolic value of stones and mounds and their incapacity to see them as anything other than building material. Stukeley became, to coin a Wordsworthian phrase, not just 'a man speaking to men' but 'a man endowed with a greater sensibility, a more lively sense of imagination'. Of course, this might just have been part of an elite archaeologists' rhetoric and it might be possible to unearth unlettered peasant excavators, just as literary scholars have discovered peasant poets such as John Clare or Stephen Duck. There is one anecdote, for example, that two of the main workmen whom William Cunnington employed on an early nineteenth-century Wiltshire dig, Stephen and John Parker, actually went out looking for antiquities on their own.

But Stukeley presented his research as if his unique sensibility were hugely important, emphasising the way in which his own subjectivity shaped his perspective upon the ancient remains. He would draw the same scene from different perspectives on the same page, thus implying that truth was kaleidoscopic and depended upon the subjective and imaginative vision of the viewer. And he also depicted in his drawings the lost or absent archaeological features which only somebody sensitive to archaeological poetics would appreciate. He included a picture of a 'Prospect of Bekampton Avenue from Longston Long Barrow', in which the missing rocks form actually the main feature, appearing as two circles. In this picture what is not visible but can only be known to the interested excavator – the missing rocks – is emphasised more strongly than the landscape features which are available to the local worker or the casual tourist. Stukeley suggested that the missing stones were symbolically more significant than the surrounding countryside. The picture captures through a negative vision the notion of loss and elegiac change inscribed in the landscape.

For Wordsworth, too, a grave or tombstone could mean different things to different people. In his *Essays upon Epitaphs*, he made a careful distinction between the bereaved relatives and the general observer of the cemetery, whether a later descendant in the village or the casual tourist. But Wordsworth dramatised most vividly the different ways the same burial mounds might be interpreted in the most poignant and heartrending of all his poems, 'The Brothers'. In this poem, the Priest of Ennerdale in the Lake District spots a visitor to the village lingering in the churchyard and assumes that he is a butterfly-like tourist, 'rapid and gay', who, following Thomas Gray's 'Elegy in a Country Churchyard', visits rural cemeteries to luxuriate briefly in profound and melancholy thoughts. But in fact the man was once a child of the parish and has just returned years later to find out what has happened to the last of his family, his younger brother James. He is examining the graves in the churchyard, which are not marked by gravestones but are just simple 'heaps of turf', to see whether a new grave has been added, which would contain the body of his brother. Too emotionally confused to confess his identity to the priest, he hopes to deduce what might be too painful to hear directly from the hints gleaned in the graveyard.

The man, called Leonard, hopes that he will not see a new grave. He hopes that his brother has not been buried and that, unlike the family in the poem 'Michael' which I discussed earlier, his family has not been integrated with the earth and stones of the landscape. So when he does see a new 'heap of turf', he tries to convince himself that it does not mean anything and that perhaps even the natural landscape itself is new and strange:

> When Leonard had approach'd his home, his heart
> Fail'd in him, and, not venturing to inquire
> Tidings of one whom he so dearly lov'd,
> Towards the church-yard he had turn'd aside,
> That, as he knew in what particular spot
> His family were laid, he thence might learn
> If still his Brother liv'd, or to the file
> Another grave was added. – He had found
> Another grave, near which a full half hour
> He had remain'd, but, as he gaz'd, there grew
> Such a confusion in his memory,
> That he began to doubt, and he had hopes
> That he had seen this heap of turf before,
> That it was not another grave, but one
> He had forgotten. He had lost his path,
> As up the vale he came that afternoon,
> Through fields which once had been well known to him.

2. Romancing Stones: The Archaeological Landscape

> And Oh! what joy the recollection now
> Sent to his heart! he lifted up his eyes,
> And looking round he thought that he perceiv'd
> Strange alteration wrought on every side
> Among the woods and fields, and that the rocks,
> And the eternal hills, themselves were chang'd.

Wordsworth's repeated phrase here, 'another grave', plays with the confusion over general or particular histories. 'Another grave' could mean unspecifically 'any other grave', a general inclusion for the casual visitor. But to Leonard, for whom each grave is numbered and known personally, 'another grave', a new addition, appears to carry only one meaning. 'Another grave' means the new grave of his brother. It means that his brother has died. It would only be by imagining a complete reversal of everything he knows, a 'strange alteration' in 'the eternal hills', that he could resist the sinister implications of 'another grave'.

The priest soon comes to disabuse Leonard of his wishful thinking. His brother has died and is indeed buried in the new grave. Not recognising Leonard, the priest tells him the stories belonging to each grave, wistfully suggesting that if there were more time and Leonard were sitting by his chimney's nook, they could entertain themselves with the tales of the whole village, 'turning o'er these hillocks one by one'. He defends the village custom of doing without gravestones.

> 'We have no need of names and epitaphs,
> We talk about the dead by our fire-sides.'

Unlike the fanciful tales circulating in 'The Thorn', the stories of the village maintain a careful integration of imagination and material reality. But what they cannot do is sustain the degree of identification which Leonard feels. While the priest can recount the story of James' tragic early death to somebody he assumes is simply a man of sensibility, Leonard cannot identify himself to the priest or express his particular relation to the story or to the grave. He leaves in silence and only later writes a letter to the priest, revealing who he is.

In many ways, this poem seems to be about the limits of archaeological excavation. The Priest, supposedly 'turning o'er these hillocks one by one' and interpreting each 'heap of turf' authoritatively, is unable to penetrate the identity and emotional state of the man with whom he is conversing. Archaeological investigation, when conducted scientifically, is shown to be inadequate, offering only limited insight. While barrows and cairns demand sympathy by their assimilation of nature and culture, the very close identification between Leonard and this particular mound is too poignant for sympathy to be easily expressed. 'The Brothers', in other words, raises questions about the nature of the archaeological imagination. Can it be shared? Can it be communicated?

The answer is that it can only be implied. Leonard's repression of his story echoes the burial of his brother's body. The poem could be said to be archaeological in the sense that, like the end of 'Ode: Intimations of Immortality', it deals with 'thoughts that do often lie too deep for tears'. It relies upon the reader appreciating the undercurrents of feeling hinted at during the course of the narrative, just as the excavator interprets a particular history from the stratigraphic layers in the archaeological landscape. Wordsworth wishes the feelings of grief to stay buried, because, held in the memory of repeated acts of recollection and repression, they then retain more poignancy and meaning. So the emotional power of the poem is derived from what it compresses in layers as hard-packed and resistant as the stony ground of the Lake District.

Archaeological poetics involves reading between the lines, appreciating what is buried, comparing present insignificance with past and now lost significance. It requires the poet or archaeologist to see things in a new way, to turn the imagination 'inside outwards' in order to ponder what is hidden below the earth rather than what is visible above. There is nothing easy or glib about archaeological poetics, about the absorption of history into nature and the integration of stones and words. It can surprise, as Stukeley proved when he looked up at the stones of Stonehenge rather than down into a natural quarry. It can bear witness to private pain, as Leonard shows in 'The Brothers', when what lay buried was too painful to articulate or share. But crucially it shapes our capacity to appreciate our historical intimate relation with the earth, to develop an understanding of the unstated and the opaque, and to celebrate and preserve the symbolic importance of things like earth and stones which outwardly look insignificant.

*

In the last few years, the largest of all the barrows in Wiltshire, Silbury Hill, has been going through a crisis. In May 2000, a great hole appeared in the summit, provoking much debate and political controversy about the internal working and preservation of the hill. The mound, as I mentioned earlier, has never been fully excavated and no human remains have yet been found inside. The purpose or function of the hill has remained a mystery. But with its collapse, the lack of clear knowledge about the precise structure of the mound became more significant, more politicised. Local activists and archaeologists accused English Heritage of being slow to respond to the situation, of not appreciating the significance and importance of the hill to the local community and of shrouding its business in secrecy. English Heritage, on the other hand, countered by stressing that it was important to gain a deep knowledge of the hill's structure before forming a plan for its conservation. They commissioned a seismic survey in order to gain 'a three-dimensional image of the interior structure'.

In June 2001 and again in December, local protesters, impatient at the time the survey was taking, abseiled down into the unstable eighteenth-century excavation shaft, the apparent cause of the collapse, to investigate it with video cameras. This action actually caused further erosion damage in the process. The protesters wanted instant knowledge, direct access to the internal workings, regardless of the consequences. English Heritage, in contrast, are taking their time. Not content with the results of the first survey, which revealed a spiral rather than terraced structure in the centre of the hill, they demanded that further tests be undertaken. They are gaining an understanding of the hill not through damaging excavation but by sonar equipment, by 'measuring the relative speeds of sound travelling through the different voids and solids'. Only once they have built up a 'reading', through sonar implications of the hill and through boreholes drilled carefully into the eighteenth-century excavation shaft, can they form conservation plans.

It seems all the more important to appreciate the density and complication of Silbury Hill when increasingly the cultural emphasis leans towards accessibility and clarity. It seems similarly important to appreciate the density of Stukeley's and Wordsworth's writing at a time now when the demand is for transparency in all things. Language must be clear-cut at all times; aims and objectives have to be transparently available for scrutiny. Political democracy is synonymous with the right to know and the right to understand. Perhaps it is in line with this sentiment that Marjorie Levinson and others criticise Wordsworth for effectively being guilty of repression. They argue, in effect, that Wordsworth buries the historical beneath the ground and ties up his meaning in obfuscation, an act of conservative displacement. But if the ground itself is considered political and historical in its density, in its layers of social integration between man and his environment, then burial beneath the ground should be celebrated, not denigrated. The lapidary does not replace or displace the linguistic but both are subject to the same forces of burial, disintegration and subsequent interpretation. The opacity of Wordworth's language, its poignant understatement, the things left unspoken, are as valuable as Stukeley's artificial hills, as the giant Silbury Hill, the 'artificial ornaments of the great plain' of Wiltshire.

So I thought, as I sat on my boulder on Fyfield Down, that this is a chapter both about stones and, latently, about my mother, poised as it is

51

between the landscape of her early life and the place of her burial, between Wiltshire and the Lake District. And it is in thinking about those connections and repressions, in inferring what I have left unsaid and in appreciating what I can never hope fully to understand, that the archaeological imagination really begins.

Unearthing Bodies:
The Disruption of History

On a hot, sultry day in August 1790, the parishioners of St Giles, Cripple-gate, in London's East End decided to dig up the body of the poet John Milton. He had been dead for over a hundred years.

A group of Milton enthusiasts were proposing to set up a permanent monument to the poet, in the church in Cripplegate where he was supposed to have been buried, nowadays marooned in the middle of the Barbican centre. Since the exact location in the church of his grave was in doubt, some of the project's supporters suggested that the matter should finally be investigated by the spade. Workmen dug down in the chancel and found a lead coffin, lying on top of the wooden coffin which was thought to be that of Milton's father. The sight of these two coffins seemed to settle the question of Milton's burial place and it was decided, out of a 'just and laudable piety', to close the excavation.

But later that evening, after a 'merry' time in the local pub, several of the men decided to return to the site, daring each other on to look inside the coffin before it was buried again. Philip Neve, who reported the incident, takes up the tale:

> They then went with *Holmes* into the church, and pulled the coffin, which lay deep in the ground, from its original station, to the edge of the excavation, into day-light. When they had thus removed it, the overseers asked *Holmes* if he could open it, that they might see the body. *Holmes* immediately fetched a mallet and chisel, and cut open the top of the coffin, slantwise from the head, as low as the breast; so that, the top being doubled backward, they could see the corpse; he cut it open also at the foot. Upon first view of the body, it appeared perfect, and completely enveloped in the shroud, which was of many folds; the ribs standing up regularly. When they disturbed the shroud, the ribs fell. Mr *Fountain* told me, that he pulled hard at the teeth, which resisted, until someone hit them a knock with a stone, when they easily came out.

Once Fountain had seized hold of Milton's teeth, a frenzy of trophy hunting broke out around the body. One man grabbed a bunch of the hair from the decomposing slime at the bottom of the coffin. Another took out the whole lower jaw, complete with teeth, and one of the leg bones, but eventually 'tossed' them back into the coffin again. Next morning, one of the grave-diggers, Elizabeth Grant, was left in charge of guarding the corpse and, following the example of the men, she decided to turn the excavation to her commercial advantage. She stood, arms akimbo, at the door of the church and charged punters sixpence a head for a view of the body. Those desperate to see it, but unable to pay the fee, apparently crawled in through a window at the back of the church and crept down to the grisly sight in the chancel.

Meanwhile, outside the church, the men were cutting up Milton's bones and hair into smaller pieces and selling them on the black market. Philip Neve acquired his relics from a man, probably called Mr Laming, who had paid Elizabeth Grant for access to the body and was now evidently trying to recoup his expenses:

> He had lifted up the head, and taken, from among the sludge under it, a small quantity of hair, with which was a piece of shroud, and, adhering to the hair, a bit of the skin of the skull, of about the size of a shilling. He put them all into my hands, with the rib-bone, which appeared to be one of the upper ribs.

Philip Neve was particularly anxious to acquire Milton's hair, because that was the most remarkable feature of the body. It startled by its abundance, its colour and its perfect preservation. 'Milton had light brown hair; the very description of that which we possess', Neve explained. 'It is yet so strong, that Mr *Laming*, to cleanse it from its clotted state, let the cistern-cock run on it, for near a minute, and then rubbed it between his fingers, without injury.'

*

I find this story of Milton's disinterment shocking, as admittedly Philip Neve also did. The participants blatantly disregarded the sanctity of the poet's body. They treated the corpse as an object for plunder, snatching violently at his hair and teeth. They turned his body into a commodity, to be chopped up, traded and hoarded. And they made it into a spectacle too, exhibited by Elizabeth Grant at sixpence a throw. (Later, in fact, according to Philip Neve, the rate dropped to twopence, as the novelty wore off and spectator demand diminished.)

But I find the story fascinating too because, while the parishioners had to dehumanise the body in order to ransack it, the value of the corpse in the East London black market paradoxically derived from the fact that it had once been a person and, more precisely, that it had once been John Milton. The punters paid to see the body's immaculate preservation and its luxuriant hair. They marvelled at how natural and lifelike the body looked, despite the hundred years of its burial. And they paid as well to own a little piece of the man who wrote *Paradise Lost*. Each fragment of jaw or rib was supposedly the repository of genius.

The excavation of perfectly preserved bodies disturbs the boundaries we maintain between what is natural and what is unnatural. In the last chapter I pondered the way in which the body naturally disintegrates into the landscape after death and is subject to the same forces of decay and historical process as is nature. I claimed that archaeology highlights what has been lost or passed away naturally and what can only be understood elegiacally, through imagining what has disappeared. But in this chapter, the revelation of immaculate bodies from the past shatters all those theories. For by cheating death and normal disintegration, mummies, bog bodies and other archaeological marvels like John Milton show that certain burial conditions can intervene in the ordinary course of nature and prevent miraculously the expected process of decay. In other words, nature does not have to operate in the way we expect it to and perhaps it is not as natural as we might think.

So if nature normally demarcates for us what is ethical or not ethical, where does that leave the ethics of studying the immaculately preserved dead? Is our fascination with archaeological mummies ethically responsible or sensationally voyeuristic? Once every few months I go to visit the bog man in the British Museum. Discovered buried in a peat bog near Manchester in 1984 and called Lindow Man, it is little more than a mass of leather and bones, just half a torso and one lower leg (Plate 3). Indeed, archaeologists have now established that the man was probably killed as part of a sacrificial ritual in the first century AD. Yet despite the dim lighting and scanty remains, crowds always gather at this particular case in the 'Celtic Europe' gallery, craning their heads over the rail in an attempt to get face to face with a man who has survived two millennia. And when I visit him, on a regular basis, I linger over the glass case, marvelling at the perfectly formed left ear, the hair plastered down on his head and the brown skin drawn tight over his sharp cheek bone, and I am awed into a type of reverence.

But my feelings on looking at Lindow Man are totally different from the sensation I experienced visiting the *Body Worlds* exhibition in the Atlantis Gallery, Brick Lane, in the East End of London in the summer of 2002. This was an exhibition of people who had died within the last two decades and whose bodies had been treated and contorted by the German doctor, Gunther Von Hagens. In 1978 Von Hagens developed a method of preserving bodies by impregating them with polymers such as silicone or polyester, a process he has termed 'plastination', with the result that the bodies retain their original colour and texture but are hard and dry for easy display. Von Hagens proceeded to persuade people to donate their bodies to him after death and to exhibit them in various states of dissection and dismemberment. The exhibition tours different European cities continually, on Von Hagens' supposed mission to educate the general public in basic anatomy and to broaden access to the process of dissection beyond the confines of medical schools.

But when I visited the exhibition the atmosphere was much more grisly sensation than sober education. Bodies were displayed in gratuitous postures, such as playing chess or riding a partly-dissected horse. One was exhibited holding his own flayed skin, installed deliberately to echo the sixteenth-century etching of Ververde, which was hanging all the wall behind it. Worst were the bits of body parts, slices of the lung or liver or leg, displayed without context and without the rest of the body. Some were healthy but others showed evidence of deformity or disease, bulging with cancerous tumours or apparently born with vital parts missing.

I felt an overwhelming, physical sense of revulsion. The show challenged every normative or ethical notion of what is natural, from the display of unnatural, deformed body parts to the whole unnatural preservation and presentation process itself.

'This is so interesting,' my friend came rushing across the gallery to tell me at one point. 'I am really missing having somebody to discuss the bodies with.'

But by this stage I was slumped, faint and dizzy, over a chair in the corner and incapable of discussing anything with anybody.

So why, I wondered when I visited Lindow Man again recently, was my reaction to the *Body Worlds* bodies so different from my regular response to bodies retrieved from the earth? Why did *Body Worlds* feel like the modern equivalent of the Victorian freakshow, bodies gawped at as extraordinary sensations? Why, on the other hand, did Lindow Man conjure up in me an awe-inspiring sense of recognition? The answer, perhaps, can be found in the fact that Lindow Man both looks perfectly human and yet also has been transformed by the bog. The context of his mummification – in other words, the centuries of being held in the bog – is detectable on his body. The *Body Worlds* cadavers, on the other hand, are unnatural sensations consumed by a voracious public, part now of a large commercial enterprise.

So perhaps the answer, I wondered, looking at Lindow Man's brown pate, lies in the familiarity of the human body, even when it has survived over centuries. Familiarity can sometimes be frightening, if it is encountered in unfamiliar circumstances. Indeed the most disturbing experiences occur when what we most trusted and felt certain about re-emerge in unexpected form. But they still have a hold upon our imaginations and press an ethical imperative. But some forms of exploitation to which dead bodies have been put are simply alienating, carry no human resonances, and appear merely grotesque and shocking. How can we be sure that digging up the dead retains that ethical imperative and does not become exploitative?

*

When I was a teenager, I developed an obsessive phobia, shortly after reading the Gothic novel *Jane Eyre*. I became convinced that, when I bent down over the bathroom basin to wash my face and then raised my head again to look at myself in the mirror, just once I would stare into the face not of myself but of a madwoman, a ghastly, haggard figure with wild hair and manic grin. I would be face to face with an alien being, myself and yet not myself, familiar and yet not familiar. And in that case, I would be only inches away from the reflected image, intimate with the demonic unknown.

So I developed strategies to defend myself against this scenario. Sometimes I would try the quick splash, flicking water up to my face while never taking my eyes off the mirror. Sometimes I would linger deep down in the water, not daring to re-emerge and confront the looking-glass. But other times, my heart racing and a tingling fear coursing down my arms, I would face down my terror and lift my head to outstare whatever might be reflected back at me. And on each occasion, I would breathe a sigh of relief as the familiar, pale, uncertain teenager looked back at me. The world was still as I thought it was. Nature, this time at least, had held steady.

*

Staring at the face of the dead preserved over centuries can be an uncanny experience. According to Sigmund Freud, who thought a great deal about the impact of history on the body, uncanny objects are frightening precisely because they are so familiar and close to us. You could say that they get under our skin. The uncanny is 'in reality nothing new or alien, but something which is familiar and old-established to the mind and which has become alienated from it only through the process of repression', writes Freud. So the body dug up out of the Lindow bog is familiar because it has not decayed but still remains recognisably fleshy and human.

But it is paradoxically the fact that the perfectly preserved dead body looks identifiably human which produces the feeling of uneasiness. For what should be dead appears to be alive. And by the same token, perhaps

57

what is alive, the spectator or excavator, should be dead. Our primitive fear of the dead is based on 'an old belief that the dead man becomes the enemy of his survivor and seeks to carry him off to share his new life with him', observes Freud as he attempts to explain the uncanniness of the dead. The uncanny return of the dead creates a breach in nature. For the natural processes of time, which one expects to decompose the rotting corpse, have been subverted so that the dead comes back exactly the same. Nature and time might not be as reliable as one previously thought. Surprised by an unexpected re-occurrence or re-emergence of something one thought to be safely buried in the past, one experiences, in the words of the critic Nicholas Royle, 'a disturbance of any sense of "familiar ground"', so that what was previously thought homely ('heimlich' as Freud says) becomes unhomely ('unheimlich'), and vice versa.

Looking at a dead face which has overcome the ravages of time and suddenly comes back into view is frightening. But it is not disgusting, because it is intimately connected with us. According to Freud, we repress what is closest to us and what has troubled us most in order to be able to cope with the experience. The fact that we repress it shows that we feel guilty about it and it means a great deal to us. The act of repression allows that experience to be preserved, in breach of the normal course of nature, and to return someday, in uncanny form, to disturb us. But the repression also means that the experience or object will come back changed in some way, like a hysterical symptom. 'Every affect belonging to an emotional impulse, whatever its kind, is *transformed*, if it is repressed, into anxiety', writes Freud. The uncanny has become 'alienated from the mind only through the process of repression'. The repression, which has altered the uncanny object into a symptom carrying the marks of the repression, allows us to face that object, however horrified we may feel. So Lindow Man's crushed, contorted head and mangled limbs indicate the weight of the sodden peat bog which bore down upon him for two thousand years. The means of his preservation have affected his appearance. The repression, which burial in the peat bog represents, has 'transformed' the body into a symbol of that anxiety, into the leathery skin and distorted face.

'Poor guy,' sighed one girl, looking down at the spread-eagled arm, when I was last visiting Lindow Man and lingering near the display.

'It's the earth which makes them like that,' her friend told her. 'You can see he's all squashed flat on one side of his face.'

Unlike the uncomfortable intimacy of Lindow Man, which Freud's explanation goes some way to explain, the corpses in *Body Worlds* were coldly disconnected from their humanity and from anything which might even originally have appeared normal or ordinary. The disconnection of the display reminded me of the theories of another great philosopher of the

3. Unearthing Bodies: The Disruption of History

body, Michel Foucault. According to Foucault, historical progress from century to century is fragmented, discontinuous, liable to interruption and surprise. Between each historical period, there is no continuity or gradual progression but instead a series of ruptures and dramatic leaps and sudden changes. So excavating a discontinuous past allows for the kind of exploitative objectivity which the Cripplegate parishioners exhibited in their treatment of Milton. Against the connectivity posited by the historians mentioned in the last chapter, Foucault relishes his disconnection from the past. 'In attempting to uncover the deepest strata of Western culture', he writes, 'I am restoring to our silent and apparently immobile soil its rifts, its instability, its flaws.' So he alights upon a historical period or 'episteme' with the same detachment that an archaeologist might chance upon a flint axe or indeed a grisly skeleton.

Foucault claims that the pressure of the historical environment determines the constitution of the body. There is nothing timeless or essentially human about the body but rather it gets its particular nature and outward appearance according to the particular historical pressures and ideology of the time. This influences its potential for transgression and its capacity for punishment. For example, criminals are watched carefully by the public among whom they originally lived and by whom they come to be judged and condemned. As a result the criminals come to internalise that scrutiny and judgement until their very identities are shaped by that spectatorship. Foucault's bodies, then, are objects of their period of history, held fast in the metaphorical rift or seam of the 'immobile soil'. They might mean nothing to us now because the historical context of their original mummification is utterly detached from our own. We can potentially look at them with the neutral gaze of the voyeur, cut off from guilty feelings of complicity.

*

Digging up perfectly preserved bodies invokes both accounts of history – the Freudian sense of guilty respect and responsibility and the Foucauldian version of cold detachment. When Tollund Man was first unearthed from a bog in Denmark in 1950, the overwhelming immediate reaction to the body was how natural he looked, how close in appearance he was to contemporary men. The recollection of Professor P.V. Glob, the main excavator of the bog bodies, strikingly emphasises the ordinary context in which the discovery took place and the familiar appearance and pose of the body:

> A telephone call was put through straightaway to Aarhus University, where
> at that moment I was lecturing to a group of students on archaeological

problems. Some hours later – that same evening – I stood with my students, bent over the startling discovery, face to face with an Iron Age man who, two millennia before, had been deposited in the bog as a sacrifice to the powers that ruled men's destinies. The man lay on his right side in a natural attitude of sleep.

But the case of the utilitarian philosopher Jeremy Bentham, who arranged before his death to have himself embalmed or turned into what he called an 'Auto-Icon', proves that the perfect preservation of the body does not necessarily make it look natural. In the article which Bentham wrote on the merits of mummification – 'Auto-Icon; or Farther Uses of the Dead to the Living' – he claimed that an embalmed body looks more like the original person than any artistic representation or artificial replica might do:

> What resemblance, what painting, what statue of a human being can be so like him, as, in the character of an Auto-Icon, he or she will be to himself or herself. Is not identity preferable to similitude?

Rather than relying upon written or pictorial descriptions of the individual after death which could mislead people, Bentham believed that the most natural and lifelike way of representing any man was to carefully embalm him and preserve him against the ravages of time. The preserved human body was the most authentic record of a life for, as he stated, 'Auto-Icons cannot be invented, cannot be forged.'

So, on Bentham's death in 1832, his friend Southwood Smith dissected the inner organs of the philosopher before an audience of medical students in the London University Webb Street School of anatomy and then proceeded to embalm the body. Bentham was positioned sitting, fully clothed in morning coat with walking stick in hand, as if just about to go out to take his constitutional. Indeed it is still possible to visit Bentham, sitting in his box, in the corridor of University College London, in Gower Street.

But the embalming process proved imperfect. Despite what appear to have been Bentham's previous experiments with drying heads in his stove, his head shrank, lost its colour and became increasingly unrecognisable as his own. As a result, Southwood Smith also commissioned a wax head to be made by the anatomical modeller, Jacques Talrich. In the end it was this wax replica head, covered with Bentham's own hair, which was attached to his body for display, while the real head, discarded as less 'natural', was wrapped in tarpaulin and paper and secreted within the body itself, wedged between the ribcage and the spine.

Glob's bog bodies appear at first uncontroversially natural. Bentham's real body, or at least his embalmed head, appears less natural than his false one. But the body at the end of James Hogg's Scottish Gothic novel, *The Private Memoirs and Confessions of a Justified Sinner*, is paradoxically *more* natural than one would expect and therefore particularly troubling. At the end of the novel, two men, out on the moors cutting peat, decide to dig up a grave in order to substantiate a story circulating among locals about a man who once hanged himself and was buried there. However, on opening the barrow and pulling on the rope around the victim's neck, they are met with their biggest surprise. Instead of a skeleton, the barrow contains the whole body, perfectly preserved, with a blue bonnet still on its head and a tartan shawl around its shoulders. 'The features were all so plain, that an acquaintance might easily have known him', the narrator goes on. 'One of the lads gripped the face of the corpse with his finger and thumb, and the cheeks felt quite soft and fleshy, but the dimples remained, and did not spring out again.'

The excavated body confirms the rumour that the devil had something to do with the suicide's demise. Only a man possessed would be unnaturally resistant to decay, potentially able to be recognised by an acquaintance even though he had been dead for one hundred and five years.

The discovery of the perfect corpse in the grave disrupts the natural process of history. The men might have expected, as William Stukeley did in the last chapter, to find in the grave an organic integration of earth and bone, nature and history. Instead they expose a perfect body which is the residue of a fragmented and unpredictable passage of time. The body, consequently, is the archaeological product more of Foucault's description of ruptured history than Freud's unexpected personal continuities. In order to account for the surprise, the men reach not for a rational or historical explanation but one drawn from magic, superstition, popular folklore. The man was bewitched by the devil. The uncanny return of the dead, according to Freud, occurs in periods when primitive beliefs in demons have been surmounted by rational logic. But according to Hogg's novel, common people continue to believe in magic and miraculous events and do not share the rational explanations of the past, promoted by an elite educated class.

But the story gets even more complicated. For before writing his novel, Hogg actually published the tale of the excavation in *Blackwood's Edinburgh Magazine*, under the title 'A Scots Mummy'. He supposedly sent parts of the plaid and waistcoat found on the body to the magazine as the final proof of the authenticity of the remarkable story. And in the novel, the 'editor' of the justified sinner's memoirs reads Hogg's account of the excavation in *Blackwood's* and decides to investigate. He travels down from Edinburgh to the borders where a character called Hogg refuses to show him the barrow. 'I hae mair ado than I can manage the day, foreby

61

ganging to houk up hunder-year-auld banes', the Hogg character says. So another shepherd agrees to escort the editor to the grave. He leads him to a barrow in a different place from the one described by Hogg in his letter to *Blackwood's*. Nevertheless, when they reach the barrow it shows evidence of recent digging and, sure enough, it soon reveals the perfect body. So fact and fiction seem to be confused. The 'familiar ground', in which uncanny excavation supposedly is undertaken, begins to crumble under the reader's feet.

When the 'editor' goes to excavate the body for the second time, he finds a written testimony of the man's life left in the coat pocket. The excavators want to keep it, hoping to discover further 'mysteries', but instead the 'editor' dries it and unrolls it and uses it as the basis for his novel. So the claims of the common diggers to the body and their traditional superstitious beliefs about demonic possession and miraculous mummification are disregarded by the editor. His cool and logical analysis wins the day. He removes the uncanny excavation of the corpse from its grounded, social, political context in common folklore and turns it into an interesting publishing phenomenon, the occasion for a novel. Snatched from the ordinary excavators, the mummified body loses its capacity to confirm the continuation of popular, rural beliefs and Freud's uncanny familiarity. It becomes instead simply a sensation, a curious exhibit for the gratification of a new bourgeoisie.

*

According to the alienating perspective of Michel Foucault, bodies are objects to be ogled and policed, determined by the institutions and regulations of their age. Mummies, however, unlike Foucault's bodies, take on significance outside their immediate historical context. They are marvelled over by a very different culture to the one which they originally inhabited. The act of spectatorship in Foucault turns the bodies into objects which are disciplined and managed. But in the case of archaeological bodies, the corpse has been turned into an object in a previous age and remains impervious to the decomposition or the dialectic, as a Marxist would see it, of history. What Marxists would call its reification – resisting the processes of history and becoming an object – in fact is the cause of the body's celebrity; mummies and bog bodies become famous just for surviving.

Modern celebrity relies upon the erasure of history. In order for the famous person to be idolised and consumed by the public, he or she must be turned into an object of wonder, disconnected from context, history and environment. We are familiar with the way in which ordinary people are transformed through the media into a 'nationally advertised brand' to create what one theorist, David Boorstin, has described as 'a new category of human emptiness'. So, in a similar way, bog bodies and permafrost mummies become famous for being famous, turned into intact objects outside history through their miraculous preservation and then further fetishised by the public excitement upon their rediscovery. The most famous mummy in Europe, the Ice Man, discovered in 1991, was moved in 1998 to the relatively inaccessible town of Bolzano, in northern Italy, but even there it attracted 300,000 visitors in the first year. As the archaeologist of the Ice Man, Konrad Spindler, observed in bewilderment, there was nothing traditionally valuable about his find, in terms of treasure or gold, but it dominated the headlines and turned the 5,000-year-old emaciated man with no genitals into a 'cult figure'.

Mummies and bog bodies were once ordinary people, but they have become famous. Having escaped history once, they take on extraordinary status, displayed as cult objects in museums, disconnected even further from a historical environment. They are celebrated simply for having survived. But such is the bizarre business of fame that this process can be inverted; in other words, bodies survive because they are celebrated. Of course there are obvious examples of this and clear political reasons for it. The bodies of kings and tyrants and totalitarian rulers have been embalmed and preserved in state for centuries. Lenin and Mao are just the culmination of a long tradition going back to the time of the Egyptian pharaohs.

What interests me, however, is not the deliberate embalming of the rich and famous, but the tales of the miraculous somatic preservation of those who are felt to be touched with greatness – the saints, the sinners, the geniuses of the past. These are the figures which, on being dug up again, are found to have outwitted the natural rotting processes of death, presumably because there is something extraordinary about them. Most frequently, the parts of the anatomy that are discovered to have been especially well preserved are precisely those places in which the genius of the person was traditionally thought to reside. So, for example, Milton's luxuriant hair, which in Philip Neve's tale has survived glossy and intact over one hundred years, was popularly thought to be the source of his poetic powers and probably preserved by them. And in the case of the Scottish poet Robert Burns, it was his whole head and not just his hair which was distinctive.

*

September 1815. The whole country is celebrating final victory over the French, after fighting them almost without interruption for twenty-three years. The troops are returning home to a very different world to the one they left behind. And up in south-west Scotland, in Ayrshire, the locals are re-assessing the reputation of their most famous son, the drunken, radical, womanising, firebrand poet who had bitten the dust at the early age of thirty-seven back in 1796.

Robert Burns died during some of the worst months of domestic unrest in the war. He was an enigma, sponsored by the establishment because they thought him a 'heaven-taught ploughman', but monitored closely by the government who were concerned about his sympathy with the French revolutionaries. So after he sweated and shivered his life away, while yet another woman gave birth to yet another of his children, his widow buried him in an obscure corner of the local churchyard, unable to afford anything more than a simple commemorative stone. But now, by 1815, attitudes have changed. With the danger of the French revolution spreading to Britain clearly over, Robert Burns can be safely celebrated as Scotland's national poet. And how better to do that than by establishing a large mausoleum over his remains?

The church wall cannot be moved to allow for a mausoleum to be constructed over Burns' existing grave. So the only possible solution is to open the grave again and move Burns' body. The quickly-formed Monument Committee move into the churchyard at first light and begin digging up the turf. They find three coffins, the Bard and his two sons, all liable to disintegrate at any moment. One touch on the lid of Burns' coffin and it crumbles to reveal the body of the poet, still undecomposed and intact. The whole sight is amazing, but it is the brow and the enormity of the head which impress those crowding in to look.

'The forehead struck everyone as beautifully arched', recalls John McDiarmid of Dumfries, who later tells his memory of the excavation to James Hogg. 'The scalp was rather thickly covered with hair, and the teeth perfectly firm and white.'

As soon as the workmen move the coffin, Burns' body disintegrates. His head, with its brow supposedly bulging with brains, rolls off from the neck. The trunk gets detached and the flesh crumbles into dust. Even so, a few of the men step forward and lift the head to examine its proportions, feeling the lumps and bumps of poetic genius.

Robert Burns' remains, carefully reassembled from this slight débâcle, are safely interred in the new mausoleum. The memory of Burns' prodigious skull persists, however, and in 1834 his grave is opened again in the presence of a professional phrenologist. One of the excavators, who was also present at the 1815 disinterment, identifies Burns' head, by now no more than a skull, and it is carefully cleaned and a plaster cast taken. It is the task of the phrenologist, Mr Armour, hired especially from London, to study the 'size and character' of Robert Burns' head, based upon this cast. He is required to pronounce upon Burns' personal traits, his talents and character based upon his observations. This plaster cast is now the property of the Irvine Burns Society, one of their most jealously guarded possessions.

Meanwhile the excavators are already attempting to measure the size of their hero's head by trying to ram their hats down upon his skull. 'The largest hat of the whole was found too narrow to receive the skull', Hogg writes in his account of the event. The following morning, a special lead box, lined with silk and velvet, is brought to the cemetery and Burns' skull, after being hauled around from one man's hat to the next, is placed carefully inside. The committee witnesses the re-interment of the 'sacred relic'.

The attention given to Robert Burns' head involves veneration but also steers close to violation. The treatment of the 'sacred relic' can easily become exploitative if its original context is forgotten or repressed. A relic, by definition, is a piece of a body which remains and which is usually disconnected from the person and from its original context. Its sacred power stems from its intact nature as a thing to be possessed. And once it has become a thing, a commodity to be consumed, it is all too easy for it to become mistreated, traded and reduced to its material constituents.

*

Egyptian mummies were originally embalmed because it was felt that there was something precious about the human body which needed to be preserved. But in time, that value became concentrated within the physical, desiccated body itself, independent of its spiritual or metaphysical implications. From the sixteenth century onwards, pieces of ground-up mummy were used as medicine, supposedly considered capable of warding off disease and death because the original body had survived with impunity. According to Thomas Pettigrew, the nineteenth-century surgeon and expert on mummies, 'no sooner was it credited that mummy constituted an article of value in the practice of medicine than many spectators embarked in the trade'. Mummies therefore became the ultimate consumable, bought and sold, applied and imbibed, because their significance had been fetishised within the body parts themselves. Pettigrew noted, presumably with some amusement, that the king of France was 'in the habit of always carrying about with him a little packet containing some mummy mixed with pulverised rhubarb, ready to take upon receiving any injury from falls, or other accidents that might happen to him'.

Pettigrew might have written disapprovingly about the trade in mummies for medicine, but he himself did not treat them very much better. Having initially been consulted by Giovanni Belzoni, the great excavator of Egypt, in the analysis of three mummies, he developed a fascination and purchased a mummy at a Sotheby's auction in 1833. He went on to develop the practice of the public 'unrolling' of mummies in front of large audiences, displaying the body on one occasion to the Bishop of Chichester and Viscount Ossultston among others. One assistant, John Davidson, with whom he unrolled a mummy at the Royal Institution, confessed to a slight sense of disappointment that there was nothing more valuable under all the wraps and bandages than the anatomical details. 'I have cause for disappointment in not finding papyrus, coin or other valuable adjunct to mummies', Davidson wrote. But Pettigrew realised the celebrity value of mummies and exploited it to the utmost, using his collection as the centrepiece exhibits for his famous mummy parties. He would invite the great and good to his house and they would mingle among the ancient mummies, sipping champagne while glancing down at blackened, decayed faces and emaciated, stick arms and fingers. 'I brought together many evenings during the season for 6 or 7 years the principal talent of the country and received all travellers', Pettigrew remembered. 'I had in my museum a constant variety of specimens to display. These meetings were most delightful and useful in bringing men together.'

Pettigrew's shameless exhibition of the bodies purely as objects of curiosity, displayed ostensibly for their anatomical detail but actually for their capacity to provoke sensation and excitement, has its contemporary counterpart in Gunther von Hagens' *Body Worlds* exhibition. But in contrast to Pettigrew's and Von Hagens' attention-grabbing disregard for the humanity of their subjects, Southwood Smith recognised the natural difficulty of divorcing man from body. When he dissected and embalmed Jeremy Bentham, he had actually to urge his audience to make the mental leap in thinking of the body before them not as the figure of the philosopher they had known and admired but as a collection of anatomical parts which could be put to good use in the study of medicine. Indeed he acknowledged his own ethical resistance to the treatment of the corpse simply as a thing rather than deeply bound up with the man he had known. 'The very particles of matter which compose this dull mass, a few hours ago were a real part of him', he told his audience. 'I cannot separate them in my imagination from him; and I approach them with the profounder reverence, and I gaze upon them with the deeper affection, because they are all that now remain to me.' But valiantly he proceeded in carrying out his friend's commands in the auto-iconisation, disconnecting all associations and emotions from the object beneath his knife. 'It is my duty', he bravely stated, 'to conquer the reluctance I may feel to such a disposition of the dead.'

Southwood Smith managed to excavate Bentham's inner organs while maintaining a sense of respect and reverence for his friend. But mostly once the archaeological body is understood as simply Southwood Smith's 'particles of matter' rather than as a person, it is ripe for exploitation. Milton's ribs and hair acquired a commercial value as objects which supposedly correlated with the spiritual value they possessed as pieces of genius. But when they were chopped into smaller and smaller pieces and, as a result, the supply came increasingly to meet the demand, the price dropped. The commercial value of mummified bodies seems to be independent of the spiritual.

Certainly when Robert Burns was excavated, there were two types of relic-hunters present. In charge of the operation were those who pretended to a type of serious archaeology, who were interested in Burns' head for the supposed insight it might yield into the source of his poetic power. Meanwhile, hovering around the edge of the grave like hyenas ready to pounce when they get the chance, were those who valued dead body parts not as pseudo-literary evidence but purely for their commercial value, as items to trade on the black market. Such was the climate of commercialism in the trade of body parts at the time that even the serious excavators did not feel themselves immune from feelings of greedy speculation. When they dug up Burns' grave the second time in 1834, they chose to do it under cover of darkness to avoid the spectators and relic-hunters. But the nocturnal setting turned them into the worst kind of exploitative anatomical resurrectionists themselves:

> Again the party conferred privately, and proceeded stealthily, one after another, by the quietest paths, and after clambering over the churchyard walls, met by appointment, in front of the mausoleum. In this, it must be confessed, there was something degrading, which reminded us of the horrid trade of body-snatching; but the most profound secrecy was indispensable, and if there be any who feel inclined to impute blame, all we can say is – our motives were good, and totally alien to those of idle curiosity.

Body-snatching, the early nineteenth-century criminal's response to a growing demand for bodies in the anatomy schools and, given the meagre supply, soaring prices paid for corpses, constitutes the logical extreme of the tradition of coldly treating bodies as objects or relics to venerate or violate. By the 1820s it is estimated that London hospitals alone required about three hundred corpses a year to train their surgeons. Rather than finding bodies that had somehow miraculously survived the ravages of time, the body-snatchers, or 'resurrectionists', as they were also known, dug up new graves in order to rip corpses from their natural environment and subject them to a very different kind of history to the expected one of gradual decay in the cemetery. There were rich rewards. In 1800, resurrectionists might earn two or three guineas a body, but by 1828 the price had risen to eight or nine guineas and occasionally as much as fourteen guineas was paid. A flourishing protection business also emerged. In 1818, for example, Edward Little Bridgman started advertising strong cast-iron anti-resurrectionist coffins, which could not be opened, for three pounds and ten shillings. Burke and Hare in Edinburgh even began to resort to murder to obtain their bodies, in order to avoid the difficulty of digging them up in the heavily fortified cemeteries.

Body-snatching altered the architecture of graveyards. It had a significant influence upon the archaeological landscape of cemeteries, still evident in the railings and iron barriers protecting old graves in Edinburgh today. But while the concerned community undertook practical measures to deter the grave robbers, which did to some extent manifest their anxiety about the trade in corpses, the full extent of the horror of the business only became apparent at moments when the corpses were recognised, when they ceased to look like a business transaction and became people once again. At moments of recognition, when the excavator or dissector was brought face to face, as it were, with a person rather than an object, the anatomisation of bodies became reinvested with a type of ethics, albeit in pretty perverse circumstances. In other words, the uncanny return of the dead, even at the moment when they were being most commodified, could carry some ethical or moral pressure.

One prime example is the case of the eighteenth-century novelist, Lawrence Sterne. He was buried in St George's Church, Hanover Square, in March 1768. But shortly afterwards the grave was robbed and his body sold to the University of Cambridge for dissection. It was arranged on the slab for the professor of anatomy, Professor Charles Collignon, to give his lecture. It seems that Collignon recognised the body, telling somebody later that 'he recognised Sterne's face the minute he saw the body'. He confessed also to a friend, the Master of Emmanuel College, that 'the body of Mr Sterne had been sent down to Cambridge and was anatomized. It was stolen from the burying ground beyond Tyburn where it was interred and was recognised by sevr. persons who knew him.' Incredibly, even though Collignon recognised the author of *Tristram Shandy*, he proceeded to dissect him regardless, salvaging his conscience by convincing himself that the body was somehow mixed up in the collection of executed criminals near Tyburn, officially the anatomists' only source of bodies for dissection. Only once the dissection had taken place were Sterne's remains secretly taken back to London and reburied, not of course 'beyond Tyburn', but in the smart area of Hanover Square, where they had first been laid to rest. The potentially criminal activity in which Collignon was engaged, cutting up a famous novelist who had just recently been given the rites and ceremony of a funeral, was repressed by him and only returned as a Freudian 'false memory'. He erroneously recalled that Sterne had been buried near the gallows at Tyburn, supposedly alongside other criminals, in order to surmount the uncanny revelation that Sterne was an innocent victim of a foul practice, a fellow human being who had been caught up in a nefarious trade.

Robert Louis Stevenson also revealed how the grisly trade of body-snatching could be challenged by the ethics of ghostly recognition. His short story, 'The Body Snatcher', follows closely the real events surrounding the nefarious activities of Burke and Hare. The story's main protagonist, Fettes, is a young medical student, a demonstrator in the laboratory of the real, historical Mr Knox, the infamous professor of medicine who bought the bodies which Burke and Hare supplied. Fettes is also the assistant to a fictional young doctor called Macfarlane. Macfarlane and Fettes become close. When they run short of bodies, they 'drive far into the country in Macfarlane's gig, visit and desecrate some lonely graveyard, and return before dawn with their booty to the door of the dissecting-room'. During the course of the story, Macfarlane murders an enemy called Gray and delivers it to Fettes for the students to dissect. While Fettes panics over the potential charge of murder, Macfarlane organises the practical aspects of the dissection. The dissection itself, when 'the members of the unhappy Gray were dealt out to one and to another', constitutes the final act of turning the body into an object and removing any sign of its humanity and therefore the morality or immorality of its demise. Fettes watches as the students cut into the body. It gradually loses the identifying characteristics of Gray and becomes simply a grisly collection of objects, the scattered remains of blood and tissue. It seems that the ultimate perverse alienation has been accomplished, as Fettes watches, with 'increasing joy', the 'dreadful process of disguise', the transformation of a human body into a thing.

But Gray returns to haunt Fettes. During a grave-robbing expedition sometime later with Macfarlane in a remote country churchyard, the lantern, their only source of light, is knocked over. They continue to excavate the body in darkness and carry it, in a sack, to their carriage. After returning some of the way to Edinburgh, they become suspicious of the body, which seems remarkably large for a farmer's wife, which they had supposedly exhumed, so they decide to light a fresh lantern and inspect the contents of the sack:

> As Fettes took the lamp his companion untied the fastenings of the sack and drew down the cover from the head. The light fell very clear upon the dark, well-moulded features and smooth-shaven cheeks of a too familiar countenance, often beheld in dreams of both of these young men. [It was] the body of the dead and long-dissected Gray.

It is a typical Gothic plot, the inner psychological anxiety – in this case guilt over the murder of Gray – becoming projected externally into a literal object of horror. Being pursued by the undead is a common narrative device, from vampires to vengeful mummies. Stevenson draws upon all these traditions from the horror tradition. But what is particularly interesting here is the fact that Gray, unlike traditional Gothic figures of terror, is not ghastly to behold. In fact, he is almost handsome, his features 'well-moulded' and his cheeks 'smooth-shaven'. Despite being 'long-dissected', he is perfectly preserved, impervious to the ravages of time and the destructive processes of history. The two men recognise him immediately, as a fellow human being rather than a corpse to be traded, as unmistakably Gray. The uncanny return of the dead here operates as a chastening moral check upon the lawlessness of the protagonists' activities. The revelation brings with it not some Gothic sensationalism, thrilling purely for its aesthetic qualities and outside any ethical framework, but rather an important sense of accountability, a reminder that actions carry consequences and take place in a social and moral context.

*

It has proved difficult to treat mummified, archaeological bodies in an ethical way. They have already defied the organic processes of history by resisting normal disintegration in the grave and thus they disturb the familiar conceptions of humanity, mortality, morality. Yet they can return the spectator to a more acute social and historical awareness by carrying upon them the marks of previous wrongdoing and thus crucially bearing witness to grievous transgression. The bog bodies unearthed in Denmark, for example, reveal the violence and victimisation endemic in prehistoric culture. P.V. Glob describes the shock of discovering that Tollund Man, despite looking as if he were lying in the 'natural attitude of sleep', had actually met a violent end:

> The air of gentle tranquillity about the man was shattered when a small lump of peat was removed from beside his head. This disclosed a rope, made of two leather thongs twisted together, which encircled the neck in a noose drawn tight into the throat and then coiled like a snake over the shoulder and down across the back. After this discovery, the wrinkled forehead and set mouth seemed to take on a look of affliction.

Indeed, the bog bodies turn out to have been preserved in the peat because they were all sacrificed there and not cremated or buried in normal burial grounds where they would have decomposed naturally. The miraculous mummification, which challenges nature, emerges as the product of an unnatural, violent demise. Glob invests the body with human emotion, made possible because of the preservation of the face with its expression, the 'look of affliction', and by humanising it in this way, he offers an ethically-charged picture of the historical past.

Archaeologists attempt to treat mummies with forensic objectivity but also with a degree of moral sensitivity. This is a delicate and sometimes ambivalent balance to maintain, which requires thinking of the body both as an object and as a human being. Unlike the bog bodies, the Ice Man, discovered in 1991, initially seemed almost non-human. The couple who first came across him thought that they had spotted some rubbish, and even once they realised it was human they described its appearance as like leather: 'a leather-brown round shaved-looking skull'. A concerted effort later was made to find a name for the body ('Ötzi') in order to invest it with some humanity. As a newspaper reporter commented, 'This desiccated, horrible corpse must be made more positive, more charming if it's going to be a good story.'

The confusion between forensic and moral approaches to mummies is evident in the prevailing obsession among archaeologists with the bog-man's or iceman's 'last meal'. Partly associated with Christ's 'last supper' and partly with the convict's 'last dinner' before execution, the last meal consumed by the men and women who were then preserved in the peat bogs of Denmark or the ice glaciers of the Alps become the absorbing interest of archaeologists. The contents of the stomach and guts are analysed and, from that data, the ancient diet is reconstructed. The last meal of Lindow Man, a broth made from mistletoe, is displayed on the board beside the body in the British Museum. Out in Denmark, both Tollund Man and Grauballe Man were investigated by Dr Hans Helbaek, who washed out the smaller and larger intestines and studied the contents, which he found to be a type of gruel based on barley, rye and other types of grain and weed. Since the meal seemed to be vegetarian and yet Iron Age man almost certainly did eat meat, the conclusion is that 'men chosen for sacrifice were given a special meal'. This account implies that Tollund Man and Grauballe Man are both sacred and condemned, marked out from the norm not only by their preservation but apparently even when they were alive, when they were selected as sacrificial victims. So the bodies seem to be normal and abnormal, sharing our humanity by their need to eat but also challenging it by their role as victims in some strange rite.

It is the common humanity that links present spectators to the bodies salvaged from the past which the poet Seamus Heaney, more than any other writer, has crucially asserted. In his series of 'bog body' poems, which focuses upon bodies dug up from the bogs in Ireland and in Denmark, he draws lines of connection both geographically, between Ireland and Scandinavia, and also historically, between the Iron Age past and the twentieth-century present. It is our capacity to feel sympathy, to sense a strong identification with a body now returned from the distant past which, he implies, ensures its ethical treatment and our moral and political awakening. By looking at the victims of Iron Age sacrifice, Heaney can confront the guilt for the violence in Northen Ireland in which he feels implicated. He confesses that his sense of pity was stirred when he first saw the pictures of the Danish bodies in P.V. Glob's *The Bog People*, more even than he consciously felt for the victims of Irish sectarianism. 'My emotions, my feelings, whatever those instinctive energies are that have to be engaged for a poem, those energies quickened more when contemplating a victim, strangely, from 2,000 years ago than they did from contemplating a man at the end of a road being swept up into a plastic bag.'

In his poem 'Tollund Man', Heaney suggests the force of this 'quickening' sympathy when imagining a visit to see the Bog Man at Aarhus. He might feel the same reverence towards the Earth goddess to whom the man was sacrificed:

> In the flat country near by
> Where they dug him out,
> His last gruel of winter seeds
> Caked in his stomach,
>
> Naked except for
> The cap, noose and girdle,
> I will stand a long time.
> Bridegroom to the goddess,
>
> She tightened her torc on him ...

The complicated syntax of these verses suggests a mutuality between the Iron Age man and the poet. Is it the bog man who is 'naked except for/ The cap, noose and girdle' or is it Heaney? And who exactly is the 'bridegroom to the goddess'? The syntax and punctuation indicate that the bog body is the bridegroom, the victim of the goddess's tightening 'torc'. But the verse form suggests that Heaney himself could take on the role: 'I will stand a long time/ Bridegroom to the goddess'.

Heaney also imagines sharing the same feeling of tragic fatalism as the Iron Age man in the moments before his execution:

> Something of his sad freedom
> As he rode the tumbril
> Should come to me, driving ...

The natural connection between the world of Tollund Man and Heaney's own world is alluded to through Heaney's use of anachronistic terms. He draws on words and phrases from Catholicism to describe the rituals of Iron Age sacrifice. Jutland is referred to as a place of 'man-killing parishes'; the bog preserves the body like embalming liquid, working on him 'to a saint's kept body'. The bogs of Denmark are witnessed with unashamedly twentieth-century eyes, so that Iron Age violence becomes Catholic republican violence and its victims equally Iron Age 'peat-brown heads' or twentieth-century 'stockinged corpses' – necessary sacrifices, in both cases, to opaque causes. Sacrifice becomes horribly normal under Heaney's Irish perspective. No wonder, we might think, that Heaney confirms the familiarity of Aarhus at the end of the poem:

> Out there in Jutland
> In the old man-killing parishes
> I will feel lost,
> Unhappy and at home.

In Heaney's final 'at home', however, we hear Freud's uncertainty about 'homeliness' in his essay on the uncanny. The homely or 'heimlich' can also mean unhomely or 'unheimlich'. There is, apparently, alienation lurking even at the most comforting moment of familiarity. Heaney is very aware of the awkwardness of what he is proposing, the possible disconnections between Tollund Man and a victim of the Troubles, the lack of proper comparison. A clue to his sense of awkwardness, it seems to me, lies in that 'sad freedom' of the Tollund Man before execution mentioned earlier. Why 'freedom'? This is, in fact, one of the many examples of oxymoron which litter the 'bog body' poems and which lend them their atmosphere of strangeness. 'Sad freedom', 'perishable treasure', 'leathery beauty', 'vivid cast', 'strange fruit': the shocking awkwardness of these phrases mirrors the sudden disruption of history which presages the bodies' emergence from the ground. But Tollund man's 'sad freedom' implies also his bewildering disconnection both from his own times and from Heaney's own. Are we all 'sadly free', unable to understand either the violent politics and customs of our own time or the savagery and hope salvaged from the past?

> Something of his sad freedom
> As he rode the tumbril
> Should come to me, driving,
> Saying the names
>
> Tollund, Grauballe, Nebelgard,
> Watching the pointing hands
> Of country people,
> Not knowing their tongue.

At the end of the poem, all that Heaney can be certain of is uncertainty. His imagined visit to Aarhus, which promised some archaeological answers and redemption, 'germinating' the bodies of Irish victims, ends in 'not knowing', feeling 'lost,/ Unhappy and at home'. Significantly the only direct future tense in the poem is the statement of future bewilderment – 'I will feel lost' – while the imagined identification with Tollund Man takes place in the subjunctive, or the future conditional: 'I could risk blasphemy', 'Something of his sad freedom ... Should come to me'. Imagined hope and connection – the germination – is set against certain disquiet – lost and unhappy.

Heaney considered the consequences of this disconnection further in the bog body poems which appeared in his collection *North*. Rather than the bewildered yet sympathetic approach to Tollund Man, the treatment of the bodies in these poems is almost voyeuristic, exploitative, violent. The bog queen is wrenched up from the ground, 'barbered and stripped', her bones 'hacked', her hair 'cut'. The Grauballe Man's head is deliberately lifted to reveal his 'slashed throat'. The 'Strange Fruit' girl has been beheaded and the excavators have 'unswaddled' her hair. Heaney concerns himself with the act of witnessing these atrocities, displaying them in museums, writing about them in poems. The girl's head in 'Strange Fruit' has been exhibited with a combination of 'reverence' and grisly fascination at the work of the 'axe'. Both she and the Grauballe Man are caught 'in the scales/ with beauty and atrocity', the violence of their death made uncomfortably aesthetic.

Heaney, writing these poems, finds himself complicit in this 'beatification'. In 'Punishment' he chides himself for enjoying looking at the long-preserved consequences of ethnic violence in the bog, while disconnecting himself from their parallel in Northern Ireland:

> I am the artful voyeur
>
> of your brain's exposed
> and darkened combs,
> your muscles' webbing
> and all your numbered bones:
>
> I who have stood dumb
> when your betraying sisters,
> cauled in tar,
> wept by the railings ...

Heaney fancies the girl and hates himself for doing so. Accordingly the aesthetic response to these bodies with their 'leathery beauty' is only possible if the circumstances of their original history are forgotten and if the comparisons with contemporary politics – republican women punished for links with the British military – are suppressed.

So where does this leave Heaney's ethical writing? He reveals the problems of forcing a sympathetic connection between Tollund Man and himself, which results in a simplification of the violence both in Denmark and in Ireland. And yet to disconnect the two experiences, to see the bodies as 'the artful voyeur' rather than as the sympathetic concerned citizen, is to exploit the archaeological past for a private moment of virtual erotic excitement. The answer, it seems to me, comes in Heaney's recognition that these issues must be confronted, that these bodies must be witnessed whatever the problems and implications. At the end of the sonnet 'Strange Fruit', the bog girl has herself transcended both the horror of violation and that of veneration through her capacity to keep looking:

> Beheaded girl, outstaring axe
> And beatification, outstaring
> What had begun to feel like reverence.

The bog girl must of course keep looking because her eyelids have withered and her eyeballs themselves disintegrated. Only the sockets hold the gaze of the viewer steadfastly. But it could be said that Heaney's poems are similar attempts to 'outstare' the 'axe and beatification', to 'outstare' both the historical specificity of the violence and its aesthetic transformation. In this poem, at any rate, the repeated word 'outstaring' does just that: it shatters the polished sonnet form by the solecism of its repetition and thereby prevents the easy transformation of this grisly head into the subject for poetry.

Heaney's ethical compulsion comes from the sense that we are all stuck fast in the same historical conditions which demand a response. The soil holds us to account: literally in the case of the bog bodies, metaphorically or emotionally in the case of the poet and indeed that of his readers. So in 'Kinship':

> I grew out of all this
> like a weeping willow
> inclined to
> the appetites of gravity.

'The appetites of gravity' ensure that we remain rooted in our history, forced to confront repeatedly the capacity for tribal violence in any community and the capacity for conniving silence. The bog, for Heaney, provides the ethical answer. In 'Kinship', he uses it to challenge Yeats' great modernist vision of disintegration and dispersal, of the abrogation of the moral sense ('Things fall apart/ The centre cannot hold'):

> This centre holds
> and spreads,
> sump and seedbed,
> a bag of waters
>
> and a melting grave.

While that 'centre' might deliver up evidence of the worst atrocities, in the form of the Grauballe Man or the bog queen, yet it 'holds' us in a challenging act of witness which ensures that each body matters somehow, that there is something valuable and important from which we can learn in the 'melting grave'.

*

During the 1970s, indigenous groups in North America and Australia began to protest against the unethical practices of archaeologists. The bones and bodies of their ancestors had been treated like any other archaeological objects, seized from graves, removed to laboratories for study and distant museums for display, taken far away from their original home soil. In America, activists took their case to Congress, where the Society for American Archaeology (SAA) fought attempted legislation for about seven years. Eventually the SAA agreed to compromise, to hold a 'national dialogue' with native American groups, and in 1990 the 'Native American Graves Protection and Repatriation Act' was passed. In Australia, the Australian Archaeological Association drew up an equivalent code of ethics in 1991, requiring excavators to consult with the living descendants of any human remains which are found. In both countries, institutions are handing back large collections of skeletons for burial or cremation. But tensions are still running high, since the spiritual or political priorities of the indigenous groups and the forensic, scientific priorities of the archaeologists drive them in different directions. Ethical archaeology is said to be based on a careful compromise between respecting the sensitivity of the native people whose ancestors are being unearthed and a commitment to extending our scientific knowledge. 'It is highly probable that increasing numbers of indigenous communities will co-operate and even encourage archaeological endeavours once they come to perceive the benefits of the knowledge that can be obtained in this way', writes the archaeological commentator Paul Bahn.

But the ethics of digging up bodies should be based upon more than simply the 'benefits' of the scientific information it offers us. It should, as this chapter has suggested, be shaped by considerations of the importance and ambivalence of history and the significance of the body to remind us of what is natural and ethical. It should be shaped by the need to bear witness and to mourn. 'In our "advanced" society', the archaeologist Don Brothwell has wisely observed, 'when matters of death and violence are all too commonplace, we nevertheless hasten it out of the way, disposing of it through well-established funerary practices. In the bodies from the past, we are reminded of its certainty, then as now.' I know that, personally, I am squeamish about just such an encounter with the dead, with the uncanny. But Seamus Heaney leads the way in pointing out the simultaneous difficulty and necessity of confronting bodies from the past, bodies which retain the marks of politics, history, violence and reverence. In Heaney's vision, which holds us altogether despite ruptures and differences, there is a meeting point, a vital 'national dialogue'.

4

Fulfilling Desires: Erotic Excavation

Sigmund Freud's study at 20 Maresfield Gardens, Hampstead, is crammed with antiquities. When he moved to the house in September 1938, to escape the Nazis who had invaded Vienna two months before, his main concern was the fate of his collection of archaeological objects. It was uncertain whether the Nazis would confiscate certain items or whether the authorities would prevent the collection from leaving the country. In the end nothing was confiscated and the whole collection was packed up and shipped to London. Freud was able to recreate his study in Hampstead apparently exactly as it had been in Bergasse 19, Vienna.

Visit the house in Hampstead today and you will see Freud's desk crowded with marble and bronze figures, erected like a barricade several statues deep between the work-space of the desk and the rest of the study beyond. There are marble heads arranged along a shelf, and two free-standing busts in the window beside the desk. A table is covered with ancient bronze axeheads and Greek vases, while three glass cabinets are packed with all sorts of antiquities, including an Egyptian ritual boat. In among the bookshelves, where Schliemann's *Ilios* and Arthur Evans' *The Palace of Minos* are prominently displayed, are numerous small Egyptian and Roman figures. As you walk through the doorway to the library, which is also filled with antiquities, you pass a plaster reproduction of the famous classical relief *Gradiva*, a woman picking her way carefully along the street, 'her gown slightly raised and her ankle exposed'.

Freud regularly drew comparisons between psychoanalysis and archaeology, turning to his collection of antiquities around his consulting room for illustration. When he was treating Ernst Lanzer, for example, the patient who has become known as The Rat Man because his deepest fear was being gnawed by rats, Freud compared the depths of the mind with the depths of earth mined by archaeologists. Through talking to the Rat Man, Freud had discovered that apparently trivial details or tasks seemed to terrify him, and it was as a result of this finding that Freud began to develop the concept of the conscious and the unconscious mind. The conscious mind, he explained to the Rat Man, was always being worn away by daily events. But the unconscious mind remained relatively unchangeable, always lying below the surface and liable to erupt at any time. To illustrate his point, he swung round on his chair and indicated all the Pompeian antiquities around the room. 'Look at these objects found in a tomb', he told the Rat Man. They were like the unconscious thoughts in his mind, originally preserved in the soil for centuries. He went on: 'Their burial was their preservation. The destruction of Pompeii is only beginning now that it has been dug up.'

In many ways, Freud's collection of antiquities served as a metaphor or substitute for other, deeper psychological concerns. The care with which Freud organised the removal of his collection from Vienna, and the precision with which he arranged all the objects in his new house in Hampstead, suggest that the collection became a substitute for his sense of home. Reminding him of the past, of the ancestors who had fashioned the figures and of the ancestors whom they represented, the antiquities arguably offered Freud a version of rootedness not available to him otherwise in the turbulent years before the Second World War.

Or one could argue that the collection was a substitute for sex. Freud once confessed to his physician that acquiring ancient sculptures was an 'addiction second in intensity only to his nicotine addiction'. Since he believed that all addictions were just substitutes for the primal addiction, masturbation, both cigar-smoking and looking at his phalanx of figurines could be understood as displacements for less acceptable desires. In that case, the story that Freud would sometimes take a new antique object with him to the dining room to fondle as he ate in the evenings takes on a new significance.

Or the collection could have been used by Freud as an alternative for engaging directly with people, with his patients. The curator of an exhibition of Freud's collection, Lynn Gamwell, described all the 'hundreds of human and animal figures' crowding round Freud's study as 'a huge audience'. 'Freud treated these figures as his companions', she wrote. But it seems to me that they could equally be seen as a barrier, erected between Freud and his patient, to prevent and deflect fluent and mutual conversation.

Or the antiquities could have been trophies displayed to illustrate Freud's taste and luck as a collector, open to a similar scrutiny to the patients' supposedly private case histories, which were preserved for public consumption.

Freud's antiquities might have been a substitute for all kinds of neuroses and perversions. But of course, archaeology itself is often a displacement for other concerns. The act of excavation is centrally bound up with all sorts of cultural anxieties and desires. The new post-processual archaeologists expose the political and ideological assumptions which permeate the apparently innocent process of digging. But it seems that

80

even they are not immune to the seductions of the soil. One trendy post-processual, Michael Shanks, consciously defended the notion of 'excavation as striptease': 'This pleasure of coming to know is not about taking and raping. This is a pleasure existing in the interplay of performer and audience.' But he also inadvertently and subconsciously used images earlier in his book of penetrating the soil – 'delving deeper' – in order to grasp what he thought were appropriate metaphors to describe the normal mentality of the archaeologist. The feminist archaeologist, Meg Conkey, was quick to draw attention to the aggressive masculinity of Shanks' writing, its emphasis upon the phallic spade and the phallic eye. Certainly the erotic associations involved in stripping away the soil seem to be never far from the male archaeologist's thoughts. 'Excavation is like undressing a woman,' my archaeology supervisor Amit Romano told me during one dig, as he kicked aside the stones that I had spent all day painstakingly brushing free from the dirt. 'I'm not interested in treasure or objects in museums. Archaeology is all in the process, not in the final result. It is very exciting gradually uncovering a pot. But five minutes after it is pulled out of the earth, I am no longer interested.'

So the earth teases the archaeologist with its promise of material evidence, the literal fulfilment of the search for answers, but offers only the imprints and traces of that evidence now vanished. It entices with the possibility of direct access with the past or literal, unequivocal knowledge but also, in its ellipses, absences and mysteries, can also be interpreted metaphorically. So too for Freud, archaeology is both a literal obsession, interesting for its own sake, and also a metaphor, adopted to suggest other, less tangible meanings.

Freud's interest in archaeology has been mainly of concern to psycho-analysts rather than to archaeologists. Consequently the metaphorical significance of excavation in his writing has attracted more attention than its possible literal origin. But Freud was as interested in literal nineteenth-century excavation and archaeological discovery as in metaphor. This is, after all, the man who said that he had read more books on archaeology than on psychology. The site of Pompeii, I believe, held a particular resonance for Freud. Here was a site which, covered so suddenly by volcanic ash, had not been subject to the usual process of what Freud called 'wearing-away' but had supposedly been perfectly preserved. Here was a site too, which right from the earliest excavations in the eighteenth century, had been associated with forbidden desires, with the mysterious and the erotic. Here, finally, was a site where bodies from the past had tantalisingly left a more vivid impress than anywhere before or since and where the excavator had literally to fill in the imprints to fulfil his desire for communication with the dead. Pompeii, in short, represented that ambivalent zone between presence and absence, between literalism and

81

metaphor, which Freud found so compelling in his excavation of the psyche.

*

When people first started to dig Pompeii out of the ash in the mid-eighteenth century, it seemed to them that they were bringing the town back to life. Unlike other civilisations from the past, which gradually disintegrate and crumble away or get covered over by later buildings, Pompeii had been literally buried under volcanic ash in two days, cut off in the prime of life, dying young and intact. Now the excavators were restoring her to a second existence. 'I stood within the City disinterred', wrote Percy Bysshe Shelley, and another poet, William Branwhite Clarke, commented that Pompeii 'has risen as it were from its grave, where it had slept nearly 1800 years; and its scenes are as fresh to the eye, as before the catastrophe which ruined it'. Cashing in on the public mood, a law student at the Inner Temple versified this new fascination with Pompeii's disinterment with almost necrophiliac excitement: 'The shroud of years thrown back, thou dost revive,/ Half-raised, half-buried, dead, yet still alive!'

The association of Pompeii with death and with a type of mysterious and erotic morbidity probably derived from the manner of its excavation. This was haphazard and involved unsystematic tunnelling of exploratory shafts down into the hardened lava and mud. An Austrian cavalry officer, Prince de'Elbeuf, was the first to order a tunnel in 1728; his tunnel emerged, in fact, in the amphitheatre of Herculaneum. In the course of his digging he found three statues and sent them back to the Elector of Saxony and head of the Holy Roman Empire to be displayed in Dresden. About twenty years later, Charles III, king of Spain and Naples, whose wife, Maria Amalia, had seen Elbeuf's statues in her father's possession in Dresden, commissioned Alcubierre, a Spanish engineering officer, to lead a new excavation. Urged by the king to find treasure for his museum, Alcubierre moved away from the rock-hard soil – originally mud and molten lava – above Herculaneum and on to the softer earth – originally ash – above Pompeii. In April 1748, he brought the first body of a victim of the volcano to the surface. A few months later, he began to clear away the earth from the amphitheatre and he also discovered one of the main high streets. Alcubierre's successor, a Swiss military officer called Charles Weber, turned out to be a distinct improvement upon the earlier archaeologist. He worked more systematically, drawing a careful map of all the tunnels and alleyways, and the buildings to which they led, and also writing up a detailed account of the excavation. In Pompeii, he located the main streets and uncovered various houses and paintings and charred manuscripts.

But under both Alcubierre and Weber, the work was slow and chaotic. The great art critic Johann Joachim Winckelmann wrote despairingly in 1771 that Alcubierre knew 'as much of antiquities as the moon does of lobsters' and that consequently many antiquities had been lost in his search for elusive treasure. Winckelmann found just eight men working on the ruins of Pompeii when he visited in 1762. He complained that the excavators were too secretive; nobody was actually allowed to see Weber's drawings. Most annoyingly, the archaeologists were more interested in finding treasure than in preserving and displaying the site. When they had finished exploring a building, they would use it to dump the rubble in which they dug out of the next house. As Winckelmann observed somewhat testily, 'I know that strangers, particularly travellers, who can take but a cursory view of these works, wish, that all the rubbish was entirely removed, so as to give them an opportunity of seeing, as in the plan of which I have been speaking, the inside of the whole subterranean city of Herculaneum.'

Winckelmann wanted the excavation of Pompeii to be carried out systematically because he felt that Pompeii potentially had something to teach people. He wrote a widely circulated letter about the faults of the current excavation and he agitated for reform. Pompeii, he thought, had been buried precisely so that the antiquarians of his age could rediscover her: 'By their being secluded from public view for near 1700 years, by the hand of Providence, it seems as if they were reserved by the Omnipotent Disposer of all things, for the instruction and improvement of the present century.' Instead of the secrecy of the Spanish and Italian excavators, the dig should have been recorded publicly and efficiently so that its findings could be made available to as wide a group of people as possible. And instead of covering over the buildings as soon as they had been searched, so that they remained dark and mysterious, the whole city should have been exposed to the general view. As Winckelmann's fellow countryman, Goethe, commented after visiting the excavation, 'It is a thousand pities that the site was not excavated methodically by German miners.'

What Pompeii was supposed to teach the onlooker, according to Winckelmann, was the transience of human existence and the importance of showing humility before God. Winckelmann, the aesthete who was to be murdered a few years later by his homosexual lover in a sleazy travellers' inn, wanted Pompeii to encourage piety. 'These antiquities afford the most striking moral reflections to the mind of the contemplative', he wrote. 'We see the transitory glory of all earthly objects.' Inspired by these moral aspirations for the excavation, the universities of Oxford and Cambridge frequently set Pompeii as the subject for various poetry competitions.

Young students, who had not actually been to Pompeii but had read about it in books written by men such as Winckelmann, submitted worthy poems filled with pious reflections about mortality and ignorant pagan arrogance. In 1819 the future historian Thomas Macaulay won the Cambridge Chancellor's Medal for 'Pompeii; A Poem'. And in Oxford, in 1827, the future clergyman Rev. R.S. Hawkes claimed the university prize with such lines as 'Devoted City! could not aught avail/ When the dark omen told thy fearful tale.' The moral was clear. The pagan Pompeians had lived a life of luxury and riot, ignoring God, and therefore the volcanic eruption had been an act of divine punishment. The fact that at the very moment that they were buried in ash, they appeared to have been out on a pagan jamboree at the theatre – theatre tickets and skeletons at the theatre had been discovered by archaeologists – just confirmed for the puritanical poets that their days rightly had been numbered.

But despite Winckelmann's and Goethe's best criticisms and suggestions, Pompeii and Herculaneum were not excavated by 'German miners' and this affected the impression of visitors to the site. In other words, instead of being systematic, open and morally instructive, the excavation was mysterious, secretive and chaotic. The digging up of these ancient cities thus appealed not so much to the intellectual mind as to the lower, more basic instincts of the public. In 1740 the antiquarian Horace Walpole, son of Britain's first prime minister, visited Herculaneum and later described the mile-long tunnels and paths: 'The path is very narrow, just wide enough and high enough for one man to walk upright. They have hollowed, as they found it easiest to work, and have carried their streets not exactly where were the ancient ones, but sometimes before houses, sometimes through them.' When the architect Robert Adam visited the excavation of Herculaneum in 1755, he was taken down to the underground amphitheatre by the light of torches, as if he were visiting a 'coal-mine worked by galley slaves'. Indeed these underground trips made viewing Herculaneum and Pompeii seem like a journey to Homer's underworld or Dante's inferno, with the sinister, dimly lit passages resembling the different circles of Hell. Certainly the sketch of Alcubierre's excavation of Herculaneum, published in 1782 in Richard de Saint-Non's *Voyage Pittoresque de Naples et de Sicile*, reveals an almost Dantean vision of the entry into the Inferno (Plate 4). Some men stand on the cliff's edge at the top, presumably at the daylight, rational level of the eighteenth century, while other men beaver away with wheelbarrows of earth, carting off the rubble left by the volcano and exposing just the top of a temple. Meanwhile other men hang over the edge, staring down into the abyss, invisible to our eyes, below. It is a striking image of the excavation of a city, which evokes popular ideas of the Underworld, the land of the dead located beneath the earth.

4. Fulfilling Desires: Erotic Excavation

Even the parts of the city that were exposed seemed ghostly. Since the archaeologists had not devised a way of preserving them, they were crumbling away as soon as they were unearthed. The artist Sir William Gell went round drawing the scenes whenever he could, with difficulty, obtain permission to do so from the chief archaeologist, in order to record them before they disappeared. The pictures he drew depicted a curious mixture of times. He showed the buildings in ruins, as they were at the time of his visit in 1819, but he also peopled them with ancient Pompeians wandering around the ruins, walking the streets once again, sitting by their baths, as if they were alive. Gell's pictures allowed the ancient inhabitants briefly to rise from the dead and haunt the streets before they disappeared from view once more.

One of the features which most fascinated visitors to Pompeii in the first century of its excavation was the discovery of the skeletons. Often these were found, not carefully composed and buried, but arrested wherever they had happened to be and doing whatever they had happened to be doing at the time the volcano struck. William Hamilton, the British ambassador in Naples at the end of the eighteenth century and key populariser of the Pompeii dig, drew pictures of the excavations with the skeletons still in place. Two of the best loved skeletons were discovered in 1766 in what became known as the Gladiators' Barracks, shackled by the wrist and still chained to the wall. These were thought probably to have been prisoners or gladiators, who had not even been released once the volcanic eruption had begun but were left to succumb helplessly to the fumes. William Hamilton pointed out gleefully that the skulls of these men were 'now placed on the shelves for the inspection of the curious'. Writers reacted with a kind of delicious horror at the thought. How could the pagan Pompeians be so cruel as to keep their fellow human beings chained up when fiery destruction was facing them all anyway?

So Pompeii became a symbol of death, a macabre mausoleum. Goethe confessed that 'the mummified city left us with a curious, rather disagreeable impression' while Sir Walter Scott returned from a visit exclaiming 'The City of the Dead! The City of the Dead!' But although these writers claimed ostensibly to feel uncomfortable about the funereal quality of Pompeii, in fact it was precisely this macabre aspect of the excavation which fascinated them. 'There have been many disasters in this world, but few which have given so much delight to posterity, and I have seldom seen anything so interesting', Goethe confessed, after visiting the city a second time. Writers queued up to express their delight in the Gothic search into the grave. The clergyman John Hughes, for example, inspired by the accounts of William Hamilton and William Gell, excitedly pointed out the unnatural, sinister implications of digging out the Pompeian dead:

> It is as if, raised by some demon spell,
> The dead should wander for a space
> Mongst aliens to their name and race,
> The secrets of the grave's abyss to tell.

And another poet, a Rev. Middleton, described the deathly quiet which hung over the city in the early nineteenth century in contrast to the noisy bustle of the days when it was alive. The only sound one could hear at Pompeii, he observed ghoulishly, was that of the archaeologist's 'mattock' striking stone which, like a gravedigger's spade, explored 'the relics of a City's tomb'.

The most interesting evocation of the deathly associations of Pompeii and Herculaneum was written not by a clergyman nor by a grand ambassador, however, but by a woman, Margaret Keogh. She was not able to travel to Italy to see the site, nor was she steeped in classical education like men such as William Hamilton. But she read all the books she could lay her hands on about the new discoveries at the foot of Vesuvius and became fascinated. Pompeii was impossibly distant for her and so it became a place of desire. In her poem, 'Herculaneum', she imagines wandering through the streets, which 'though involved in gloom and misty clouds' are nevertheless 'beautiful thus robed in shrouds'. Keogh was suffering from a kind of Byronic melancholia, in which indulging in gloomy thoughts seems deliciously poetical. In her poem 'Pompeii', the ancient city becomes for her a symbol of everything she longs for. She feels dead whereas Pompeii is paradoxically vivid and alive; she is grey and sad while Pompeii is sunny and happy:

> I seek but to divert a mind
> Whose thoughts were wounded by a world unkind;
> They now take refuge with the glorious dead,
> Friends meet for one whose hopes from earth are fled.
> Ah! in thy sunny land might I but dwell -
> The wish is futile – Italy, farewell!

Margaret Keogh was partly frustrated by the fact that she was a woman. Men could travel to Pompeii and include it on their Grand Tour, while women had to stay at home and read about it. So Pompeii became, for women like Keogh, a forbidden place of desire, a city of transgression. In her subversive transformation of the deathly Pompeii into a seductive lover, Keogh was actually falling into a long tradition of secret Pompeian eroticism.

*

4. Fulfilling Desires: Erotic Excavation

I remember very vividly my first encounter with the ancient city of Pompeii as a nineteen-year-old student one summer vacation. Having explored the large public spaces, which are always thronged with tourists – the forum, the temple of Jupiter, and the main street with its ancient equivalent of pavements and zebra crossings – I wanted to venture further afield. I turned into a side street, ducking into a small house, a maze of courtyards and unexpected rooms and archways. It was suddenly quiet, hushed, deserted. The curator, who had been sitting hunched on a window-sill, shuffled towards me.

'You like I take you to a special house?' he asked me. 'It's very nice, very beautiful pictures, very special.'

I leapt at the opportunity. I was going to see something extraordinary, not available to the general public, perhaps an ancient fresco perfectly preserved. So I followed as he beckoned me through the rambling streets, further and further from the forum.

We reached the destination, a small building with little cubicle rooms, each leading off a central corridor. Around the walls of the corridor was a painted frieze, depicting sexual coupling in every position and combination. There were men with women, women with women, women underneath, women on top, women frontwards, women backwards. The building, I realised, must have been an ancient brothel. The frieze had been either used as pornography, to excite the clients as they waited their turn, or as a kind of menu of options along the lines, I suppose, of 'I want a bit of the second from the right.'

'You like the pictures? Very nice, very beautiful,' my guide asked me urgently, as he fingered his fly and touched my breast.

'No,' I insisted, my nineteen-year-old sensibility still eminently shockable. 'I do not like the pictures.'

'Wait,' he cried after me, zipping himself up, as I beat a hasty retreat, away from the promised opportunity to see the special, hidden Pompeii and back to the safe, public forum. 'I show you more pictures. Another house. Very special.'

It is hardly surprising that the private Pompeii of pornography and casual sexual encounter was not for me. Deserted ruins and opportunistic curators added up to a mildly threatening combination for a young woman travelling alone and I hurried back to the wide open space of the city's forum where there was safety in numbers and chastity in art. Yet, hardly daring to admit it to myself, I was subconsciously drawn not to the pornography as such but certainly to the labyrinthine, furtive possibilities of Pompeii. I had discovered Pompeii's dark side, something that responds to our secret demand for titillation and horror, for all the things that are forbidden, and I wanted to know more.

87

*

From the earliest days of the excavation of Pompeii, archaeologists un-earthed pictures and objects which both shocked and excited them. The first bronze Priapus – the god of fertility with characteristically exagger-ated penis – was dug up by a peasant in 1748. And soon diggers were discovering a whole mass of explicit paintings of sexual intercourse and more and more votive phalluses. It was embarrassing and it was intrigu-ing. What more might be found? And what should they do with the stuff? Pompeii seemed to be the place where they might be liberated to look at the most erotic material, permitted by the fact that it was exhibited abroad and that it was antique and vaguely scholarly. And yet even in Pompeii, it was felt appropriate that the erotic art should be often buried and hidden and looked at furtively.

Pompeii became one of the key European sites of hard-porn in the eighteenth century. Notorious debauchees, jaded by what was on offer in their home countries, were drawn there. The Marquis de Sade, for exam-ple, stayed in Naples for about eight months from 1775-76, and gathered a large collection of ancient sex toys. Later the association of Naples and Pompeii with erotica was to filter back when he chose the Naples area as the site of the journey of debauchery in *Juliette*. Casanova visited in the 1760s and confessed in his memoirs that he felt particularly happy and at home in Naples, although he had been on the point of 'disgracing' himself in the museum at Portici. 'There is no remedy against the degradation of the mind', he reflected, but did not enlighten his readers by being any more specific.

One of the chief aficionados of Pompeii's erotic potential was William Hamilton, the British ambassador in Naples. His wife, Emma, a renowned beauty who would strike antique poses on request for visitors, was to conduct a famous affair with Nelson. But Hamilton, cuckolded, had by that time already sought relief in archaeology. From the early 1770s, he had been collecting what he termed 'curiosities' picked up at the site, vases often with sexually explicit illustrations and a vast number of ornamental phalluses. Visitors to Naples were invited to view his collection and the men would make private jokes about what they saw. One of the visitors to Hamilton's collection was William Beckford, the author of the notorious Gothic shocker *Vathek*, who, like Byron, was later to be exiled from England as a result of a sexual scandal. Another visitor was the father of the novelist Fanny Burney, who wrote somewhat euphemistically that the 'curiosities both of art and nature in Mr Hamilton's possession are num-berless and inestimable'. Some of these visits were supposedly chaste and scholarly; Dr Burney, for example, was investigating early music and thought for some reason that the antiquities might inspire him. Other friends pretended to take a scholarly interest in the collection but actually made ribald remarks about what they saw in private. After writing to one friend about an ancient fertility rite still being practised in a local village – the annual fete of St Cosmo's Great Toe or phallus – Hamilton signed off with a bit of familiar bawdy joking between mates: 'That your Great Toe and your purse may never fail you is the wish of, dear Sir, your most faithful humble Servant William Hamilton.'

At the beginning of February 1775, William Hamilton read out an account of his discoveries at Pompeii to the Society of Antiquaries in London. The society was a bizarre mixture of serious scholars and gentlemen *bon viveurs*, and Hamilton's paper offered nuggets for both groups. There were detailed plans and drawings and there was a catalogue of the exploration of each house for the scholars in the crowd. But there was also inevitably the phallus. Hamilton explained carefully for his audience:

> The Priapus, cut in stone, and placed in a niche on the outside wall of this house, is called here the sign of the Brothel, which they suppose to have been kept in the house; but it has more probably been placed there in honour of the Deity so called, in the same manner as we see frequently now, against the houses of this country, a St Francis, a St Anthony etc. It is evident, from the very public situation, that such a representation did not in those days convey any indecent idea.

As the worthy antiquarians sat electrified in their elegant headquarters in Burlington House, Piccadilly, Hamilton created for them a masterpiece of tease, hinting at obscenities while denying them at the same time. But he was to oblige his male audience much more directly and explicitly a few years later, in 1784. He had already sold his collection of vases, amulets and what he called *ex-voti* to the British Museum in 1772 for a substantial £8,400, and had begun to publish the multi-volume edition of his antiquities. Now he wrote a letter to his friend Joseph Banks purely on the ancient Pompeian obsession with the phallus and the continuing preoccupation in southern Italy at the present time. The account was illustrated with engravings, explicit pictures showing male genitalia, cocks with penises instead of beaks, phalluses being weighed and clenched hands making obscene phallic gestures. It was blatant, simple and direct. Hamilton clearly thought the sexiness of Pompeii was located in the objects unearthed there. He listed them in exhaustive detail.

Even today Hamilton's letter to Banks can only be looked at in a special, carefully guarded section of the British Library. I spent a few weeks sitting at seat 169, leafing through Hamilton's account and other Pompeian erotica, while the library staff carefully monitored my behaviour and that of the other readers at the ten 'naughty' desks in the library. We had to return the books to the staff whenever we left the room and not leave anything open on the desk which might corrupt the casual reader passing by. And we had to keep our hands above the desk at all times where they could be seen. What I was looking at was probably no more sexually explicit than anything I could have picked up from the top shelf of a newsagent's, had I been so minded. Indeed, some of my week was spent wading through the memoirs of the Marquis de Sade, in French, with no pictures. But still it had to be read at the 'naughty desk' which lent the task a frisson it might otherwise have lacked.

*

By the nineteenth century, the authorities in Naples decided that the stream of obscene material coming to the surface in Pompeii needed to be controlled in some way. In 1819, Francis I, duke of Calabria and the future king of Naples, visited the Portici museum with his wife and daughter, shortly before it was scheduled to be moved into a new building and was shocked to view some of the items on display. He therefore suggested to the curator Michele Arditi that it would be better to restrict the erotic items to a single room so that access to them could be limited to 'persons of mature age and of proven morality'. Arditi took the hint and picked out a hundred and two 'curiosities' for isolation. He called the collection the Cabinet of Obscene Objects. Four years later it was renamed the Cabinet of Hidden Objects (Gabinetto degli oggetti riservati) and acquired a mythical, fantasy status. In order to see the exhibits, men had to apply to the Ministry of the Interior; women, needless to say, were forbidden to view them at all. Numerous applications were made, such was the notoriety of the collection, but even when permission was granted the bureaucracy was slow and there was a long delay before the permit was actually issued. Some permits had to be printed in order to keep up with the demand and even then men were frustrated, waiting interminably for their slim chance of being allowed 'di vedere per una sola volta il Gabinetto degli oggetti riservati del Reale Museo' as the permit put it.

The opportunities for actually seeing the famous Pompeiian pornography were so few that an industry grew up in the description and depiction of the Cabinet's contents which relied as much on fantasy as on reliable knowledge. In 1840 the Frenchman Louis Barré published the contents of what he termed the 'Musée Secret', arguing that it was important to know about the customs of the ancients and in particular to understand the mysterious but nevertheless interesting subject of their sexuality. He hastened to downplay the titillating factor of his book. The sole interest was scientific and archaeological, he maintained: 'Partout, nous avons voulu rester calme et serieux.' But even then he admitted teasingly that some self-censorship had gone on. Some anatomical details had been reduced in size and others had disappeared altogether. Readers were left once again to imagine wildly what might actually be seen if only they were given the opportunity.

The details which Barré's cautious and relatively chaste publication carefully glossed over were lavishly supplied by another Frenchman, César le Famin. Unlike the small engravings which appeared in Barré's book, le Famin's *Musée Royal de Naples, Peintures, Bronzes et Statues Erotiques du Cabinet Secret, avec leur explication* was in glorious colour and graphic detail. Le Famin tried to dress his publication up as scientifically necessary and important. The moderns had tried to repress the obscenity of the ancients, he argued. They had tried to represent them as gentle and pure, when actually, before the positive influence of Christianity, they were rude and sinful. In this sense, he maintained, 'modesty is just hypocrisy' and the ancients were in some way more honest than those in the early nineteenth century.

However le Famin's honesty, or at least his factual veracity, is debatable. One of the most lurid of his illustrations, 'Spinthria – Danseurs de Corde', is of a man and a woman copulating while balancing on a tightrope and drinking wine (Plate 6). The fresco is 'remarkable for the purity of the drawing and the brilliance of the colours', according to le Famin, and also 'one of the most obscene'. It is also significantly unsourced, termed simply 'fresque de Pompei', and has never been found. Did le Famin just make it up? Had he become so carried away by all the erotica that he had been allowed to see that he began to fantasise more and more extravagant scenes of his own? Le Famin tried to prove the authenticity of the fresco by quoting a rude poem by the Latin poet Martial which was very close in subject matter and therefore, he implied, could have been the inspiration for the ancient artist. Of course, this allowed him to titillate his readers further by having them pore over the Martial. He also quoted a modern French writer, de Senancour, to support his case. What is amazing is that, despite its very uncertain provenance, Famin's fresco found its way into what might be called the canon of Pompeian erotica. Four years later, Barré included a much more discreet black and white version, together with a note about le Famin, his source for the picture. Le Famin, according to Barré, had little evidence for the authenticity of his claims but, as Barre coyly put it, readers could judge for themselves and excuse his own silence on the matter.

Baron Denon abandoned even a façade of historical accuracy and scholarly interest in his publication of Pompeian erotica. His book, *L'Oeuvre Priapique de Dominique Vivant*, contains only pictures; there is no accompanying earnest text to counterbalance the pornography. Some of the pictures draw heavily on well-known images from Pompeii. The famous statue of Pan copulating with a goat reappears, but in Denon's version the pair are depicted outside in a rural setting as if they were alive and the sculptural origin is forgotten (Plate 5b). A typical Pompeian icon, a Maenad clutching a Priapus or fertility god, usually represented as a pillar with head and genitals, appears in the book, but again in Denon's version the Priapus is depicted with all his torso as if he were very much alive and virile. Another picture, of a woman lifting up her skirt to reveal her bottom, recalls, in her pose, the picture of Venus on one of the vases in the Secret Room collection. But Denon's woman is clearly modern. In each case, Denon is subtly mixing antiquity and modern culture, and the result is to make the images more piquantly and blatantly sexy. There is no equivocal aura of scholarship or inaccessibility about the images in his book. Instead, each Pompeian sculpture comes alive, like a modern Pygmalion, through Denon's vivid imagination and is made available for the male debauchee.

Keeping the real Pompeian erotica hidden from the public provoked these pornographic books by Barre, le Famin and Denon. In fact, because they were not bound by any authentic originals which could be checked, they could become wilder and wilder in their imaginings, making results all the more stimulating. The excess of the depictions was directly related to the prohibition on public access to the Pompeian collections. But while those pictures were now based upon gossip and imagination, rather than on first-hand knowledge as it was for Hamilton, de Sade and Casanova, they still placed emphasis upon explicit depiction, upon blatant sexual content. There was nothing flirtatious or teasing, nothing of the thrill of stripping back the soil to expose these curiosities. But while this was one tradition of Pompeian erotica, revelling in fleshy anatomy, there was another that placed more emphasis upon absence, evasion, repression and burial. It was this which more directly seduced Freud.

*

In the 1860s the new chief excavator of Pompeii, Giuseppe Fiorelli, developed a novel archaeological technique. He found that if he poured plaster-of-Paris into the holes which had been left in the ash layer by the bodies of the victims before they decomposed, he could recreate the Pompeians. The plaster was poured in and left to harden and then the ash was broken away to reveal a statue of the original body (Plate 7). The hardened ash provided a mould for a new type of sculpture. Even the facial expressions were captured. Victims emerged from the process fighting for breath, grimacing with pain. The statues worked like a ghostly photographic negative. They filled in solidly what once might have been there, making concrete the haunting human life now lost. It was an archaeological sensation and everyone started talking about it. The French archaeological writer, Gaston Boissier, for example, recorded the excitement in 1896: 'It has been found possible to assemble in the little museum, placed at the entrance of the town, several people who are reproduced just as they were when death struck them; some wrestling against it in despair, others yielding without resistance. It is a striking sight, and one of the greatest curiosities of Pompeii.'

One of Fiorelli's other main contributions to Pompeian archaeology was to make rambling around the site more possible. Up until he took over as director of excavations in 1863, the city of Pompeii was more like a building site, blocked by the debris of previous excavations. According to Boissier, 'he who formerly visited Pompeii was stopped at every moment by mountains of cinders and islands of rubbish which hindered locomotion, blocked the streets, and interrupted his walks'. Fiorelli decided to tidy the place up, to go back over the areas which had been previously 'excavated', and to allow the houses and streets to be viewed not as potential stores of treasure but as the recreated city from the past. Pompeii, for Boissier, was now to be commended for its capacity to accommodate the walker, the *flaneur*: 'It is all spread out before our eyes, with its smallest alleys, its meanest houses, and its most humble shops, and walking through it one may obtain a very true and complete idea of life in ancient time.'

It was Fiorelli's Pompeii – the city of the simultaneously absent and present figures, the city for the archaeological rambler – which Sigmund Freud visited in 1902. There he almost certainly saw the ghostly plaster figures in the museum at the entrance and wandered through the labyrinthine streets. He wrote afterwards to his great friend Wilhelm Fliess that he was studying the street names of Pompeii and they were beginning to infiltrate his dreams. Each night he travelled the main thoroughfares of the buried city like the arteries of his brain. And each day he attempted to uncover the hidden traumas in his patients' unconscious while surrounded by an ever-expanding collection of antiquities from the site.

He had already, of course, found that archaeology in general provided a useful metaphorical explanation for what he was doing in the consulting room. Like the archaeologist, the analyst worked from small clues to construct a large theory, allowing himself a degree of speculation and creative fiction in the process:

> Just as the archaeologist builds up the walls of the building from the foundations that have remained standing, determines the number and position of the columns from the depressions in the floor and reconstructs the mural decorations and paintings from the remains found in the debris, so does the analyst proceed when he draws his inferences from the fragments

of memories, from the associations and from the behaviour of the subject of the analysis.

Like the archaeologist, the analyst also relies upon the fact that his patient has actively repressed or buried particular memories so that they have been preserved and can be later studied. In a famous image in *Civilisation and Its Discontents*, Freud compares the mind to the ancient city of Rome. 'In mental life', he argues, 'nothing that has once been formed can perish – everything is somehow preserved and in suitable circumstances can once more be brought to light.' A city like Rome, which is rich in archaeological remains, is very similar to the mind. In every street there are layers of history visible as the buildings of one era are built on top of another. Like the geological sedimentation of rocks, each period can be clearly detected in the vertical structures of the city. First, Freud says, there was the oldest Rome, a federation of settlements on the seven hills, the *Roma Septimontium*. Then there was the Rome of the Republic and the Rome of Julius Caesar. On top of these are built the Rome of the emperors, the Rome of the early Christian church and the Rome of the Renaissance. The ruins of past ages are not separated safely off from the present but, Freud says, 'dovetailed into the jumble of the great metropolis'. Some remains have been unearthed but others still lie buried in the soil of the city or under the modern buildings. Being buried in that way keeps the past intact.

However, in order for the analogy between Rome and the psyche to seem even more convincing and illuminating, Freud argues, we would have to imagine that the ancient city was not left buried beneath the modern with just a few fragments visible above ground but that it was simultaneously present and whole amidst the new buildings. In other words, we would have to imagine a miraculous state of archaeological preservation:

> Now let us, by a flight of imagination, suppose that Rome is not a human habitation but a psychical entity with a similarly long and copious past – an entity, that is to say, in which nothing that has once come into existence will have passed away and all the earlier phases of development continue to exist alongside the latest one. This would mean that in Rome the palaces of the Caesars and the Septizonium of Septimius Severus would still be rising to their old height on the Palatine and the castle of S. Angelo would still be carrying on its battlements the beautiful statues which graced it until the siege by the Goths, and so on.... Where the Coliseum now stands we could at the same time admire Nero's vanished Golden House. On the Piazza of the Pantheon we should find not only the Pantheon of today, as it was bequeathed to us by Hadrian, but, on the same site, the original edifice erected by Agrippa; indeed, the same piece of ground would be supporting the church of Santa Maria sopra Minerva and the ancient temple over which it was built.

4. Fulfilling Desires: Erotic Excavation

Freud paints a bizarre picture of all the most famous buildings in Rome over the last three millennia sharing the same space and re-emerging undamaged to stand at the same time. And like these ancient buildings, Freud believed that formative experiences, even those dating back to earliest childhood, could not be erased. 'Everything is somehow preserved and in suitable circumstances it can once more be brought to light.'

Freud's example of the city of Rome highlights the limits of the archaeological analogy for the mind, for the city has crumbled and decayed over time whereas painful memories do not. Pompeii, however, seemed a unique case because of its unusual state of preservation. 'Only in such rare circumstances as those of Pompeii', Freud wrote, could the direct analogy be made between the 'psychical object' and the 'archaeological object': 'All of the essentials are preserved, even things that seem completely forgotten are present somehow and somewhere, and have merely been buried and made inaccessible to the subject.' Yet it was in that 'somehow' and 'somewhere' that the difficulty lay. For while Freud was developing his theory about the preservation of the traumatic memory, aided by its burial in the psyche, he also found in his work with patients that the hysterical symptom was in fact a displacement or a distortion of the original experience, not its immaculate resurrection. The symptom was a kind of 'mnemic symbol', an imprint of the original trace, a further development upon the original form. The task of the analyst was to interpret the distortion, to try to imagine the original experience from the painful imprint which it had left. It was the psychoanalytic equivalent of imagining the victims of Pompeii from witnessing Fiorelli's plaster casts.

Fiorelli's haunting, ghostly bodies were to play a role in Freud's most striking attempt to connect his passion for Pompeii with his psychoanalytic studies, in his essay on Jensen's short story, 'Gradiva'. Indeed he first read the story in the same year that he visited Pompeii. But his essay was also fleshed out, so to speak, by another elusive body part from Pompeii and the archaeological and literary attention it had received.

*

Back in the early 1770s, long before Fiorelli's experiments with plaster, the imprint of a woman's breast was discovered in the hardened ash in the Villa of Diomedes in Pompeii. The ash had solidified around the woman's body, so after her corpse had decomposed, the outline of her form remained. The mould was displayed in the museum in Naples; William Hamilton saw it when it was first exhibited and was moved by it. But when Theophile Gautier, the friend of the French decadent poet Charles Baudelaire, saw it in 1851, he found it decidedly sexy, a source for his erotic fiction. Hamilton's tastes were more for the unequivocally phallic and explicit; Gautier preferred the striptease, the evanescent, the mysterious. The hero, Octavien, in his novella 'Arria Marcella', sees the breast in the museum and is mesmerised. Bowled over by his new love, he is overcome by emotion when he visits the house in Pompeii where the woman's imprint was discovered and distances himself from his two unfeeling comrades. They go off for lunch and the conversation turns to the most appropriate and inevitable topic in Pompeii, namely what kind of woman each fancies. While one friend is attracted by beauty and youth and the other is excited by a woman's resistance, Octavien confesses that he is not seduced by reality but that he is drawn to the ideal woman of poetry or art, and had once yearned to embrace the Venus de Milo.

His sexual fantasy is fulfilled in Pompeii, not with the Venus de Milo but with the woman whose breast so obsesses him. Unable to sleep that night, he stumbles out into the ruins of Pompeii and discovers that he has been transported back in time, to the days when the woman, Arria Marcella, was alive. Having passed a little shop selling phallic amulets and little golden Priapuses, which Gautier is careful to point out and explain, Octavien is enticed into Arria Marcella's house, where after a sumptuous meal he is finally invited to kiss her breast and to make love to her: 'Nothing more was heard save the confused sounds of kisses and low moaning.' But the lovemaking is interrupted by an austere Christian who reproaches Arria: 'Have your ashes still not cooled since the day you perished beneath the volcano's rain of liquid fire?' Arria is exorcised by the old Christian, a 'gasp of agony' escaping from her 'broken breasts', and Octavien finds himself holding nothing in his arms but the black hardened ash which he had seen in the museum. Filled with melancholy and unable ever to retrace his steps back in time to her again, Octavien finally marries an Englishwoman. He tells her nothing, but she always suspects that his heart belongs to another.

Gautier's story celebrates the erotic inaccessibility of Pompeii. Octavien was excited not by the nicely available Englishwoman, but by the unavailable, dead Arria Marcella. He fixated upon her breast because it was both the one thing he could see in the museum and yet it was also teasingly missing, leaving only its imprint in the ash. Arria could only be conjured up in his fiction; the eroticism inherent in the elusive imprint in the lava was echoed in the seductive twists and turns of the story, as the woman accepted – and then later slipped away from – his embrace. In many ways the story is a classic fairytale in which a statue comes to life and then crumbles again; Gautier presents his readers with a strict polarity with the breathing present and the marble and ash past. But in its deliberate confusion between the desire for sexual love and the desire for a vanished culture which is excited by its material traces, Gautier's tale paved the way for Freud's more complex recreation of Jensen's story, *Gradiva*.

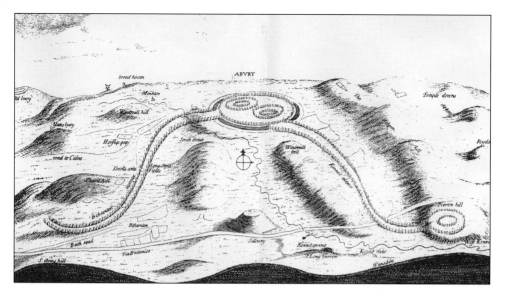

1. 'A Scenographic View of the Druid Temple of Abury in north Wiltshire as in its original', from William Stukeley, *Abury, A Temple of the British Druids* (1743).

2. 'Silbury Hill, July 11th 1723', from William Stukeley,
Abury, A Temple of the British Druids (1743).

3. Lindow Man.

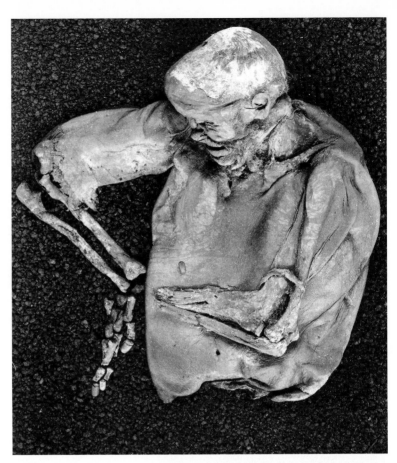

4. 'Excavation of Herculaneum', from Richard de Saint-Non,
Voyage Pittoresque de Naples et Sicile (1782).

5. 'Pan and the Goat'.
(a) *above* Original, from The Secret Room, Archaeological Museum of Naples.
(b) *below* Fantasy, from Baron Denon, *L'Oeuvre Priapique de Dominique Vivant* (1850).

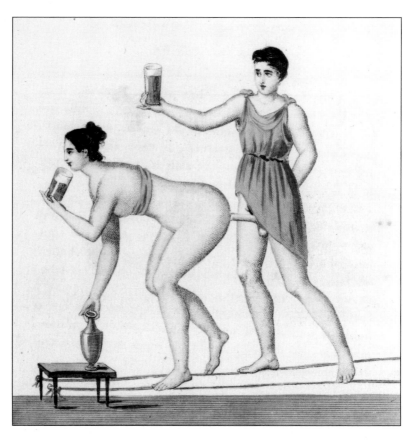

6. 'Spinthria, Danseurs de Corde', from César Le Famin,
Musée Royal de Naples (1836).

7. Some of Fiorelli's casts from Pompeii.

8. 'View of the Tombs of Achilles and Patroclus on the shores of Troy', from J.B.S. Morritt, *A Vindication of Homer* (1798).

9. Testing the tomb of Achilles on the plain of Troy with Sehmas.

10. Trojan idol with swastika on her genitals, from Heinrich Schliemann, *Ilios* (1881).

11. Rev. James Douglas excavating a barrow.

12. Ground Zero, New York.

13. Digging at El Ahwat, Israel.

14. Mayan sacrifice in the darkness of Actun Tunichil Muknal, Belize.

15. The Garbage Museum, Stratford, Connecticut.

4. Fulfilling Desires: Erotic Excavation

Freud's essay, entitled 'Delusions and Dreams in Jensen's *Gradiva*', draws together both his knowledge of Fiorelli's recent work in Pompeii and also his reading of previous erotic descriptions of the site, such as Gautier's, in order to aid his interpretation. He is concerned, too, with the capacity of the mind not merely to repress desires but also to displace and distort them to produce the hysterical symptoms mentioned earlier. Freud's essay lingers over questions about the connection between the literary and the psychoanalytic and over the value of the repressed memory or the buried desire. But these questions are centrally embedded in the ambivalent and seductive archaeology of Fiorelli's Pompeii.

In Jensen's story, a German archaeologist, Norbert Hanold, is captivated by the sculpture in the Vatican Museum, which he calls 'Gradiva', meaning the 'girl who steps along', and arranges to have a cast made for his study back in Germany. He becomes obsessed especially by the marble girl's gait and imagines that she must have lived in Pompeii where she would have had to pick her way over the stepping stones found in the streets there. Visiting Pompeii a few years later, he spots what he thinks is Gradiva crossing the street in front of him. Half wondering whether she is a ghost, he follows her only to discover that she speaks German. After speculating that he has regressed two thousand years back into the buried city of Pompeii, Hanold finds that Gradiva is actually Zoe Bertgang, his neighbour back in Berlin. They were childhood sweethearts and she has continued to love him, but he has been so absorbed in archaeology that he has ceased to notice her. The trip to Pompeii reawakens his love and they end the story planning to return to Pompeii for their honeymoon, both effectively 'dug out of the ruins'.

The 'Gradiva' story became a classic account of repression for Freud. He showed, in his analysis of it, that Hanold had repressed his real affectionate feelings for Zoe Bertgang by plunging himself into his study of archaeology. But because archaeology was really just a displacement for his emotions, it became itself eroticised and he fell in love with a marble statue that bore a strange resemblance to his childhood love. In Pompeii the delusion which he laboured under – that he was drawn not to a living woman but to a sculpture and that Gradiva had lived in Pompeii before its destruction and was now a ghost haunting the city – is dispelled and he is gradually dragged back to the world of reality. For a time, Zoe Bertgang plays along with Hanold's delusions – pretending to be resurrected from the dead – in order to win his love and allow for the gradual liberation of his repressed affection into an openly acknowledged and conscious attachment.

Pompeii plays a crucial part in Hanold's delusion and eventual reintegration into human society. The sculpture of Gradiva is the key way in which Hanold represses his real feelings – he falls in love with a marble dead woman instead of a living one right next to him. But subconsciously he is only attracted to her because of his real feelings for Zoe; following her into the dig at Pompeii is actually a way of reawakening his love. So archaeology both represses and liberates his sexual desire or, as Freud explains it, 'the arousing of the repressed eroticism came precisely from the field of the instruments that served to bring about the repression'. In this process, the footsteps of Gradiva, her peculiar way of walking lightly on her toes, are crucial. Hanold is captivated initially by the skipping step of the statue. And once he has met Zoe in Pompeii, he is mainly concerned to see if her feet leave prints. We might be tempted to think of Freud's comparison between 'fragments of memory' and the archaeologist's study of 'depressions on the floor' left by columns in the past, mentioned earlier. In other words, it is the elusive quality of the girl – the traces left behind by her feet, her ghostly absence – which most haunts him. Repression is all about an emotion which is felt but not acknowledged. By converting Zoe into a dead statue who has just left the ghostly imprint of her form beneath the ash of Pompeii, Hanold was able to cope with his conflicting, troublesome feelings, making them less tangible and urgent and more suggestively seductive. But Zoe, in partly playing along with Hanold's delusions by suggesting that she is indeed a ghost and partly gradually revealing her very different, living identity, succeeds in drawing Hanold out of his fantasy and into a fulfilling and loving relationship.

According to the critic Rachel Bowlby, Freud's essay ultimately constitutes a repudiation of archaeology. Zoe draws Hanold away from the obsession with the archaeological past, with dead sculpture and up towards the living. She writes that 'what is most authentic' is not the marble Gradiva, the 'version deep down and buried' but rather 'the modern girl steps out and away from the lower depths to which the statue must now be definitively relegated'. This is Zoe taking control, striking a blow for the living and for feminism. But Fiorelli's bodies, which are and are not types of statues, and which are both the resurrected dead and yet only their ghostly imprint, actually disrupt the neat polarisation between archaeology and the 'everyday' which Rachel Bowlby sets up. Zoe's game, in which she playfully pretends to be a ghost and yet is also sensuously corporeal – Hanold checks her footprints, after all, to see if her weight presses into the mud – fits the ambivalence of the dead in Pompeii, who both can and yet ultimately cannot be seen. The desire which Hanold feels for Zoe will always be bound up with uncertainty, with the erotic tease of absence which lies at the heart both of sexual relations and of archaeological investigation.

Freud's analysis of Jensen's story crystallised the long association of Pompeii with the repressed, unacknowledged but powerful part of our minds. After his Gradiva account, the curious operation of the mind would be forever linked with the burial and excavation of the city. 'There is', he wrote, 'actually no better analogy for repression than the burial that was the fate of Pompeii and from which the city could reappear through the work of the spade.' While initially Pompeii appeared to be the best analogy for the mind because of its perfect preservation and the fact that all the artefacts were still tangibly present and visible, in fact it was precisely its elusiveness and seductive *near* presence which proved the most appropriate analogy. What teases both the archaeologist and the analyst is the illusion of fulfilment, of gaining answers about the past. But it is an illusion which is not supported in reality, because the mind, tugged both ways by desire and shame, distorts and displaces the objects of its thoughts until they become altered beyond recognition and sources themselves of further desires. So too Pompeii's ash and lava appeared to capture the fleeting lives of the ancient Pompeians but in fact only retained their impresses, leaving the spectator feverishly to imagine the original and to fetishise the very hardened lava and solidified footprints left behind.

*

Excavation in Pompeii is still continuing. Areas are being continually opened up, and new discoveries – the latest is an ancient five-star hotel – are announced on the news. Meanwhile only a tiny part of Herculaneum has been excavated, since the modern city of Naples has been built on top of the site and the houses would need to be cleared of their inhabitants before any further digging would be possible. Visitors to Herculaneum can still see some of the eighteenth-century tunnels, going back into the cliffs on the edge of the site and receding into mysterious darkness. Some of the evidence about the topography of Herculaneum is actually still based upon the unreliable eighteenth-century accounts, when exploratory shafts were dug down which have since been filled in and built over.

Amid great publicity in the year 2000, the Secret Room of the Archaeological Museum in Naples was opened to the public. All the items, which had acquired an imaginative power precisely because they were hidden away, were put in a special public exhibition. 'Pan and the Goat' – which excited Denon so much – is displayed in an alcove, one of the treasures of the collection (Plate 5a). The explicit brothel copulation scenes are all collected on one wall while the mythological sex scenes are hung on another. There is a glass case of terracotta votive phalluses and breasts and another case of *tintinnabula* (penises with bells on). There is even a case of the eighteenth-century Borgia collection of ancient erotica, several of which are known to be fakes, the products of modern fertile imaginations. Each display is accompanied by a written explanation in Italian and English, and indeed the collection is the best presented gallery in the museum.

So will Pompeii lose its capacity to shock and excite? Perhaps when the last remnants of the city have been unearthed and all the erotic frescoes and objects have been revealed, there will be nothing left to enthral us. 'It is only the time taken shedding clothes which makes voyeurs of the public', the critic Roland Barthes famously wrote of the Parisian striptease show. 'Woman is desexualised at the very moment when she is stripped naked.' Like a striptease, perhaps the excavation of Pompeii excites us only when parts of the city still lie buried and unexplored and when aspects are deliberately hidden from our view and just temptingly suggested or described. While the prohibition on access to the Secret Room was increasingly difficult to justify and its public opening marks a new phase in the openness of the excavation, does it seriously alter the imaginative power of Pompeii?

I made a special trip to Naples to find out. At the moment, the answer seems to be no. While the Gabinetto degli oggetti riservati is now officially open to the public, there is still a certain mystique attached to the gallery. Although I did not need any exclusive permission or authority to see the Secret Room, I had to go to a separate desk and collect a special pass after I had bought my general entrance ticket to the museum. The pass – I was visitor number 1 that Monday morning – specified a time of entry to the gallery – 9.30 am in my case – and limited the visit to a strict twenty minutes. The gallery was shut off from the rest of the museum by a large, wrought-iron gate. A curator sat by it, permanently on guard, checking passes and timing visits. At present tour groups seem to be barred from the gallery and it is only those who know to ask for a pass – again the frisson of exclusivity – who can view. For my twenty minute visit, I was joined by just one South African couple and the three of us were guided round by a young Italian woman, who gave us a very serious and informed lecture about the quality of the art and the cultural significance of the collection. But not content with this, having travelled all the way from Britain just to see this gallery, I managed to persuade one of the guards at a weak moment later in the morning to let me slip through the gate again and I crept round, alone, making notes, taking sly photographs, feeling naughty.

I hope that the gallery will continue to be run in this way. While this state of affairs continues, Pompeii will remain a place of hidden and forbidden desire, a place which inspires lurid fantasy because the hard facts are not readily available, a site of repression and half-acknowledged memory. It will continue to be a place that seems to be forever out of reach, evanescent, teasing, Gothic. And as such, it will always offer one of the most potent, dark and exciting symbols of archaeology.

5

Fundamentalism:
Digging Our Trojan Origins

My summer mission in 2003 is to visit Troy. When I tell my friends, it is
as though I had confessed to a desire to see Narnia or Camelot.

'Where is Troy?' they ask me. 'Is it in Greece? We've never really
thought about it as a real place before.'

I want to see Troy, on the north-west coast of Turkey, because a team
of German archaeologists from Tübingen University have been excavating
there since 1988. Rumours are circulating that they are finding a city
which is even closer to Homer's original than previously thought. Beyond
the citadel of Troy, known as Hisarlik, which has always seemed too small
to measure up to Homer's elaborate descriptions, they are discovering
evidence of a large city down on the plain. And a mile away at the sea,
there is further excavation, revealing harbours and more construction.

So at 6 am on August 18th, as the red sun slides over the horizon, I meet
the man leading the archaeological campaign, Professor Manfred
Korfmann, over breakfast at the excavation headquarters. It is a military
operation in which everybody knows their place. The students move from
the mess where breakfast is served to the outside tables for cigarettes and
tea with timed precision. The second-in-commands, all thin and anxious,
scurry round, from office to laboratory to the field, directing the workers
in their different divisions. And Korfmann sits in control of all activities,
large and charismatic, khaki waistcoat and a shock of blond hair.

By 6.30 am, I am touring the citadel with a member of his team,
Professor Koppenhofer. He shows me the different cities of Troy, built over
thousands of years and spiralling out from the centre of the citadel like
tree rings. At the heart of the complex, now covered by a specially designed
protection roof, is the palace belonging to the city known as Troy II,
destroyed by fire in about 2450 BC. A few rings out are the massive
fortification walls and bastions of Troy VI, the city flourishing about 1500
BC, around the same time as Mycenae in Greece. Walking further out, we
stand for a while and watch the excavation team put in repairs to Troy

VIII's Greek temple precinct wall, built over the site by one of Alexander the Great's successors in 300 BC.

On the north-west corner of the citadel, near the fourth-century sanctuary, we stop and look back up the hill at the massive walls of Troy VI. The sea, with the harbour which Manfred Korfmann has excavated, is behind us.

Up until now the conversation has been all dates and excavation techniques but, for a moment, Erdmute Koppenhofer lets his professional, scientific demeanour slip.

'These are the walls of the city which Homer describes,' he says to me quietly. 'I sometimes imagine Helen standing on these walls, looking down on the ships and pointing out the different Greek chiefs to King Priam.'

It is a significant confession. For the archaeological study of Troy has been dogged over the centuries by the question of its relation to Homer's work. It has become a place where fact and fiction meet. But, even more interestingly, it has become a place where even the very status of fiction or of fact has been tested and explored. Homer's poems have been dismissed at times when the historical evidence did not seem to support them. And archaeological remains around the plain of Troy have been discarded when they failed to match Homer's description. Some of the earliest excavation techniques were developed because of the *Iliad* and the *Odyssey*, and thus archaeology in the region might be said to have a problematic origin in poetry.

Back at our second breakfast at excavation headquarters at 10 am, after Korfmann has announced my presence to the assembled archaeological team during his daily briefing, we get talking. Korfmann has identified Troy as the city called Wilusa, mentioned in ancient Hittite texts. The Hittite empire was based in what is now modern Turkey with its centre around Hattusas, just north-east of Ankara. So references to Wilusa offer an Eastern perspective on the city, as opposed to Homer's Western perspective.

'People ask about Homer and the *Iliad*,' Korfmann says, reaching for some olives and more tea. 'I'm happy to answer queries from Homeric scholars, but that is not the interest or motivation behind the dig. I am interested in Troy as an important ancient city in a strategic site. The Hittite account of Wilusa is a historic text concerned with facts, whereas Homer is poetry.'

'Oh, but surely you are a little swayed by the fact that this is the city Homer described,' Koppenhofer dares to suggest.

'Well, I must admit that my favourite place on the site is the walls overlooking the sea, where Helen might have stood,' Korfmann smiles. 'I do sometimes stand there, looking down over the plain.'

I am pleased that Korfmann is sometimes very moved by the myth of the place. And I am pleased that we are having this discussion. For the story of Troy, we might say, is the story of the debate about the relationship between fact and fiction. It is the tale of what happens when fact and fiction become confused, when one is used wildly to justify the other.

*

After Koppenhofer's tour of the citadel at Hisarlik and our second breakfast, I catch a ride with Sinan, one of Korfmann's doctoral students. We drive about twenty minutes further south, through fields of cotton and tomatoes, to the village of Pinarbasi. It has a single café in the centre of the village, shaded by vines and filled with about eight men reading newspapers and passing the time of day. Sinan and I settle at a table with two villagers and order some glasses of tea. Our negotiations may take some time.

What we are trying to arrange is for somebody to guide me to the hill outside Pinarbasi which became the centre of archaeological attention long before the mound at Hisarlik. Indeed it was first visited by Robert Wood, the antiquarian, who was a member of the Society of Dilettanti and its first director of Archaeological Ventures. Up until this time, Troy had been considered a fictional city, no more real than William Shakespeare's Bohemia or Thomas More's Utopia. The closest anyone had got to portraying a geographical or historical city was Alexander Pope in 1720, who included a bizarre and geographically-impossible map with the second volume of his translation of the *Iliad*. It was exuberantly fanciful, peopled with warriors and ships and tents and other characters from the *Iliad* busily doing things, and yet readers pored over it, using it to make sense of the poem as they read it.

Robert Wood's trip to Pinarbasi in 1750 marked a turning point in the value given to historical, archaeological facts in the eighteenth century. His mission was to 'visit one of the most celebrated scenes of ancient story in order to compare their present appearance with the early classical ideas'. No longer content with Homer's fictional account of the place, the Society of Dilettanti wanted concrete facts. What was the terrain like? Was there anything of the city of Troy still remaining? Could you still see the rivers Scamander and Simois between which the Greeks and the Trojans fought their battles? Was there room for the Greeks to have docked their ships and pitched their tents, while laying siege to Troy for ten long years?

Wood set out to Turkey attempting to answer these questions. Armed, amazingly, with Alexander Pope's map, he began a long process of sketching and measuring the landscape. Pinarbasi was selected as the site of

Troy, chiefly because it was encircled by the river Scamander (the modern Mendere) and because it was the source of numerous springs. But Wood discovered that the terrain did not quite match Homer's description. It was too far from the sea and the rivers did not follow the course described in the *Iliad*. The only possible explanation for this was that there must have been a series of major earthquakes since Homer's time. 'I have seen several parts of Ida and also of Tmolus which have been evidently separated from the two mountains by the shock of an earthquake', he wrote in his account, finally published in 1775. 'And there are in the plains of the Scamander many pieces of massy rock, that are manifestly detached from the place where they originally stood.'

Robert Wood's explanation was quite clever and sophisticated. The idea that the landscape changed over time, with coastlines receding or advancing and mountains rising or sinking, was only just being developed by the early geologists. He had probably come across James Hutton at the Royal Society of Edinburgh, to which they both belonged, and had discussed these ideas. Hutton went on to publish *Theory of the Earth* in 1795, a hugely influential geology book which described for the first time the way in which the earth was evolving constantly, through volcanic eruptions and earthquakes, as well as quieter, gradual erosion. A new geological understanding meant that, just as a text could alter over time as it was edited and reinterpreted, so the earth, which previously had seemed to ground everything reliably and timelessly, could change too. The alliance between archaeology and geology, which today seems obvious, was at that time novel. Wood's consideration of Hutton's ideas in his description of the Troad was brave and imaginative.

But when it came actually to drawing his map, Wood backed down. He could not draw the flexibility of the landscape into the map but stuck rigidly to what were presumed to be facts. Historical speculations could not influence the work of the cartographer. 'As alterations of this nature have not been punctually recorded, and are not easily to be ascertained, I have not marked out any variation of ground in the following Map', he wrote, desperately trying to justify himself. 'I put it in the Reader's power to judge, by recurring to the journal of the siege in the *Iliad*, how far the bounds and distances observed by the Poet are consistent with the opposite plan, which I here exhibit.'

In the café in Pinarbasi, several glasses of tea later, negotiations are coming to a head. Jihan and Bahri, who have drunk tea with us, will guide me as I follow in Wood's footsteps, checking whether the texts of the eighteenth-century cartographers are 'consistent' with the facts on the ground. The whole village, gathered for the day in the shade of the café, watches as we set off, threading our way through fields of crops and goats, to a series of springs bubbling up a few fields below. I dip my hand in each one expectantly, to test the temperature.

The temperature of the springs is significant, because this became a vital piece of evidence in the case for the Trojan identity of Pinarbasi (or Bournarbasi, as it was known then) mounted by Wood's main critic, the Frenchman, Jean-Baptiste Chevalier. 'The present state of that once renowned region had never been explained with any sort of accuracy', he wrote later in the preface to his account of his findings which was read in French before the Royal Society of Edinburgh in February 1791. 'Instead of elucidating the subject, Wood seemed to have involved it in greater obscurity than ever.' Chevalier claimed to have discovered two springs feeding into the Scamander which according to Homer were hot and cold. On testing them, Chevalier confirmed that they did indeed differ greatly in temperature. He also showed that the river Scamander had been diverted by a modern canal, but that it was still possible to identify its original course, which fitted the description in Homer. All these discoveries meant that Chevalier, unlike Wood, was fitting the landscape back into the description in Homer. The village of Pinarbasi, located near the hot and cold springs, was clearly Troy.

But when I test them, the springs at Pinarbasi all feel cold. Perhaps sensing my disappointment, Bahri, who turns out to be a farmer, dives into one field and picks some tomatoes which he washes in one of the springs. Drizzled in the water of Scamander, they taste good. We retreat from the midday sun to Jihan's home to drink ayran, a yoghurty drink made fresh from his goat's milk that morning. Jihan is young, dressed in trendy shorts and T-shirt, the village policeman when he's on duty. He proudly shows me his goat and his two cows and his rabbits.

An hour later and it's time to climb the mountain that Chevalier thought contained the walls and palaces of Troy, the hill called Ballidag or 'mountain of honey'. It is huge, far higher than the mound at Hisarlik, with steep cliffs plummeting down to the Scamander river below.

We stop at the summit. Jihan mimes somebody writhing around bound by their wrists.

'Here. Helen. Dead,' he gestures in universal sign language.

I thought that Helen returned to Greece with Menelaus, but Jihan and Bahri are passionately adamant. The most beautiful woman in the world ended her days on their hill.

I look out over the plain. Some seven miles away I can see the sea, the seven miles which so perplexed Robert Wood. And on the shore, a curious pimple. I gasp with excitement. This, I realise, must be what was known as the tomb of Achilles.

*

105

The tomb of Achilles became the focus of Chevalier's attention. Excavating Ballidag did not even occur to the Frenchman. In this period, archaeological excavation, apart from the one in Pompeii, was not conducted in antique lands, where antiquarians were supposed to admire objects from the past, not dig them up and study them. But stirred by William Stukeley's account of barrow-digging in Wiltshire, Chevalier went to work on the big burial mounds which lined the shore of Asia Minor (Plate 8). These were always said to be the tombs of the Greek heroes, of Achilles and Patroclus and Ajax. Well, the French asked themselves, if these are the tombs of the heroes, are their bones still visible inside?

The Turks were naturally suspicious of western antiquarians who, they thought quite rightly, were out to steal their treasure. So the owner of the land where Achilles' tomb lay refused Chevalier and his employer, Conte de Choisseul Gouffier, permission to dig. But while he was away, his brother, thinking he might profit from any finds which were unearthed, hastily allowed the excavation to go ahead.

Digging itself was not undertaken by men of Choisseul Gouffier's and Chevalier's standing. They employed a local Jew, Solomon Ghormezano, to dig for them. He took two months, working only at night so as not to alert the suspicions of the Turkish authorities.

According to the story Chevalier circulated, at the centre of the mound, Ghormezano finally discovered what they had all been looking for. An urn, richly decorated and containing ashes and human bones. 'This Urn', Chevalier reported, 'which is now in the possession of the Conte de Choiseul, is encircled in sculpture with a vine branch, from which are suspended bunches of grapes done with exquisite art.' What Choiseul Gouffier did with the original urn is unknown. The general public never got to see it. Instead, the artist and antiquarian Fauvel made a copy of it, and it was this copy that was displayed in Paris.

The French were turning archaeology into a nationalist enterprise. Never mind that they could not prove that the bones in the urn were those of Achilles. Never mind that the urn displayed in Paris was not actually *the* urn unearthed by Solomon Ghormezano. It was enough to suggest that the urn symbolised the spirit of Achilles, the original and fiercest hero, and that it had been unearthed by a French expedition. According to Chevalier and the others, the French had been the one nation to appreciate Greek heroism and were therefore its natural heirs.

The British, at that point at war with Napoleonic France, naturally moved in to attack Chevalier's conclusion. Their cause was defended by Jacob Bryant, famous for endorsing the notorious eighteenth-century forger, Thomas Chatterton. Bryant never actually travelled to Troy, but this fact did not deter him at all. He studied the landscape features described by the Frenchman, drew maps and compared them with

106

Homer's poem even more punctiliously and painstakingly than Chevalier. Chevalier's over-riding concern had been not to allow for flexibility or change over time, but to demand that the text of Homer fit the landscape consistently. Bryant demanded this consistency even more stringently and outmeasured the French. He used Chevalier's much-vaunted accuracy against him, calculating distances and numbers with so much precision that the resulting picture became ridiculous. He produced, in effect, a cartographic satire to bolster his theory that Homer had never been to Troy. 'I mention these computations, in which however I place not the least truth', he wrote with biting sarcasm. 'They form an artificial system, designed to determine the times of ancient events, and reconcile the histories of the first years. But those histories are not to be reconciled, and they are rendered more and more contradictory by the very means used to make them agree.'

The travel writer and artist William Gell, on the other hand, decided not to re-measure the plain of Troy but rather to excavate in his turn. He visited the Troad in 1804 and inspected the tomb of Achilles. There was, he noted, little evidence of actual deep digging having been conducted and 'no appearance now remains of any such research, nor is there any trace of human labour, except a small hollow among the circular foundations at the summit'.

Naturally, with all these claims and counter-claims about the contents of the tomb in the eighteenth century, I am excited when I first catch a glimpse of it from Ballidag and anxious to explore it myself. Manfred Korfmann arranges for one of the Turkish students, who is part of the archaeological team drilling holes in the plain beside the tumulus, to act as my escort the next morning. This means breakfast even earlier, at 5.30 am.

'You will leave at 6 am and it will still be dark', Korfmann tells me over supper with grim relish.

It is an archaeologist's challenge and I meet it, rising from my bed out on the hotel balcony even before the muezzin begins his early morning call to prayer. By the time the red ball of the sun starts squeezing up into sight, we are already packed into the expedition van and bumping over the old, cobbled military road down to the shore and the strange hillock which is Achilles' tomb.

My escort's name is Sehmas and his father is a farmer in Mardin, south-eastern Turkey. We naturally start talking about Seamus Heaney, farming, digging and poetry.

'Between my finger and my thumb/ The squat pen rests./ I'll dig with it,' I recite, smiling. 'You must read your namesake.'

'I will read him, as his father was a farmer too. And I am digging every day,' he replies.

It seems appropriate to be accompanied up the tomb of Achilles by somebody called Sehmas. For the mound was really the place of poetry and legend before Chevalier's excavation. Alexander the Great came here, before conquering Asia in the fourth century BC, to pay respects at the spot where he imagined the bones of the great warrior were interred. And two thousand years later Lord Byron made a pilgrimage here, to lie on the grave of the Homeric hero.

But Byron's visit was spoilt by Bryant's literal, scientific accuracy. The plain of Troy, which for a time had seemed so rich with history, now suddenly seemed empty. Years later Byron recalled the disappointment of his experience in Troy.

> I stood upon that plain daily, for more than a month, in 1810; and, if anything diminished my pleasure, it was that the blackguard Bryant had impugned its veracity. I venerated the grand original as the truth of *history* (in the material *facts*) and of *place*. Otherwise, it would have given me no delight. Who will persuade me, when I reclined upon a mighty tomb, that it did not contain a hero? – its very magnitude proved this. Men should not labour over the ignoble and petty dead – and why should not the dead be Homer's dead?

Sehmas and I inspect the top of the mound (Plate 9). There is a small hole, covered by scrub undergrowth, but when we prod it with a stick, it measures only about three feet. Hard to imagine Solomon Ghormezano stumbling upon Achilles' ashes in so shallow a trench.

We walk back to the archaeological team through the cornfields talking of poetry. The excavators are drilling holes to analyse the soil sediments and so determine how far the sea once came over the plain. It is tough work – yesterday they drilled their three-hundredth hole – and Sehmas is keen for us to make our way back slowly.

'I never knew Alexander the Great and Byron were here,' he tells me. 'All these weeks drilling holes and I didn't know.'

Manfred Korfmann is with the drillers to greet us.

'There is nothing in the mound,' he tells us. 'I investigated it some years ago. It was probably just a natural mound as there is stone right through it. Only later it might have been shaped into a cone as a type of monument.'

'But people believed that there was something there,' I say, 'and that's what matters.'

Bryant disproved the very facts upon which Chevalier grounded his fantastical theory and after that, nothing remained. Byron's pleasure, both in the landscape and apparently in Homer, had disappeared. A culture which puts great emphasis upon material evidence finds difficulty in maintaining belief. It falls prey to the possibility of forgery and hoaxes. The Romantic period is full of examples of relics being produced to sub-

108

stantiate a story. Sir Walter Scott's house in Abbotsford has a cabinet packed with sacred objects with a story attached – a snippet from Bonnie Prince Charlie's coat, for example, or a button snatched from the battle-field of Waterloo. If people think that a story must have evidence, they will be more likely to believe the forger once he produces these things. But once these objects are seriously questioned and debunked, then the whole story collapses. There is no alternative notion of truth or authenticity for the forger to fall back upon.

By contrast, only a more ironic and flexible notion of literary truth would allow visitors after Bryant to appreciate the plain of Troy. Byron's travelling companion, John Cam Hobhouse, always maintained a note of deflecting scepticism in his travel journal, and noticeably allowed all the topographies of Troy to coexist:

> Monsieur Le Chevalier determined upon the discovery of Troy and suc-ceeded. The Pergamus of Priam, ruins of temples, foundations of walls, the Scaean gate, the hot and cold sources of the Scamander were ascertained, laid down and irrevocably named.... Another traveller, however, apparently of a totally different complexion, restored us to our ancient uncertainty; and, when we travelled, the village of Bournabashi was no longer Troy; the springs of the Scamander and Simois had disappeared, and the encampment of the Greeks had again sunk into the nonentity to which it was before reduced by the trident of Neptune and the streams of seven vines.

He must have been a great tonic to the melancholy and reflective Byron.

*

When Heinrich Schliemann came to excavate Troy in 1870, he was arguably trying to follow in the tradition of Chevalier and Bryant. No prevarication. No Victorian doubt or literary sophistication. Either there was a real founda-tion to Homer's epic or there was not. This was a back-to-basics archaeology, proving the worth of stories through the spade. But while the eighteenth-century fundamentalism had implications for the status of fiction in the period and led to some comical absurdities and rivalries between nations, Schliemann's nineteenth-century fundamentalist archaeology led to far more sinister conclusions. His interest in pseudo-scientific factual evidence was to result in grotesque ideas which were entirely fantastical but horribly endorsed by his archaeological discoveries, as I shall explain later.

Schliemann claimed that he first decided to excavate Troy when he was just a boy. His father gave him a book – Georg Ludwig Jerrer's *Universal History* – which included a picture of Troy burning. The boy looked at the picture and decided that Jerrer must have seen Troy, otherwise he could not have portrayed it so vividly. But his father told him that Jerrer had never seen Troy, that he had just imagined what it must have looked like.

'But did Troy really have such huge walls?' Schliemann asked his father.

'Oh yes, it did,' his father replied.

'Well father,' Schliemann retorted, 'if such walls once existed, they cannot possibly have been completely destroyed; vast ruins of them must still remain, but they are hidden away beneath the dust of ages.'

The father and son argued this point for some time, about whether cities could vanish, about whether places hymned in poetry and painted in art must have a factual, literal origin.

'And finally,' said Schliemann, 'we both agreed that I should one day excavate Troy.'

The story is that Schliemann never forgot this conversation and consequently never lost his determination to excavate Troy in order to substantiate the popular myth. But first he had to gather the funds to pay for the dig and the academic learning to give it a veneer of respectability. He had left school at the age of fourteen with no qualifications, and had to climb his way up. So he worked in business for forty years and built up substantial independent wealth, with interests in California, Petersburg and Japan. Meanwhile, he had allegedly heard a drunk man reciting Homer while on his first job as a grocer's apprentice, and so formed the ambition to learn the language Homer wrote in. He in fact began teaching himself Greek, so that he could read Homer in the original by the age of thirty-four. By the time that he had thrown in his job in business at the age of forty-two, he was fully prepared for the assault on Hisarlik.

Schliemann's whole life was apparently focused upon searching for Homer's Troy. Even his fantasy life had a single theme. When he decided to marry for the second time, he specifically looked for a Greek wife. Indeed, he wrote to a friend, seeking help in his search for a bride who 'must be enthusiastic about Homer and a rebirth of my beloved Greece'.

It is hard to disentangle myth from reality in the story of Schliemann's life. The only source for the stories of Jerrer's pictures of Troy or the drunk man reciting Homer is Schliemann himself. He began his dry archaeology book, *Ilios: The City and the Country of the Trojans*, with a personal story about his early life and passion for Homer and Troy. He clearly wanted to promote one version of how he came to excavate Troy in 1870, a version in which he was an outsider, a self-made man and a genius, who was simply inspired by the poetry of Homer. According to this version, the text of the *Iliad* was his only guide; it was through reading Homer that he was inspired to go to Turkey, to look for Troy in Hisarlik, not Pinarbasi, as his predecessors had done, and to dig down until he found the appropriate treasure worthy of a heroic age. In other words, his motivation to dig was entirely due to his imagination, stirred by tales of Achilles, Agamemnon and Hector.

Schliemann's contemporaries were convinced by this version of events and claimed to recognise the role that imagination had played in his excavation. For some this made for bad archaeology. William Borlase, Schliemann's English translator, observed in the magazine *Fraser's Review*: 'Imagination is a very important qualification for an archaeologist to possess but in proportion to the strength of this power, a counterpoise of judgement is necessary, otherwise the imagination gets loose and runs riot.' He warmed to his theme: 'Dr Schliemann is, undoubtedly, an able man; but he must be credited with a vast amount of this sort of unbalanced imagination in order to explain the creations which he has produced out of the explorations of Hisarlik.'

But others defended Schliemann. In fact, they argued, it was Schliemann's imagination that had given him the vision to look for Troy in the first place. Good archaeology needs a vivid fantasy. Chief advocate for Schliemann was Rudolf Virchow, the founder of the German Society of Anthropology, Ethnography and Prehistory, who assisted in the surveying of Hisarlik after 1879. 'The Burnt City would still have lain to this day hidden in the earth, had not imagination guided the spade', Virchow wrote. Schliemann had revived science by his passion, according to Virchow. He had brought together truth and imagination so successfully that now archaeology had been injected with a new vigour and Homer could be read differently: 'The search for truth has at last so far relegated the intuitions of poetry to the background, that I felt myself forced to remind my friend, that the poet was not a poet only, that his pictures must also have had an objective foundation, and that nothing ought to deter us from bringing the reality into relation with the old legends.'

There were various key moments in Schliemann's excavation, when it seemed that imagination had particularly 'guided the spade', and perhaps clouded the judgement. On Professor Koppenhofer's tour of the citadel of Troy, we stop at one point and contemplate what has become known as Schliemann's trench. It is deep, bare, flat and much less cluttered than the rest of the site.

'Schliemann was convinced that Homer's Troy must date back to the earliest period of settlement and would therefore be found near the bottom of the hill, in the lowest stratum,' Koppenhofer says carefully.

'So he threw out all the layers above this one, right?' I ask.

'Yes,' replies Koppenhofer. 'We are looking down at Troy I, which dates back to about 2920 BC. But what Schliemann threw out was the later layers, like Troy VI, which were actually much closer to what he was looking for.'

'So crucial evidence was destroyed for ever in Schliemann's drive to find the purest, earliest, original layer,' I muse.

As we continue round the citadel, I keep asking Koppenhofer about the location of Schliemann's discovery of gold. For besides looking for the earliest city at the bottom of the citadel, Schliemann was also looking for a wealthy one, worthy of reverence. In his third season, in 1873, he duly found it. According to his story he was digging a rich seam, with various precious objects, bronze and copper, when he thought he spotted gold. In order, as he put it, 'to secure the treasure from my workmen and save it for archaeology', he called an early breakfast break so that the site would be clear and he could investigate his find alone. While the men were eating, he supposedly carefully cut out the gold from the soil with his knife.

'It would have been impossible', he went on, 'for me to have removed the treasure without the help of my dear wife, who stood at my side, ready to pack the things I cut out in her shawl and to carry them away.'

Schliemann dressed his wife in the jewels – bracelets, necklaces, dangling earrings and a golden headdress – which he called 'Helen's gold' – and photographed her. Since his wife was Greek, it seemed as if Helen herself had been brought back to life. This was not archaeology devoted to finding more about the past dispassionately or scientifically, but the search for an unbroken line between the present Schliemann family and the family of Priam, the people of Homer's imagination. The simple question – 'Did Troy exist?' – provoked the apparently simple answer – 'Yes, and it looked just as we imagined it.'

In recent years, Schliemann has come in for a lot of criticism, even more than during his lifetime, and a series of revelatory biographies and articles has been published. Everyone wants to dig the dirt on him, it seems. What annoys readers is that while Schliemann tried to ground Homer in literal, concrete evidence, his own life was one long fabrication. One of the key distortions, according to a recent critic, Susan Heuck Allen, is the notion that Schliemann came along to an empty landscape, Homer in hand, and by poetic inspiration and genius picked upon Hisarlik and discovered Troy. In fact, a British archaeologist, Frank Calvert, had been entertaining the idea that Hisarlik was Troy since 1860, had bought up some of the land there and had actually started to dig a few exploratory trenches seven years before Schliemann. He also gave Schliemann advice about techniques of excavation and led him to the site, persuading him that it was Hisarlik. What prevented Calvert from excavating further was lack of funds. The implication of this is that the imagination for which Schliemann is famous (or infamous) depended rather prosaically upon money. Schliemann glossed over his past history, erased Calvert from the picture and suggested that he was led by Homer or that 'imagination guided the spade'. But now it seems that the business deals in California and Russia played a crucial role in determining *whose* imagination guided what was 'found' in Troy.

The discovery of the 'jewels of Helen' has also been thrown into doubt. For one thing, it has been proved that, contrary to Schliemann's account, Sophie Schliemann was not 'at my side, ready to pack the things I cut out in her shawl and to carry them away'. In fact, she was not even in Turkey at the time but in Athens. So rather as with Solomon Ghormezano, who dug alone at night, there were in fact no witnesses to Schliemann's find, since he had supposedly sent the workmen off for breakfast and even his wife was not present. Could the treasure be a fake? Either Schliemann had bought the treasure from elsewhere and planted it in the site to be dug up, or perhaps he had gradually collected it over a number of months and chosen to reveal it all in one place. The fact that Schliemann is known to have lied about Sophie's presence has led critics to question his reliability as a source for the find overall.

Schliemann's story is one of treasure and deceit, as one biographer, David Traill, has put it. His life combined fact and fiction, just as his excavation methods did. While his work was devoted to bringing poetry or fiction closer to the material evidence needed to support it, his biography reveals that a great deal of the material evidence behind the claims about his life recedes before the fantasy. Yet as one critic, David Turner, has observed, 'much of the fictional in Schliemann's life is probably the most important *fact* of his life'. Schliemann lived half in a world of stories. Perhaps he half believed the myths he developed. Perhaps he really wanted his wife to be with him as he unearthed Helen's gold, and so it seemed to him retrospectively as if she had been with him not just in spirit but in person. 'Meaning', Turner maintains, 'is far more important than the register of mundane tabulated facts.'

It is fair, however, to say that the role of imagination which Schliemann claimed for his excavation was probably fabricated. As scholars like Allen have shown, his visionary persona was carefully constructed through editing his past history, and the myth of him as a lonely excavator, inspired by a love of Homer, was a calculated one. The cynical now believe that it was not 'imagination guiding the spade', but the love of personal fame. The 'register of mundane tabulated facts' is, after all, essential to the archaeological process and cannot be swept aside or ignored.

*

There was, however, another type of imagination motivating Schliemann's researches, one not calculated or carefully thought out at all, but altogether dirtier, more atavistic, more sinister. It went to the heart of the role of archaeology in the late Victorian period, and puts a very different gloss on the 'purity' or 'authenticity' of Troy.

In 1866, before he began excavating Troy, Schliemann visited a special exhibition held at Crystal Palace in London. The exhibition was of a Palaeolithic site from the Dordogne and had been inspired by a book, *Prehistoric Times*, written by the eminent historian, Sir John Lubbock. Lubbock's book had popularised the notion of prehistory, first developed in Denmark at the beginning of the century, and had certainly coined the terms 'Neolithic' and 'Palaeolithic', for different periods within the Stone Age. Inspired by Charles Darwin's *The Origin of Species*, which had used the findings of geologists such as Charles Lyell to posit the notion that man's history went back a lot further than the Garden of Eden, Lubbock similarly traced civilisation back into the mists of time. 'A new branch of knowledge has arisen which deals in times and events far more ancient than any which have yet fallen within the province of the archaeologist', he wrote. 'Archaeology forms the link between geology and history.'

The crucial question for Lubbock was whether that primitive history was better or worse than the present day. Was he dealing with a bunch of barbaric people, or with the purity of primitives so beloved by Romantic writers? In the opening to his later book, *The Origin of Civilisation*, which of course subtly picks up the title of Darwin's book, he alluded to this ambivalence in a striking image drawn itself from archaeology:

> The condition and habits of existing savages resemble in many ways, though not in all, those of our own ancestors in a period now long gone by; they illustrate much of what is passing among ourselves, many customs which have evidently no relation to the present circumstances, and even some ideas which are rooted in our minds, as fossils are embedded in the soil.

On the one hand, Lubbock argues that foreign people and our primitive ancestors are different from us. They are more savage and inferior, fit to be ruled in 'an empire like ours'. But on the other hand, he also says that they are paradoxically like us. Their customs are familiar, they are clearly related, and therefore they are worth studying. The familiarity of our savage ancestors is like a nagging idea in the mind, like 'a fossil embedded in the soil'. Ostensibly Lubbock claims that we share some ideas with our ancestors and that therefore they were perhaps more advanced than we might think. But the dark implication of his argument, and the suggestion of the image he adopts, is that deeply embedded in the mind of every Victorian is a savagery which is impossible to root out. Hunting for prehistoric ancestors might have seemed to offer a primitive purity. But in fact it gave rise to an atavistic savagery based on a new notion of purity: racial purity.

114

5. Fundamentalism: Digging Our Trojan Origins

Schliemann's discovery of Helen's gold grabbed the headlines. But there was another series of finds which actually started to intrigue the specialist archaeologists and ethnologists of the time still more. This was the succession of pottery finds decorated with the swastika symbol. Schliemann identified several hundred swastika symbols on the pottery which he dug up. One of the key swastikas, which he chose to focus upon, appeared as decoration carved on the body of an idol, a goddess figure (Plate 10). 'It is now time', Schliemann wrote in his book *Ilios* in 1880, 'to explain the curious signs which we have seen on the vulva of the lead idol.'

In his book of 1880, Schliemann hid behind the opinion and wisdom of his associates. He quoted the Oxford professor and Oriental scholar Friedrich Max Müller, and Rudolf Virchow. Both these men were trying to play down the iconic significance of the symbol. The swastika was universal, they argued, and should not be commandeered for some sort of political or racial argument. 'The occurrence of such crosses in different parts of the world may or may not point to a common origin. But if they are once called *svastika*, the *vulgus profanum* will at once jump to the conclusion that they all come from India, and it will take some time to weed out such a prejudice', Müller warned. 'While from these indications we are justified in supposing that among the Aryan nations the *Svastika* may have been an old emblem of the sun, there are other indications to show that in other parts of the world the same or a very similar emblem was used to indicate the earth.'

But by 1884, when he published his next book about Troy, *Troja: Results of the Latest Researches and Discoveries on the Site of Homer's Troy*, Schliemann was a lot bolder. Now he included quotations and whole essays from those with confirmed racially-prejudiced theories. The crucial point was to prove that every swastika was connected and not just a random artistic product of any and every culture. Each swastika was the emblem of a specific Aryan race, which was biologically related across time and space, now demonstrably stretching back to Trojan times. Schliemann quoted R.P. Greg, who had been studying the swastika for six years and had read a paper on the subject to the Society of Antiquaries in London in 1882. Greg argued, according to Schliemann, that every occurrence of a swastika told the same story: it was 'exclusively of early Aryan use and origin'.

The comments of the Oxford professor, Archibald Sayce, on *Ilios* formed the preface to *Troja*. Schliemann's discoveries at Troy 'acquire for us a double interest', Sayce maintained. They offered direct access to 'the later Stone-age of the Aryan race', a period previously available only through unreliable folklore and now tangibly present in the pottery finds men could handle. But also, he continued, 'they will serve to settle the question, which is at present perplexing the minds of archaeologists and ethnolo-

115

gists, as to whether the people of the later Stone-age in Western Europe can be regarded as Aryans, or as representatives only of the races which inhabited this part of the globe before any Aryans arrived here'. Since swastikas had also been found on pottery in northern Greece, Sayce maintained that the Trojans had originally crossed over to Troy from Europe. So they were safely Western, Greek in origin and Aryan, rather than worryingly Asiatic. He traced a racial blood-line directly from the Trojans to his own people in the late nineteenth century and wrote of 'hailing the subjects of Priam as brethren in blood and speech'.

Schliemann was not simply content with these two accounts of ethnic origins, based upon iconography. He was also interested in the new specifically racist and anti-Semitic notions associated with Aryanism, which were being developed by other archaeologists. For being Aryan crucially meant not being Jewish. It was a deeply loaded political issue gathering momentum all the time. Schliemann had actually cited the theory of one of the most prominent anti-Semites, Emile Burnouf, that the swastikas 'represent the two pieces of wood, which were laid crosswise upon one another before the sacrificial altars, in order to produce the sacred fire'.

What Schliemann was referring to was the book by Emile Burnouf, director of the French School in Athens, called *The Science of Religions*. In this book, Burnouf attempted to prove that Christianity was essentially an Aryan religion, and that the swastika, as a symbol, anticipated or represented the Christian cross. The sign means salvation, according to Burnouf. So when Jesus was put to death on the cross, the old Aryan symbol of the swastika was recalled and easily applied to him. Retrospectively it seemed appropriate that the means of his death, the cross, was also the means of our salvation, the cross-shaped swastika.

The swastika symbol was being co-opted in the current obsession with Aryanism and its religious and racial significance. Racist historians at this time were developing an idea of the Aryans, or Indo-Europeans, as the pure, anti-Jewish ancestors of the West. In *The Origin of Civilisation*, John Lubbock had contrasted the mental capacity of the Aryans to develop imaginatively and metaphorically with that of Semites: 'All Aryan races have a complicated mythology, which is not the case with the Semitic races.' And Schliemann included in *Troja* the thesis of Karl Blind that the Indo-Europeans had blond hair and blue eyes, which, Schliemann maintained, were the characteristics of the Trojans. Trojans were really Indo-Europeans or Teutonic Thracians. In other words, the Trojans were racially the ancestors of the Germans, justifying Teutonic superiority over all other races: 'Those Thrakians – blue-eyed, red-haired, according to an indication by Xenophanes, 500 years before our era – were a most martial and a highly musical people, much given to Bacchic habits, but also to philosophical speculation.'

Now, however, these writers who were developing theories about the Indo-Europeans had a symbol to focus on – the swastika – and an emotionally resonant site in which to place their ancestry – Homer's Troy.

Everything came to a head at a special exhibition in Paris in 1889. Organised by the Polish archaeologist Michael Zmigrodski, the exhibition included several hundred drawings of excavated objects decorated with the swastika. To promote the exhibition Zmigrodski gave a lecture on 'the history of the swastika' at the International Congress of Prehistoric Anthropology and Archaeology, gathered in Paris. Schliemann was in the audience, along with many other people connected with his excavation at Troy, Emile Burnouf, Archibald Sayce and Thomas Wilson (curator of the Department of Prehistoric Anthropology in the Smithsonian, Washington and author of the later essay *The Swastika: Earliest Known Symbol and Its Migrations*). 'Our race is a family of the highest nobility, and has for its armorial shield, the swastika', Zmigrodski told his listeners.

The swastika was both a sign of racial inheritance – the same icon had apparently been used over centuries and could be usefully traced to determine biological ancestry – and also given intrinsic nobility and meaning. It was the cross upon which the Jews had crucified Jesus, as Burnouf had bluntly put it. It therefore reminded Aryans constantly of the need to maintain anti-Semitic hatred.

Zmigrodski was tuned into the question of the origins of the race, one of the burning issues of the day, and Schliemann's excavation could not have come more opportunely. Writers who were already deep in discussion about the origins of the Indo-Europeans seized upon Schliemann's discoveries at Troy for their own purposes and turned it into something dark and sinister. One writer in the *Archaeological Journal* commented, for example, that the presence of the swastika 'would seem to indicate the common Aryan descent of all the successive inhabitants of Hisarlik'. Professor Sayce in Oxford was similarly pleased. Schliemann's archaeological finds had proved his long-cherished racial theories. 'Thanks to Dr Schliemann's discoveries, we now know who the Trojans originally were', he wrote. 'The heroes of the *Iliad* and the *Odyssey* have become to us men of flesh and blood.' Edward Thomas, an Oriental scholar whom Schliemann also cited, got caught up in the anti-Semitic, religious fervour. He wrote an article about the new archaeological finds, describing the 'crypto-import' and the 'mystic' quality of the swastika design.

There were, of course, big problems with the Aryan swastika theory, niggling details that just would not add up. For one thing, the swastika looked very different in different cultures. Sometimes it went clockwise and at other times anticlockwise. Sometimes it had straight arms and at other times curvy ones. Sometimes the broken legs were attached and at other times they were not. Another problem was the distribution of the swastika. Swastikas had been dug up in Troy and India but there were none in the lands in between, in the old Persian empire for example. Could India and Troy be connected or did the design develop in two places independently? Was there one original swastika-painting Aryan culture which dispersed later, or were swastikas just a natural design for all sorts of peoples and cultures?

The supporters of the Aryan swastika, fired up by Schliemann, attempted to explain these scruples away. Zmigrodski suggested that if the swastika changed over time – shifted from being clockwise to anti-clockwise, for example – this was an example of corruption and miscegenation. Originally there was just one type of swastika, just as there was one pure Aryan race. When the Aryans encountered other cultures as they gradually dispersed east and west across the globe, they were sadly infiltrated by other ideas and art forms, just as their blood became weakened and mixed through inter-racial marriage. So the swastika degenerated to other alternative, clockwise or anti-clockwise versions. Zmigrodski accordingly went on to reduce Schliemann's two hundred swastikas to just sixty-five 'pure' Trojan, or Aryan, examples.

Another racist, the Count Goblet d'Alviella, admitted that there was a bit of a problem with the evidence. The swastika had been unearthed in India and Troy. Could the two countries be connected? Alviella conceded that some scholars thought that they could not, that the religions of India and Greece were too different to allow for the migration of the same symbol between them. And besides, no swastikas had been found in Persia, the land in between. But this, Alviella maintained, was no substantial barrier to his theory. Several other Indian symbols had been borrowed from Greece and 'why should the swastika form an exception?' It was, he said, 'less a question of ethnography than of archaeology'; the racial theory held good and it just required archaeologists to dig up more evidence to confirm it. He added that Schliemann had made a vital contribution because his swastikas were even earlier, more original and more pure; the swastika was, at Troy, 'closer to its cradle and even nearer to its original signification'.

It is not clear from all this debate that Heinrich Schliemann himself was anti-Semitic. His books about Troy read like mosaics of other opinions, and he does not often venture his own views, apart from the heartfelt personal memoir about his childhood ambition to excavate Troy. In fact, as he writes in *Troja*, he was often overwhelmed by expert advice, following the publication of his earlier reports, and it was difficult to accommodate everyone and fit every paper and letter into his subsequent books. But on the other hand it is hard to believe that Schliemann was so naive that he did not realise what he was doing. He did attend Zmigrodski's big swastika jamboree, with all its attendant xenophobia. And he was steeped in the Indo-European theories of Lubbock, Burnouf and Müller. It seems safer to posit a subconscious additional significance to his obsessive desire to penetrate to the 'virgin-soil' of Troy, to find the 'pure' world of Homer. The Victorian archaeological imagination, at least in Schliemann's case, was hopelessly compromised by the need to find, or invent, lost ancestors and to throw out the debris of a history they would rather not acknowledge.

What Schliemann could not have foreseen was the way in which his supposedly objective, back-to-basics excavation indirectly encouraged the pseudo-scientific accounts of racial origins and purity that increasingly became an industry in the early twentieth century. Burnouf and Zmigrodski had begun the process of linking Trojan archaeology with a racist ethnography. Karl Blind, Archibald Sayce and Count d'Aviella had given a boost to the campaign. But Houston Chamberlain, born British but married to the daughter of Richard Wagner, set the seal on the connection by publishing *Grundlagen des Neunzehnten Jahrhunderts* in 1899, a smash hit which ran through eight editions in as many years and was finally translated into English and published in 1910 under the title *The Foundations of the Nineteenth Century*. In the book, Chamberlain maintains that the German or Teutonic people are the masters of the nineteenth century and that they have attained their supremacy because they have inherited the best aspects from three racial groups: art from the Greeks, government from the Romans and Christianity from the Jews. Crucially, however, behind even these three historical cultures, is the original Aryan race from which they all stem. It is a place of purity and innocence, a 'race of shepherds who walked abroad almost naked' and yet also strangely primitive: they 'knew neither cities nor metals'.

What is striking about Chamberlain's book is the confidence with which he maintains the most outlandish and bizarre theories. Jesus, for example, was not Jewish because God was really his father, not Joseph. Each of his deeply prejudicial, racially-motivated opinions about the past is delivered with an objective, scientific certainty. As Chamberlain points out at the start of his book, this work will be the product of science, not of art. 'We must leave the airy heights of philosophic speculation', he writes, 'and descend to the earth.' With the well-developed connection between racism and archaeology, it is surprising he did not descend beneath the earth.

When Adolf Hitler came to develop his theories about the Aryan race, it is clear that Chamberlain was very much present in his thoughts. The terms in which he describes the origin of the German people and the contribution of Aryanism to their supremacy echo those in *The Foundations of the Nineteenth Century*, not least in the notion of 'foundation' as a way of talking about race. In his manifesto for Nazism, *Mein Kampf*, he writes: 'If we were to divide mankind into three groups, the founders of culture, the bearers of culture, the destroyers of culture, only the Aryan could be considered the representative of the first group. From him originate the foundations and walls of all human creation, and only the outward form and colour are determined by the changing traits of character of the various peoples.' The distinction that Hitler made between the 'foundations' of the race and the variation of its 'outward' traits, which resulted from the decadent mixing of races, derived directly from these late nineteenth-century pseudo-scientific accounts of Aryanism.

So it was only natural that, when Hitler came to look for a symbol around which all these ideas about racial purity could congregate, he chose the sign which had most exercised Burnouf, Zmigrodski, Chamberlain and others. He was, after all, a fan of Heinrich Schliemann. 'I myself, meanwhile, after innumerable attempts, had laid down a final form; a flag with a red background, a white disk, and a black swastika in the middle', he recalled in *Mein Kampf*. 'After long trials I also found a definite proportion between the size of the flag and the size of the white disk, as well as the shape and thickness of the swastika. And this remained final.'

Hitler voiced cold conviction about the flag, about the swastika, about race. In the future, signs would carry a clear-cut message, mixing Schliemann's love of facts with a pseudo-scientific expectation that everything can be explained. Hitler even decoded the symbolic message in the Nazi design: 'As National Socialists, we see our programme in our flag. In *red* we see the social idea of the movement, in *white* the nationalistic idea, in the *swastika* the mission of the struggle for the victory of the Aryan man, and, by the same token, the victory of the idea of creative work, which as such always has been and always will be anti-Semitic.'

Some archaeologists tried to resist the Nazi reductive method of reading archaeological signs. The American W. Norman Brown tackled Hitler on archaeological and anthropological grounds in a hard-hitting pamphlet entitled *The Swastika: A Study of the Nazi Claims of its Aryan Origin*. He pointed out that the swastika had dispersed over vast distances and that excavation had uncovered a huge variety in the design. More importantly he threw into question Hitler's identification of culture with physical race. Just because a culture used an artistic design like a swastika, that did not mean that it was all physically one race, Brown argued. A nation should be determined by its language, not by its blood. Even in Germany, 'the German language is spoken not merely by those whose forebears were German, but also by some whose ancestors were Czechs or Celts or Prussians.' Archaeology, therefore, could not be appropriated for some pure racial agenda; even in Scandinavia, supposedly the home of Aryans, 'all evidence, including that of pre-historic archaeology, vouches for the presence of other physical types side by side with the Nordics'. Brown, like Hobhouse over a hundred years before him, was fighting a battle for a nuanced understanding of 'evidence', one based upon the ambivalent import of 'language' and 'texts' rather than upon facts and blood and objects. Events, however, were against Brown. Archaeology had been co-opted for a frightening, political cause and the scruples and sophistication he put forward had no place in the black-and-white (and red) world of Hitler.

*

Schliemann's excavation at Hisarlik had revived the popular enthusiasm for the fact, the solid object. After decades of general prevarication about Troy's historical existence and years of the common belief that Homer's was a work purely of imagination, Schliemann had dug down into the earth and come up with tangible treasure and concrete objects which apparently proved a racial genealogy from the Trojans to the present day. His supporters repeatedly urged the scientific nature of his archaeology and the important implication of his discoveries for the relative merits of material versus textual evidence. Professor Sayce in Oxford was one of the most outspoken: 'By the side of one of the jade axes which Dr Schliemann has uncovered at Hisarlik, the *Iliad* itself is but a thing of yesterday.' Since Schliemann's excavation, poetry was unnecessary. Scientific archaeological methods could now be applied to supposed relics of the heroic Homeric age with unquestioning certainty. Sayce pondered excitedly the possibility now of even measuring 'the nature and capacity of the skulls' of the Homeric heroes, presumably to assess their racial purity.

One writer who was keen to measure the skulls and test other lines of Homer's poetry against the actual objects dug up from the ground was the maverick philosopher and novelist Samuel Butler. For some time he had been captivated by the new theories of Charles Darwin and he always wanted to reduce speculation to literal fact. He had been thinking about the debates concerning the authorship of the *Iliad* and the *Odyssey* for several years, so when he heard about the excavation at Troy, he naturally wanted to see it for himself.

He travelled to the Troad in 1895. Schliemann was dead, and Wilhelm Dörpfeld was leading the excavation. It seems from Butler's account in his notebook as if he did not actually meet Dörpfeld; it was Easter, the cold wind was blowing strongly and perhaps the digging season had not yet started. At any rate, he was taken to Hisarlik by Frank Calvert's nephew, left his horse at Dörpfeld's hut and wandered in among the excavations, accompanied only, it seems, by a local guide, Gakoub. It was too cold to camp at the site and there was nowhere to stay nearby, so Butler had only a few hours to view everything. 'I should have had to spend several days upon the spot with Dr Dörpfeld or some other equally competent person before I could satisfy myself one way or the other about the series of cities which Schliemann declares himself able to detect', he confessed in his diary.

Butler disguised his jealous admiration for Schliemann and Dörpfeld with a grudging scepticism. The remains that he was shown, the ditches and walls, 'did not carry the conviction' which he was expecting and he 'saw nothing that impressed me'. The walls did not look early enough, and he was forced to take 'these burnt buildings being remnants of an earlier city on trust'. Butler had to rely upon outside explanation when looking at stones from the past and so, in his disappointment about the limits of excavation, he hit out at Schliemann's supposed incompetence. Schliemann, he wrote smugly, never saw the real walls of Troy which he was now seeing, because Schliemann 'began to excavate from the middle of the mound hoping to find the treasury of Priam and actually covered the true Iliadic walls with the earth of Priam'.

Yet, beneath the cross complaints, Samuel Butler was secretly excited. He was treading the same ground that Homer and his heroes walked, feeling the same biting wind and looking down over the same plain from the citadel of Troy which Helen had viewed. While the excavation itself just highlighted his amateurish ignorance – 'I felt all the time as though it might very well be my own fault that I could not see the force of what was pointed out to me' – the significance of the landscape, which now grounded Homer's story in indisputable fact, fascinated him. Indeed, Butler even tried to outdo Schliemann in the reduction of Homer to geographical, archaeological fact by claiming he could detect the origin of some of Homer's descriptions and therefore could tell even where Homer lived: 'Bearing in mind the utterly undue prominence given to Mount Ida throughout the *Iliad*, ... I incline to think that he came from some such place as Erjilar ... I imagine he found his way to the city of Dardanus, where he probably wrote his poem or at any rate conceived it, and became thoroughly familiar with the country around Troy.'

Butler was keen to establish Homer's childhood home because tracing the domestic clutter behind the Homeric epics, the *Iliad* and the *Odyssey*, was one of his great projects. In fact, he went to Troy at a time when he was devoting most of his attention to establishing his belief that the *Odyssey* was written not by Homer but by a woman, and that she lived in Sicily. This thesis was based upon the conviction that a writer only writes about what he knows, that he cannot imagine things or just dream them up. So if one charts which facts in the epics are conveyed with the most graphic details and intimate knowledge, then one can learn what the writer knew and therefore who he was and where he lived. This theory of

Butler's is the absurd conclusion one reaches if one follows Schliemann's literary criticism through excavation to extremes. According to Butler, the *Odyssey* is full of domestic details about weaving and laundry and household management; its portrayal of Penelope is sympathetic while its knowledge of navigation is weak. Therefore it must have been written by a woman, a 'highspirited, headstrong girl'. Similarly, its landscape features are reminiscent of Sicily. Butler made several visits during the 1890s to Trapani in Sicily, where he found everything just as 'Homer' described both Scheria, the land of the Phaeacians, and Ithaca. He even tried to substantiate his claims by exploring a cave near Trapani, 'abounding', so he said, 'in Stone-Age remains'.

Schliemann had set the agenda for a new understanding of revelation. His excavation was now a metaphor for other major achievements in new scientific or cultural understanding. Freud had compared his breakthrough in psychoanalysis to Schliemann's archaeology, writing to his friend Wilhelm Fliess that it was 'as if Schliemann had dug up another Troy which had hitherto been believed to be mythical'. And Butler compared his major discovery of the 'authoress of the *Odyssey*' and her origins in Sicily, with Schliemann's finding of Troy. 'I believe that I have unburied Scheria as effectually as Schliemann unburied Troy', he wrote. 'I do not see why it is more meritorious to uncover physically with a spade than spiritually with a little of the very commonest common sense.'

Butler's 'spiritual' excavation, which allowed readers to 'find' the ordinary things described in Homer, became an important influence on James Joyce's epic novel *Ulysses*. Joyce had probably heard from him about his trip to the excavations at Troy and had certainly read his 'literal prose' translation of the *Odyssey* which was inspired by his new archaeological understanding of Homer. Butler claimed to have firsthand knowledge of the material culture which Homer describes in his epic – the brooches, hair pins and leg greaves – and this influenced his translation; it gleamed vividly with objects. Joyce's *Ulysses*, the account of one day in the life of Leopold Bloom, followed Butler in offering an archaeological section of Dublin on 16 June 1906. Every item is recorded, just as it might be by an archaeologist in centuries to come: street names, pubs, newspapers, advertisements, betting slips. Even the most trivial details are given weight and attention in the novel; an archaeologist cannot tell the relative value of different objects when he is excavating. And nothing can even be lost or destroyed effectively, since excavation basically just involves rifling through the rubbish of the past. Bloom bets on a horse 'Throwaway' and later flings the betting slip into the river Liffey. But while he forgets about it, the novel does not and the whereabouts of Throwaway, in its course down the river, is carefully charted.

Joyce's gathering of the fragments of Dublin seems to have been without political agenda. By the time of writing *Ulysses*, he was in self-imposed exile and the book was, in effect, a work of archaeology, the loving recuperation of the Dublin he had left behind. But Joyce's friend, Ezra Pound, gathered his scraps of past civilisation for a far more virulent purpose. T.S. Eliot had written, in *The Waste Land*, that 'these fragments I shore against my ruin' and Pound also seems to see the work of archaeological salvage, which his poetry amounts to, as an act of courage against the degeneration caused by bankers, usurers, Jews. His epic-long, difficult poem, the *Cantos*, compared at one point to the postbag of history, contains fragments of past literature, including the odd words from Sappho's poetry which had just been dug up at Oxyrynchus in Egypt. But in among the scraps is one telling symbol, the swastika, the cross which 'turns with the sun':

> Περσεφόνεια under Taishan
>   in sight of the tower che pende
> on such a litter rode Pontius
>   under such a canvass
> in the a.h. of the army
>   in sight of two red cans labeled 'FIRE'
> Said Von Tirpitz to his daughter: beware of their charm
> ΣΕΙΡΗΝΕΣ this cross turns with the sun
> and the goyim are undoubtedly in great numbers cattle
> whereas a jew will receive information
>   he will gather up information
>   faute de ... something more solid
>   but not in all cases
> ΣΕΙΡΗΝΕΣ   had appreciated his conversation
>   ΧΑΡΙΤΕΣ possibly in the soft air
>   with the mast held by the left hand
>   in this air as of Kuanon
> enigma forgetting the times and seasons
> but this air brought her ashore a la marina
> with the great shell borne on the seawaves

Against the siren voices of treachery, which betray through their antique aura, their apparent but bogus origin in Homer, the swastika holds firm, linking present politics back in time to the original Homeric origins as unearthed by Schliemann. By holding tight to the swastika, as Odysseus held tightly to the mast, the siren voices can be heard and countenanced; like Persephone, the pure race of western civilisation can survive all threats and rise again from the dead.

Pound was writing this poem, the first of the 'Pisan Cantos', in post-war

Italy, where he was incarcerated for his role in promoting the Mussolini regime. There is no record, disappointingly, of his particular interest in Mussolini's enthusiastic programme of excavation. Mussolini was pouring huge amounts of money into the archaeological investigation of Rome, anxious to uncover the ancient Roman remains and thus to establish, for propaganda purposes, the links between his fascist regime and the glorious Roman empire. He adopted as his symbol the 'fasces', the axes bound with rods which bodyguards of the Roman magistrates carried – axes arguably similar to the ones unearthed by Schliemann in Troy. According to Virgil's *Aeneid*, the Trojans were the original ancestors of the Romans; the Romans, through Mussolini's efforts, were the natural ancestors of the fascist regime of the 1930s. And therefore Pound's swastika, shoring up the ruins in Pisa, brought together past and present, Troy and Rome, Schliemann and Mussolini.

So Schliemann's dig, especially once it had been popularised and developed by later writers and thinkers such as Houston Chamberlain and Samuel Butler, provoked a new type of fundamentalism. It was, in part, a fundamentalism in terms of methodology, an obsession with grounding narrative and hypothesis in scientific fact, which could slide naturally into the fascist method of proving racial characteristics through cold scientific theories. But it also established Troy as the site for a fundamentalist object fetishism, with racist implications.

It is probably in response to this development that W.B. Yeats wrote his sonnet, 'Leda and the Swan' in 1922. It describes the violent rape of Leda by the god Zeus, disguised as a swan. The rape resulted in the birth of Helen, who was supposedly the cause of the Trojan war. But Yeats compresses the story, so that the animalistic thrust of the swan produces instantaneously a Troy already destroyed, the war already over, its heroes killed:

> A shudder in the loins engenders there
> The broken wall, the burning roof and tower
> And Agamemnon dead.
>   Being so caught up,
> So mastered by the brute blood of the air,
> Did she put on his knowledge with his power
> Before the indifferent beak would let her drop?

Yeats' Troy is Schliemann's, identifiable through its material remains: the 'broken wall', the 'burning roof and tower', or in other words, Troy II, the Burnt City. But it is also latently Schliemann's in its violence and brutality. The swan carries the fate of Troy, the origins of the race, in its blood: the 'brute blood of the air'. And the fascist respect for the superior race is there in the swan's 'power', in its 'mastery' of the vulnerable Leda. Old myths survive through the modernist excavation of material fragments, through the essential bits of Homer – the wall, the roof, the tower – identifiable by scientific, archaeological tests. But that modernist excavation, by the 1920s, was tainted with ideology, sucked into Hitler's and Mussolini's fascist idolisation of power.

*

Not all of Schliemann's discoveries at Troy ended up lost in Hitler's propaganda machine. Until recently, it was thought that the treasure, Helen's gold, had indeed been lost in the war. After touting his treasure around to different national museums – the French, the British and the Americans were all given the chance to bid for it – Schliemann eventually had smuggled it out of his house in Athens and sent it to Berlin in 1881. There it became a central part of the collection of the Ethnographical Museum, later renamed the Museum for History and Prehistory, and there it remained until the Second World War. Fated never to shake off its anti-Semitic, national socialist associations, from 1926 onwards it had in fact been curated by the Nazi Party member Wilhelm Unverzagt, in a building located directly opposite the Gestapo headquarters. But when the Russians liberated the city in 1945, the collection went missing. Rumours circulated wildly about where the treasure might have gone. Had the gold been melted down? Was it lying in some vault in Leningrad? Did it now form part of the collection of some Texan oil millionaire?

But in 1993, with the end of the Cold War, the Russians finally confirmed that the treasure had been smuggled out of Berlin and stored in the basement of the Pushkin State Museum of Fine Arts in Moscow for the last fifty years. There were a few months of doubt, as it was suggested that this treasure might actually have been the copies which Schliemann had made of his collection in order to fool the Turkish authorities and distract them from the real items which he was clandestinely exporting. But after expert inspection, the message came back. These pieces were 'authentic'. Helen's gold, the kernel of the Trojan excavation, had been refound.

In 1996, the gold was publicly exhibited. It is displayed in the room at the centre of the museum which is dedicated to antique art from 'ancient Greece, Rome and the Northern Black Sea Region'. Theatrically draped over the plaster bust of a woman, the gold diadems, necklaces and earrings gleam in the spotlight, dazzling and dramatic against the black backdrop. But elsewhere in the room there are exhibited objects discovered at the site of Greek colonies in the Crimea and the Caucasus. There is, for example, a statue of Neocles, a local ruler who is dressed in Greek clothes but whose face reveals local ethnic features. These artefacts, the guide to the museum informs the visitor, 'acquaint us with the distant history of the peoples which inhabited the Northern Black Sea Region and the southern steppes of Russia many years ago'.

It is difficult not to be affected by the proximity of these two collections, housed now in the same room. One collection – Schliemann's gold – consists of art from just south of the Black Sea; the other collection – arguably the earliest traces of Russian culture – consists of objects from just north of the Black Sea. The implication is that only the sea divides the two cultures, not major ethnic differences. In other words, Moscow is implicitly laying claim to Schliemann's gold by suggesting that there is a continuous historical racial line linking the Russians with the ancient Trojans. The archaeological remains from Troy are still being used to promote certain ideological arguments about racial origins, continuing a tradition of politically motivated excavation with nationalist or racist implications which dates right back to the earliest expedition to dig Troy in the 1790s. It may look beautiful, but Schliemann's gold is still 'dirty'.

*

Back in Troy, however, things seem very different. Manfred Korfmann gives me a lift back from Achilles' tomb and the drillers to the excavation headquarters, but we take a detour round the whole plain. We drive over to Besik Bay, where Korfmann excavated in the 1980s, before starting on Troy. And we look at the fields and the woods and the rivers, which he has surveyed and known now for twenty years.

'Look at this field,' he gestures as we cross a river. 'This used to be a forest. Now it has been cut down and cultivated.'

Korfmann has persuaded the Turkish government to declare the whole plain of Troy a National Park. This means that no more housing development or tree felling is possible here, and in the future he hopes to control the amount of pesticide which the farmers put down in the fields.

'We are not just interested in the archaeological sites, in the stones and rocks,' he says. 'The whole land is precious and must be protected. We want to keep a sense of how it all relates for future generations.'

And as we round the next bend and linger behind yet another slow-moving tractor, he grows even more visionary.

'I think that Troy is a unique place,' he says. 'It has famously been the site of so many battles, so many horrible wars, because of its strategic position. Not just Homer's Trojan war, but also Gallipoli. And other smaller wars too. But I like to think we could transform that and make it famous as a place of peace. Peace in nature; peace in society; peace between nations. It is where East meets West, where Islam meets Christianity. Forget Camp David, Troy could be a place of major negotiations and peace treaties in the future. That is what I am working towards.'

Given the history of a fundamentalist kind of archaeology in Troy, and given the rise of political fundamentalism at the moment, Korfmann's wish may seem a tall order. But it is an admirable and hopeful vision on which to depend.

Rock Bottom: Digging and Despair

There is, perhaps, no more disturbing and uncomfortable moment in theatre than the scene in Shakespeare's *Hamlet* in which the prince chats to the gravedigger. The digger, played traditionally by the theatre company's clown, is preparing a grave for Ophelia, who has just drowned and whose solemn funeral procession arrives midway through the scene. While he digs, the comic gravedigger turns over with his spade the remains of those previously buried in the churchyard. Skulls and other bones are thrown up from the bottom of the hole and unceremoniously cleared to make space for the new grave. Hamlet watches with a mixture of horror and fascination at this casual treatment of the dead. 'Did these bones cost no more the breeding but to play at loggets with 'em?', he asks his friend Horatio. Shocked and intrigued, he decides to quiz the sexton about his profession.

What Hamlet wishes to know is the ultimate destination of all human life. What happens to us after death? Will we be remembered? Is there anything unique about each life which will last beyond the grave and which will make it meaningful and worthwhile? The sexton, who spends his life delving among the dead, seems the obvious person to ask. But what Hamlet gets is an unremittingly literal set of answers, which reduces every uncertainty about life and death to its material constituents. On asking the sexton whose grave he is digging, he is told that it is for neither man nor woman but for 'one that was a woman, sir; but rest her soul, she's dead'. The corpse has already lost its specific identity and is merely a 'dead' body. And questions about the fate of a body after death are answered in similarly literal, physical terms:

Hamlet: How long will a man lie i' th' earth ere he rot?
Gravedigger: Faith, if a be not rotten before a die – as we have many pocky corses nowadays that will scarce hold the laying in – a will last you some eight year or nine year. A tanner will last you nine year.
Hamlet: Why he more than another?
Gravedigger: Why, sir, his hide is so tanned with his trade that a will keep out water a great while, and your water is a sore decayer of your whoreson dead body.

The gravedigger confirms Hamlet's hunch that there is no more to life than disintegrating flesh and decaying water. Right from the beginning of the play, Hamlet has wished that 'this too too solid flesh would melt/ Thaw and resolve itself into a dew'. Contemplating self-extinction, he is both comforted and horrified by the idea that nothing lasts, even the solidity of the body. He has spoken throughout the play of a vision of a world in which nothing holds steady, in which even corpses waste away, turning back into the dirt from which they were formed and released into the atmosphere in a 'fine revolution'. Since we are all nothing but a 'quintessence of dust', he believes, there is nothing special about anyone which will be preserved. The general disintegration in the grave makes all distinctions and concerns in this life meaningless. 'A man may fish with the worm that hath eat of a king, and eat of the fish that hath fed of that worm', Hamlet teases King Claudius. This just goes to show that 'a king may go a progress through the guts of a beggar'.

But Hamlet's nihilistic vision of the pointlessness of life comes into sharpest focus when he encounters the gravedigger. Vague notions about man being possibly no more than a 'quintessence of dust', which Hamlet might have derived from reading books, develop more vivid import when he is confronted with the result of the gravedigger's excavations. Then he can see skulls as objects, 'knocked about the mazard with a sexton's spade' and thrown or 'jowled' around. He can contemplate the change in fortune death brings, when men who were once perhaps powerful lawyers can find their heads 'full of fine dirt'. And coming face to face, famously, with the skull of Yorick, the old court jester, he can even smell the decay: 'My gorge rises at it. Here hung those lips I have kissed I know not how oft.' The physical nature of death and decay is unavoidable when revealed by the spade. While spiritual notions about the significance of man, flighted to heaven by angels, might be possible when mooted in the comfort of the court or the library, out among the graves – where the clown performs what might be thought of as urgent rescue archaeology, excavating the past before it is evacuated for the present – the prosaic reality of material disintegration and insignificance is all too obvious.

The connections between archaeology and scepticism run deep. Delving among the scattered physical remains of the dead involves a concentration upon the literalness of the dying process which runs counter to any possible religious interpretation. It is perhaps hard to retain a sense of the worth of human life when faced with withered fragments of bone and tooth and hair in the grave. And it becomes worse when those remains are mingled with the dust, perhaps even indistinguishable from the dirt around them. 'Ashes to ashes, dust to dust' goes the funeral service, but only archaeologists give that dust as much significance (or insignificance) as they give to the dead.

6. Rock Bottom: Digging and Despair

Often the importance of dirt for archaeologists, as for Hamlet, takes on a bleakly comic aspect. The removal of the earth during an excavation becomes a pressing consideration, which offers both logistical problems and also a vital standard of measurement. At an excavation I worked on in Belize in the hot, humid, rainy season, one lost sense of all significance other than that based upon earth and water. We emptied buckets of heavy, rain-sodden earth dug from the site onto a huge and growing mound of earth twenty metres away across the field. And we survived the midday heat with our carefully guarded four litres each of drinking water. As the humidity level soared, nothing mattered other than shifting earth from one plot of ground to another and calculating how much liquid was left in the bottle. By the end of the day, my two-metre square excavation plot might have dropped five centimetres and supposedly the mound of earth nearby had risen five centimetres. I found myself thinking of Winnie in *Happy Days*, buried up to her waist in sand in the first half of Samuel Beckett's play and buried up to her neck in the second half. In that play, the passage of time in the theatre is indicated by the rise in sand level. So my days in Belize were demarcated by the amount of earth I had shifted. As Beckett's darkly absurd vision suggests, when the world has become emptied of meaning, progress can only be measured by the bizarrely literal, ever-rising pile of dirt.

But at other times, excavation which cannot distinguish the human from the inhuman, and the significant from the insignificant, assumes tragic rather than comic overtones. Then the search for something which might suggest that we are more than dust and dirt takes on an extra desperate urge, when the preciously human is threatened by the sheer weight and indifference of the earth. Archaeology might, in that situation, yearn for a greater spiritual dimension even at the moment when it exposes its limitations and literal reduction.

Despair has often accompanied the archaeological dig. Excavation could be said to mark the moment when we lose religious faith, when we are most vulnerably exposed to the sheer meaninglessness of human endeavour and indeed human life at all. Some excavators might deal with that despair by developing a kind of gallows humour, playing metaphorically with the bones like 'loggets', revelling in the nihilism. But ultimately it seems that scepticism about the worth of any human life, thrown up by the hapless archaeologist, should generate as much ethical questioning and debate as melancholic resignation and depression.

*

It is the early seventeenth century, around the time that *Hamlet* is first performed. Old Queen Bess has finally died after a phenomenal forty-five-year reign, and James, the new Scottish king, has just ascended the throne. Beyond the court, two new phenomena in the English landscape are having a powerful effect upon the developing archaeological imagination. As a result of Henry VIII's religious revolution and the dissolution of the monasteries, the countryside is now littered with ruins. The abbeys and monasteries have been swiftly ransacked, pillaged and destroyed, their crumbling walls and foundations the only testimony to their former power. In the city of London epidemic diseases cut swathes through the population. Vast pits are dug in churchyards and outside the newly created pest-house to cope with all the contaminated bodies of the victims.

Suddenly there is a wealth of material for antiquaries to study. New ruins to inspect, new graves to open and contemplate, new objects to unearth. But the material is tainted by scepticism and sickness. To get at it, the antiquaries must breach the rules of everything that was previously thought holy. They need to march into the old monasteries and take what used to belong to the monks. They need to peer into graves and rifle through the remains of the dead. So in both cases, be it the striking desecration of sacred houses or the visible desecration of the body, the sacred house of the soul, the effect is the same: to shatter religious certainty and to open up doubt about whether anything can remain precious and dependable.

*

The man who might be said to be the first official antiquary in England, John Leland, made his name directly as a result of the dissolution of the monasteries. Appointed by Henry VIII in 1533, he was commissioned to gather information about the books and documents housed in all the old monastic libraries before they were stolen or destroyed – in his words, to 'bring them owte of deadly darknes to lyvely lighte'. In the event, his natural archaeological interests stretched further than manuscripts and he produced a verbal map of the country, an itinerary of ancient features of landscape. Castles, abbeys, churches and monasteries were carefully noted. Near Pontefract in Yorkshire, he was shown the field beside a churchyard where there had been limited excavation and 'straunge thinges of fundations hath been found'. In Ripon he noticed that, in the ruins of an abbey that had been pillaged during the reformation, there were three old crosses standing in the crumbling chapel, indicating that 'sum notable men were buried there'. The dissolution or 'suppression' of the monasteries had allowed certain antiquities to come to light. In Kingston in Yorkshire, various 'trowehes of leade with bones' were found in a vault under the altar, while in Exeter he saw some Roman inscriptions set in a wall of a building which had previously belonged to the black friars.

But while Leland's investigations among the ruined abbeys revealed the transience of everything as it disappeared back into the soil, they did not lead him actually to articulate his doubt in his *Itinerary*. He was, after all, preparing his report for the man who had ordered the demise of the monasteries he mourned. Perhaps the only hint of the despair he felt may be detected in the fact that seven years after his travels in 1550 he 'fell beside his wits' or went mad. He was tended by his older brother and died two years later. He never saw his extensive research, scribbled on piles of paper, in the public domain. In later years the draft papers were passed around and read by enthusiastic antiquarian followers such as William Camden, but they were not actually published for nearly two hundred years, finally appearing in 1710.

William Camden, writing some fifty years after Leland, was equally shameless about opportunistically drawing upon the ruined monasteries for ancient material. 'There are some, I hear, who take it ill that I have mention'd Monasteries, and their Founders', he wrote. 'Let 'em be angry if they will since there never were more certain indications and glorious monuments of Christian piety and devotion to God.' Appointed the King of Arms in 1597 for his services to antiquity, he had to pick his way carefully and diplomatically. But mostly his curiosity got the better of him. Near Ely, for example, he charted the fluctuating fate of an abbey, destroyed by the Danes, rebuilt by the bishop of Winchester and subsequently destroyed again by Henry VIII. 'This place', Camden wistfully quotes Malmesbury, who had seen it before the dissolution, 'is the very picture of Paradise.' Priories, once the glory of the landscape, were either ruined or in the hands of Henry's cronies. And their treasures were sometimes to be found while raking through the ground: 'pots', 'slivers of bone', 'three silver plates'.

John Oglander, unlike Leland or Camden, was much more open about the depressing implications of any archaeological exploration of religious ruins. An obsessive chronicler of all historical aspects of the Isle of Wight, including the minute details of any Oglanders who might have been buried there, he had even gone so far as to organise excavations in a few places. He opened some ancient barrows, for example, which he thought must have been Roman and found 'manie bones of men formerlye consumed by fyor'. But crucially in 1607 he also hired men to dig in the cornfields where the abbey of Quarr once stood, in order to search for its foundations. The men found nothing, so absolute had been the destruction of the abbey. On the dissolution of the monasteries, a merchant, Mr Richard Mills, had bought the abbey from the king and sold all the monument and stones. Since he had no children he then sold the plot to a Mr Fleming for a mere

£3,000, the denuded land being now worth no more. It all highlighted the arbitrary and empty nature of things, Oglander concluded, now that what was previously valued had been stripped away: 'Sutch is ye unconstancye of Fortune, which with ye ayde of her servant Tyme, pulleth downe greate thinges, and setteth up poore thinges.'

*

The 'fine revolution' of the monasteries, sobering to contemplate as Oglander finds it, is as nothing to the terrifying nihilism evident in the London plague pits. While disease is a permanent hazard in this whole period and there are many pamphlets published regularly 'against the fever pestilence', two major plagues hit London in the early seventeenth century. The first, in 1603, is raging at the time Shakespeare is producing his great tragedies; the second, in 1625, almost sees the demise of the metaphysical poet John Donne. In 1603 in the city of London, over 30,000 people die of the plague in a year when the total number of non-plague-related deaths is only 7,500. In the bleakest months of the epidemic, James Bamford, vicar of St Olaves and an eyewitness, estimates that one in every six people in his parish is sick or dying of the plague.

Eighteen years later, in 1625, the death toll is even higher. This time over 35,000 die of the plague. And during the Great Plague in 1665, at the height of the epidemic, 38,195 die in one month alone. Faced each time with a triple crisis of mounting piles of dead bodies, graveyards full to capacity and the virulent spread of infection, the City authorities take drastic action, issuing draconian plague laws which attempt, unsuccessfully, to segregate the dead, the sick and the living. Gravediggers, on their orders, dig vast pits at Mount Mills (off the modern Goswell Road) and at Finsbury Fields; the London pest-house is established in Bath Street, north of Old Street (now a school and health centre); and churchyards abandon the etiquette of individual graves and open up vast caverns. Daniel Defoe's church, St Botolphs in Aldgate, opens a huge pit along the wall bordering Houndsditch, 40 feet long and 20 feet deep, which takes over 1,000 bodies in the space of a fortnight. Carts bump through the winding streets to the cry of 'Bring out your dead', collect the bodies from the contaminated houses, pick up the corpses that have collapsed in the lanes outside, and rumble down to the pits to fling their day's load into the gulf. Soon so many people die in a single day that the cart-bearers cannot even guarantee that each body will be thrown into his local parish plague pit. Some are transported through the streets all day and finish in a burying-ground on the other side of the city, lost and anonymous in a pile of other corpses.

The horror of the pits attracts curious spectators. Of course, many of the visitors are relatives, eager to catch a last glimpse of their loved ones as they are tipped onto the pile. One of the city plague orders, issued by the council who are desperately trying to retain control of the situation, actually forbids mourners from following the carts to the grave in an effort to prevent the spread of disease. But this regulation proves difficult to police. At Finsbury Fields (now Finsbury Square), which is open to the wider countryside, unwalled and unguarded, each time another body is interred the families surge forward past the custodians to watch and lament. But there are other people who persuade the guards to let them into the graveyards simply to satisfy their horrified fascination with death at such a vast scale. These are the archaeologists of despair, men excavating and documenting the moment when bodies become objects of disgust.

Daniel Defoe, writing semi-fictionally, describes an evening when he is led by 'curiosity' to visit the great pit in Aldgate. By this stage, the Aldgate pit has about four hundred bodies in it. He watches a mourner who has somehow slipped past the sexton and is waiting to witness his wife and children being buried. The cart arrives with some sixteen or seventeen bodies. Some are wrapped in sheets or rags; others are naked. The cart is backed up to the edge of the chasm, and the bodies are 'shot into the pit promiscuously', their coverings slipping from them in the fall. Within minutes the buriers have thrown earth over them, so that all that is visible are heaps of dirt down in the depths. 'I was indeed shocked with this sight', confesses Defoe. 'Just at my going out of the church, and turning up the street towards my own house, I saw another cart with links, and a bellman going before. Being as I perceived very full of dead bodies, it went directly over the street also toward the church. I stood a while, but I had no stomach to go back again to see the same dismal scene over again.'

*

The plague pits were a terrifying sight because they removed any illusion that the body after death might be treated with reverence and respect. Once in the pit, all differences and distinctions enjoyed by the victim when alive disappeared. There was no longer anything precious about him – he became transformed instead into a thing, into 'a lumpe of clay', as Thomas Dekker, chief poet of the 1603 and 1625 London plagues, put it. So swiftly did bodies follow each other to the grave that there was no time for a funeral service or even an adequate covering of earth upon one corpse before the next corpse arrived. In his poem, 'Newes from Gravesend', Dekker described the uncomfortable speed of plague burials which supposedly got even the worms dizzy and confused:

135

> To which comes many a Pilgrym worme,
> Hungry and faint, beat with the storme
> Of gasping *Famine*, which before
> Onely pickt bones, and had no more,
> But now their messes come so fast,
> They know not where, or which to tast;
> For before (Dust to Dust) be spoken,
> And throwne on One, more Graves be broken.

In the pits, bodies were mingled chaotically, one on top of the other, like an archaeological section. There was no organisation by type, class, wealth, importance – all were treated as no more than 'lumpes of clay', equally awaiting further disintegration. A well-to-do woman might find herself pressed up close to her former groom; a rich man might end up the 'pillow' for a beggar. Bodies might be crammed 'in one little hole', jostled so together that limbs and organs might visibly be 'thrust out to be eaten up by paltry worms'. In his pamphlet about the 1603 plague, 'The Wonderfull Yeare', Dekker paints a vivid picture of the sheer weight of corpses pressing down upon each other in the pits and sharing the same worms.

> But (wretched man!) when thou shalt see, and be assured ... that tomorrow thou must be tumbled into a Mucke-pit, and suffer thy body to be bruisde and prest with threescore dead men, lying slovenly upon thee, and thou to be undermost of all! yea and perhaps halfe of that number were thine enemies! (and see howe they may be revenged, for the wormes that breed out of their putrifying carcasses, shall crawle in huge swarmes from them and quite devoure thee) what agonies will this straunge newes drive thee into?

In an image which recalls Hamlet's concern about the king going through the guts of a beggar, here Dekker also suggests the worrying and strange intimacy of decay. Worms breed and feed on other corpses and then crawl over and feed on you. One body's dust is thus mingled with another in the putrefying guts of the maggots and worms in the grave.

So both the ruined monasteries, which might have vanished without trace, and the plague pits, with their 'putrifying carcasses', offered the would-be archaeologist much to reflect upon concerning the worthlessness of human existence. The whole of London, after all, according to Dekker, was like one 'vast silent Charnell-house ... thickly mingled with heaps of dead mens bones' and therefore one could not choose but to study it. It was a sight to inspire despair, to awaken a desire for the oblivion of death, to provoke a loss of religious faith. 'What soule, but would wish to be out of her body, rather than to dwell one day in such a Charnell-house?'

John Donne, torn between a religious and a secular explanation for life, could see immediately the theological implications of the plague pits and the overflowing churchyards. If there were so many bodies crammed into the cemeteries that often limbs and skulls would re-emerge from the soil a few days later and the dust of the disintegrating corpses might blow round the alley-ways of the city, how could any Christian retain the sense of the worth and value of each individual? 'Every puff of wind within these walls, may blow the father into the sons eys, or the wife into her husbands, or his into hers, or both into their childrens, or their childrens into both. Every grain of dust that flies here, is a piece of a Christian', he argued agonisingly in a sermon delivered shortly after the worst of the plague, in January 1626. No victim of the plague was allowed to rest in peace. The tranquillity of the churchyard was each day disturbed by fresh digging and so, as in *Hamlet*, even after death the body was subject to further indignity and revolution: 'The dead were buried, and thrown up again before they were resolved to dust, to make room for more.'

Having survived the plague in 1625 but facing his own death from stomach cancer just five years later, Donne contemplated the terrifying possibility of physical extinction which he had witnessed in others' graves during those months of the mass epidemic. He wrote his last sermon, *Death's Duell*, while looking upon a picture of himself, dead, in his winding sheet. It was a bizarre act of self-excavation which produced initially all the agonies of nihilism and despair. Life itself, he concluded, is a type of death, since we are absent from God and subject to the vagaries of matter which are in perpetual flux. The tone was elegiac: 'This whole world is but an universall churchyard, but our common grave; and the life and motion that the greatest persons have in it is but as the shaking of buried bodies in their graves by an earthquake.' But if life is no more than the equivalent of burial in a churchyard, then what are we to make of burial itself? Is not death a double type of total annihilation? Donne seems to acknowledge this, wringing his hands over the prospect of the 'most deadly and peremptory nullification of man'. In the grave, man disintegrates utterly to dust, so that he is indistinguishable from other human remains, from grubby maggots, from the earth itself. It is as if he had never existed:

> But in this death of incineration and dispersion of dust, wee see nothing that we can call that mans; If we say, can this dust live? perchance it cannot, it may bee the meere dust of the earth, which never did live nor never shall. It may bee the dust of that mans worm which did live, but shall no more: It may bee the dust of another man, that concernes not him of whom it is askt. This death of incineration and dispersion, is, to naturall reason, the most irrecoverable death of all.

Even the most holy or Christian man is reduced to 'ruine' or 'rubbidge' or 'dust'. Nothing survives. Nothing is sacred.

137

Donne's sense of despair in the face of the annihilation of the body in death was echoed by the most famous archaeological writer of the seventeenth century, Thomas Browne. Browne used the occasion of the excavation of a quantity of burial urns in Norfolk in 1658 in order to reflect upon the meaning of life and the vanity of elaborate funeral rituals. In a field in Walsingham, about forty or fifty urns were dug up which Browne identified as Roman but which were undoubtedly older, probably Saxon. They were packed with ashes and bones – skulls, ribs, jawbones, thigh bones and teeth – which showed evidence of cremation. There were no grave-offerings buried with them, such as vases or lamps or bottles, and there were no inscriptions. This discovery was by no means unique. Browne described similar excavations of urns in recent years in Ashbury and Massingham and Anglesey. But all these archaeological findings had drawn the same blank response; nothing was known about them: 'Meanwhile to what Nation or person belonged that large Urne found at Ashburie, containing mighty bones, and a buckler; what those large Urnes found at Little Massingham, or why the Anglesea Urnes are placed with their mouths downward, remains yet undiscovered.'

Two startling thoughts struck Thomas Browne when contemplating the excavated urns. One was just the extreme limits of our understanding of other people. Faced with these human remains, he felt neither awe nor sympathy but ignorance, an alienating indifference. How little we will ever know of any past life, was the conclusion. And how little we will care. Browne's second thought was really the chief cause of this disturbing indifference. He was indifferent to the burial because it no longer resembled anything human. Man was reduced, utterly transformed, to a handful of dust, to a few bones which could fit into a pot. He mused upon this 'fine revolution': 'How the bulk of a man should sink into so few pounds of bones and ashes, may seem strange unto any who considers not its constitution, and how slender a masse will remain upon an open and urging fire of the carnall composition. Even bones themselves reduced unto ashes, do abate a notable proportion.'

Browne arrived at the same conclusion as Donne, that everyone will be extinguished as if they had never been: 'In vain do individuals hope for Immortality, or any patent from oblivion.' But his sense of the nullification of man came not from the physical disappearance of his remains but from the mocking pointlessness of their preservation. He was troubled by the sense that the bones of these long dead people had been preserved but any significance they might once have possessed – who they were, where they came from – had been utterly lost. 'Had they made as good provision for their names, as they have done for their Reliques, they had not so grossly erred in the art of perpetuation. But to subsist in bones and be but Pyramidally extant, is a fallacy in duration. Vain ashes, which in the oblivion of names, persons, times and sexes, have found unto themselves a fruitlesse continuation, and only arise into late posterity, as Emblemes of mortall vanities.' According to Browne, a written inscription would have proved really lasting. Material remains, on the other hand, teased the excavator with a promise of significance only to refuse ultimate knowledge and understanding. Whoever had once lived in Walsingham and had been reduced to ashes was, in point of fact, lost to history and as if he had never existed.

To answer this archaeological vision of the 'dispersion' of death and the extinction of identity, both Donne and Browne tried to argue for a form of resurrection. Though the body might be blown as dust into every eye, Donne thought, yet somehow it would be gathered together and raised at the last trump because of the 'contract' which God had made with man. We must trust God's judgement on these matters, not our human capacity to understand. But Donne's consolation was based upon a leap of faith, a word, a contract, not on anything tangible or rational. The intense focus upon the materiality of the body in its state of disintegration undercut the hope for an abstract promise, until it seemed as if there might be a direct connection between faith and scepticism, resurrection and annihilation. 'So I might enjoy my Saviour at the last, I would with patience be nothing almost unto eternity', Browne confessed. In Browne's writing, this paradox was celebrated. Annihilation brought resurrection, but equally the hope of eternal life and significance paradoxically revealed the certainty of decomposition and oblivion in the grave. 'The certainty of death is attended with uncertainties, in time, manner, place', Browne concluded. 'The variety of Monuments hath often obscured true graves; and Cenotaphs confounded Sepulchres.' Excavation, which apparently unearthed non-negotiable facts – urns, bones, artefacts – only revealed an emptiness of meaning, the nothingness of life. Every sepulchre could in fact be said to be a cenotaph for all the real value it contained.

*

Thomas Browne was all too aware of the possible comic implications of his archaeological discoveries. 'To be gnaw'd out of our graves', he observed, 'to have our souls made drinking-bowls, and our bones turned into Pipes, to delight and sport our Enemies, are Tragicall abominations.' The transformation of the body into a grave object for future excavators to unearth denied it seriousness – as Shakespeare put it, laughed it 'out of countenance'. So Hamlet also resisted the devastating implications of the grave with a kind of gallows humour. But why should the grim discoveries of the gravedigger, about the nothingness or meaninglessness of human life, be a source of humour? Why is Shakespeare's sexton so often played by the company clown?

Some idea of the connection between archaeology, scepticism and absurdity can be detected in a strange fashion which emerged in the nineteenth century particularly among a group of clergymen. Collectively known as barrow-diggers who formed the backbone of the various county archaeological societies, they would go out – when they were not preaching in church or saying the last rites over their dying parishioners – enthusiastically to excavate local burial mounds. Rev. James Douglas, the chaplain to the military barracks in Chatham, Kent, in the late eighteenth century, acknowledged quite unashamedly the paradox of his two roles as archaeologist and churchman. A rare watercolour, recently acquired by the Society of Antiquaries, depicts James Douglas in his parson's robes, pickaxe in hand, standing in a grave (Plate 11). Underneath is the following verse:

> An Antiquarian & a Soldier bred
> I damned the living & dig'd up the dead.
> A Parson now my steps I here retread
> I bless the living & Inter the dead.

The picture is a study in comic incongruity. Two men near Douglas examine a skull through a magnifying glass, one with a big bone stuffed into his back pocket. Another man sieves the dust beside the grave, while a dog pisses into an ancient vase or cup. While the poem might suggest that Douglas is now repenting of his former life, 'retreading' his steps and 'blessing the living', the picture above it suggests that he is well and truly embedded in the dig-and-be-damned tradition.

The obsession with barrow-digging seemed blasphemously absurd partly because of the sheer number of graves which were excavated at this time. Rev. Bryan Faussett, the first of the serious barrow-diggers, dug 836 Kentish barrows between 1757 and 1773, including 106 graves in eleven days at Gilton and 308 graves in eighteen days in Kingston. Inspired by Faussett, Rev. James Douglas probably excavated at least 90 barrows in Kent between 1779 and 1782. He even employed the soldiers at his barracks as labourers in order to allow him sometimes to dig as many as 50 barrows in a day. Sir Richard Hoare and William Cunnington, a pioneering duo of barrow-diggers, are estimated to have excavated 465 tombs in Wiltshire and Dorset between 1803 and 1818. Rev. John Skinner, who was often a spectator at Hoare's famous excavation parties, himself opened 26 barrows in Somerset between 1815 and 1818, six of them in a single afternoon. And Rev. Stephen Isaacson, who became one of the most prominent barrow-digging poets, helped Thomas Bateman dig up over a hundred mounds in Derbyshire between 1849 and 1860.

The statistics are staggering and confounded any attempts even at the time to treat the excavation seriously. On one epic day in July 1771, when Bryan Faussett excavated no fewer than twenty-four mounds, most of the graves contained nothing more significant than a set of bones in varying states of decay. Sometimes there might be the 'blade of a knife' or 'fragments, as they seemed, of an iron buckle', but mostly his careful notes, after remarking teeth, skull and bones, end with the curt comment: 'Nothing.' His great-grandson confessed that, though his descendants were proud of his effort, they did also feel that 'there is very little to show for the number of acres spent upon it'. It is certainly true that British barrow-digging was characterised by its lack of glamour or riches. You were more likely to find, if you were lucky, 'tusks of boars' or 'unbaked urns of rudely shape' than jewels or precious metal.

Even if, unlike Faussett, the barrow-digger took his time, he was not more liable to unearth any excitements. Rev. Charles Woolls spent eight days in April 1838 opening just one barrow by Crawford Bridge at Spetisbury in Dorsetshire, finding himself on the morning of the sixth day with a 46-foot-long trench and the excitement of reaching a slightly different kind of earth, flinty rather than clay. The diggers dug on, now fuelled by a 'breathless anxiety', the silence punctuated with shouts when they thought they had chanced on 'some relic of antiquity incased in dark clay'. At the centre there were some crumbs of charcoal, the possible signs of cremation. They dug on, now going through layers of gravel, brown mould, more clay and green sand. Finally one of the labourers' spades went through the bedrock. He had reached the river Stour and water sprang up through the hole, by now fourteen feet below the crown of the barrow. He beat a hasty retreat up the ladder which lent against the wall of the chasm. The excavation – which had found only charcoal and 'urn shaped dark clay' – was called off.

There is no doubt that barrow-digging was closely linked at times to feelings of melancholy and despair. The discoveries within the tumuli, after all, revealed the insignificance of the human body, the lack of distinction between its bones and animal traces and flinty stones, the paltry possessions of a whole community in the past. The barrows themselves even taunted the digger with their vast emptiness. A huge mound, for example, which Thomas Bateman spent a week investigating on Middelton Moor in 1848, yielded no evidence of ancient burial, merely some animal bones and a flint arrowhead. What had been the original reason for building the mound? Defying these questions, the barrow challenged the excavator with the pointlessness of human endeavour. One was free to choose. Either one could celebrate the mystery of the barrows and the possibilities which they offered the imagination or, if one acted as a typical barrow-digger and concentrated upon the material objects contained in the mounds and the amount of earth to be removed, one could flounder in agonies of doubt. As William Miles, who excavated the Deverel Barrow in 1826, put it, tellingly alluding to Hamlet's despairing soliloquy: '[the barrows] give a free untethered flight to the imagination, in bold impunity of being contradicted; but to the more cautious investigator, who uses facts for ballast as he ventures out to navigate a sea of troubles and encounter arguments which clash so strangely, these points by no means smooth the course he has to steer'.

Nobody seemed more responsive to the nihilistic message of these barrows than the Somerset clergyman, John Skinner. In May 1814 he excavated a chambered tumulus a mile away from his village in Somerset. The locals were interested to start with, crowding round the trench with excitement as he hacked away at the soil with a pickaxe. But they found Skinner's discoveries – bones and flints – hard to understand or treat respectfully. The blacksmith took home a skull in which for a long time he kept nails, while others smashed into the mound at night and grabbed a whole bunch of bones. 'Unless there were some security against the visits of the lawless inhabitants of the neighbourhood, who seem to spare nothing either human or divine, it is very disheartening to do anything which we may so soon have the mortification of seeing destroyed', Skinner noted mournfully in his diary. The farmer who owned the land was disappointed at the lack of treasure and so refused permission for any further digging. Skinner was condemned to a life of parish visits and tedious dinner parties with the local gentry. 'I went to Mr Boodle's to dinner', he noted in his diary one September. 'I found far less to interest me in his Parlour than I had done in his Parish; sed de nihilo sit nihil; one may make something of a Barrow, but it requires a second Swift to extract anything from dry broomstick.' The parishioners were unsympathetic; there was nobody who could understand his antiquarian interests; he was thwarted in his desire to dig. Life seemed pointless and not worth living. So it was not, perhaps, surprising when one morning in October 1839, Skinner took his gun, walked into the beech wood near his home, and shot himself dead.

While days of shovelling earth and inspecting flints and bones exposed to Skinner the depth of his despair, on the whole the barrow-diggers were more driven to a self-deprecating humour. Their sensibility was one which appreciated painstaking literalism and comic bathos. Faced with grubby stony remains under piles of soil which signified nothing, they could only hope to juxtapose the prosaic reality of their occupation with mock romantic verse in a bizarre and ironic mixture. The result was a Victorian vogue for barrow-digging poems. Rev. Stephen Isaacson's 1845 poem,

6. Rock Bottom: Digging and Despair

Barrow-Digging by a Barrow Knight, is a classic of the genre. The poem recounts the tale of one day's digging in the manner of a medieval ballad or an early modern quest romance. It begins with the excavators gathering over dinner to talk over antiquity and to plan the next day's expedition. This allows them to whip up their enthusiasm in order to overcome the physical hardships of archaeology:

> And all exclaimed, their grog while swigging,
> There's naught on earth like barrow digging!

The next day they rise at five, sally forth and select a mound to dig, able to identify 'with practised eye' which hillock will contain objects worth studying. They reach the kist, or burial chamber, and investigate it for some time before hunger overtakes them. It is not entirely clear what they actually find. A deposit box is brought forward to house the day's finds, but it is left uncertain whether these really include an 'urn', a 'bronzed dagger', a 'spear' and a 'bone of hero', or whether these are the stuff of the romantic illusion of the poem. What is clear is that the bones are reburied, the mound is closed up again, a label is left to indicate that the barrow has been opened (by T. Bateman), and the diggers return home, happy with their day:

> 'Mid barrows and tumuli
> Though we may roam,
> Or wherever you may lie,
> There's no place like home.

Isaacson's poem is unashamedly absurd. It glamorises a mundane activity, suggesting that excavation is the equivalent of a heroic quest, and yet it also reduces archaeology to the anti-climactic level of practicalities, until breakfasting, lunching and gathering up tools become more important than what is actually discovered. In fact, the barrow-digger seems to be extraordinarily obsessed by food, happily detailing the contents of his lunchbox while sitting beside the skulls and bones which he has unearthed. The contents of the barrow, such as they are, are rather shabby and disgusting. Isaacson points out, for example, that the large quantity of rat bones which the diggers discover proves that a human burial must be close by, that there must be a skeleton:

> Beyond, for excavation ripe,
> With spade in hand and shorten'd pipe,
> An amateur of sterling worth
> Watches each shovel-full of earth,
> As heedfully as mouse does cat,
> Intent to find the bones of rat,

For these afford a certain trail,
Which LOWE-EXPLORERS never fail.

So barrow-digging exposes the degradation of the human body. The spade reveals the fate of everyone after death, gnawed by rats, dwindled into dust and mud, calcified and insignificant. Indeed, the local villagers who watch the excavation misinterpret it altogether and think that a human bone is but a sheep's thigh and an arrow-head is 'nout but flint'. And even the barrow-diggers seem to make little distinction between the human remains and all the other grubby contents of their shovel, 'wandering', as they do, 'midst bones of rats, sword, dagger, celt'. Why do they do it? Apparently only to appreciate the nothingness of human life, the fact that we will all ultimately be reduced to what can be fitted into a deposit box. As Isaacson blithely rhymes, the barrow-diggers look at the bones of the man at the centre of the mound and 'sadly cheerful contemplate the day,/ When they like him shall turn to kindred clay.'

The diggers are 'sadly cheerful' because they bizarrely offset the melancholy conclusions of their excavation – the nothingness of human life – with an upbeat jollity. The poem is full of absurd rhymes: 'sexton' / 'text on'; 'Hall of Haddon' / 'true diggers gladden'; 'liquor' / 'vicar'. There are comically incongruous scenes, such as the one in which the men sing about the joys of digging while they stride out, shovels and pickaxes in hand, or carefully measure the position of a skeleton as if it were the all-important holy grail. Isaacson makes wildly exaggerated claims for the importance of barrow-digging, humorous because belied by reality. At one point he compares the excavator's task to that of the prime minister at the time, Lord Canning. Later he deplores the fact that Socrates was not a barrow-digger, because, if he had been, then the 'Athens Archaeological Journal' might have contained notes on the barrow of Hector. Is this supposed to be ironic? The answer is probably yes and no. Yes, Isaacson seems to be aware of the absurd nature of his enthusiasm, joking about the mock seriousness and the complicated nature of the expedition compared to its minimal returns. But no, he is probably scarcely more ironic than is Hamlet. For both see the sober message of the grave. Both suggest that, 'in a barrow', one can 'find mines of philosophy'. And both, with underlying serious intent, convert the pointlessly ridiculous nature of life (and death) they find there into a comic dramatic verse.

Rev. Charles Woolls certainly noticed the parallels between Hamlet's absurdist views of life and death and the practice of Victorian barrow-digging. In 1839, shortly after he had 'assisted an exceedingly agreeable party in opening a Barrow', he published a comic dialogue entitled *The Barrow-Diggers: A Dialogue In Imitation of the Grave Diggers in Hamlet, with numerous explanatory notes*. Instead of Hamlet and Horatio, there are, in Woolls' version, an antiquary and his disciple; instead of the gravedigger, there are three barrow-diggers who are doing the hard labour for their archaeologist masters. But the conversation is very similar, albeit with a British barrow-digging twist. The antiquary, like Hamlet, contemplates a skull: 'That skull had a tongue in it and could sing once .... That might be the pate of a Druid, which this ass now o'erreaches.' He discusses how long a body might lie ere it rot with the barrow-digger, who notes that 'Geology and Zoology are one in the delvings of bone grubbers'. And rather than leaping into the grave with melodramatic gesture as Hamlet does in order to compete with Laertes' attempt to mourn his sister, the antiquary decides to close the barrow up again since nothing really has been achieved and nothing can be known or understood about the dead:

> *Antiquarius*: How long have we been here?
> *Discipulus*: Eight days! No more be done!
> *Barrow-digger*: Must there no more be done?
>   We've made an inverted cone.
> *Antiquarius*: No more be done,
>   Respect sepulchral rites, inhume those bones
> Shards, Flints and Earth replace, and heap up here
>   A pile of dust upon the sleeping dead,
>   Till of this flat a mountain you have made.

It might be said that barrow-digging poems, such as Isaacson's and Woolls', make 'of this flat a mountain'. In other words, they make something out of nothing. Struck by the emptiness of life after a long career of grubbing about under barrows, the poets transform despair into comedy and the paltry activity of excavation into fantastical, satirical pastiche. 'And if I laugh at any mortal thing', wrote the romantic poet Lord Byron with great perception, ' 'tis that I may not weep.'

*

The Victorian barrow-diggers turned the bleakness of being unable to distinguish ancient human remains from dust into comic absurdity. But in the last few years, the reduction of bodies to dust, and even less than dust, has taken up a far more grim and topical place in the public imagination. The devastating terrorist attack on the World Trade Center in New York on 11 September 2001 resulted in the collapse of the twin towers and massive loss of life, all within the space of a couple of hours. Firefighters and volunteers rushed to the scene to rescue the possible survivors. But what was initially termed a 'rescue' operation quickly became renamed a 'recovery' operation. There were no survivors. Indeed, it gradually became apparent that there were not even as many bodies to be recovered as there were known to be victims. As the men trawled through the rubble, trying to identify body parts among the mountains of steel and concrete, Ground Zero – the sixteen-acre rock-strewn and smoking chasm where the twin towers had once stood – effectively became one of the largest and most tragic archaeological sites. The excavation, carried out under the full glare of floodlights and cameras, highlighted most poignantly the intimate connection in archaeology between something of significance and nothingness, between hope and despair.

For eight and a half months, the workmen dug down into the ruins and sifted the debris, looking for the remains of the dead. There were 2,752 casualties at the last estimate. They prised apart the concrete and the metal and the crushed bodies. They laid out the piles of grey ash for firefighters to search through. And they carted off rubble and dust to the medical examiner's office and to the Fresh Kills landfill site on Staten Island for further sifting and DNA analysis. According to one firefighter, 'You look for anything that resembles a human. Anybody, anything. Could be clothes, could be bone, a shoe.'

Progress was measured statistically. 1.6 million tons of rubble removed from the site; 105,000 truckloads of material; about 1,800 more individuals still to find. What was most heartrending was that it was also measured archaeologically, in the sense that the levels of the dirt left to dig acquired a stratigraphic meaning, took on tragic significance. In March 2002, with only the basement of the south tower left to dig, one firefighter, Keith J. Dillon, summed up the desperation as the debris ran out.

> It's not over, but it's definitely winding down. You've got a great number of people that you want to find, and you've got a certain amount of dirt that's left. And there's a gap. That gap is going to be a sorrowful one. But we can't make more dirt.

Out at Staten Island, trucks and barges laden with the debris arrived around the clock. Fresh Kills, the largest landfill site in the world, had been finally shut down in March 2001, following a politically-motivated deal struck between Mayor Giuliani and the Mayor of Staten Island. But faced with over a million tons of debris at Ground Zero, the New York City government decided to reopen the site closest to the water and the New Jersey coast. Michael Mucci, Deputy Director at the Bureau of Waste Disposal in New York's Sanitation Department, was there for six months, helping to supervise the operation.

'It was just a load of pulverised rock and stone,' he tells me, back at the Sanitation offices in downtown Manhattan. 'It didn't look like anything recognisable. There were no computers, no telephones. Just rock.'

But even so, the debris from Ground Zero, already sifted by the firefighters and archaeologists at the site, was fed through a series of sorting machines at Fresh Kills. And in the process, over 2,000 body parts were found. At the moment, they have been freeze-dried for preservation, in the hope that scientific techniques will develop in the future to allow for the proper identification of the remains. 'It was all undertaken very carefully and sensitively,' says Mucci.

But the relatives of the victims are not satisfied. Diane Horning, who has set up the pressure group, WTC Families for Proper Burial, believes that the remains of her son, and the other unidentified victims, are being 'left in a garbage dump'. Everything which was sifted through the one-quarter-inch grate should have been released for proper burial. But instead she claims that once the recovery operation closed in May 2003, the minutely sifted dust was termed 'topsoil' and 'bulldozed back into the rest of the debris from the site'. Horning is campaigning for the sifted material, or what she calls the 'ashen remains', to be returned to Ground Zero and buried there as part of the World Trade Center memorial, where the 12,000 remains salvaged at Ground Zero itself and currently at the city's medical examiner's office are due to be buried. According to Horning, this will not be difficult. The material known as 'topsoil' apparently takes up only the space of one acre, twenty feet high.

When I travel out to Staten Island to look at Fresh Kills, I can quickly see Diane Horning's point. It is very bleak. As only the relatives of the victims are permitted to enter the landfill site now that it has been officially closed, I am forced to stand at the different entrances to the massive 2,200-acre area and peer through to the heaps of soil and rock and regrassed, featureless hills containing rubbish. Every so often, trucks pass me into the site, laden with 'landscape debris' and 'topsoil', clearly just consolidating the mountain of garbage. My explorations take me to the entrance beside a slip road to the expressway, where lorries thunder past and there are no people, and also through the vast parking lot of a disused cinema. At that entrance, the guard sidles up to me.

'You'd get your best view from the Staten Island Mall,' he offers helpfully, his five teeth showing through his grin.

So I catch two buses in order to reach Staten Island Mall and cross over the highway to the garbage truck depot in order to peer over the fence at the mountain of dirt which blocks my view of the sea. Beside me, discarded refuse lorries and a line of bulldozers gradually rust into oblivion.

At present, the families of World Trade Center victims must obtain permission to visit Fresh Kills from Keith Mellis at the Sanitation Department's Bureau of Public Information. He gets requests all the time.

'People get upset that their relatives are effectively buried in a rubbish dump,' he tells me. 'They want closure. They want somewhere they can go whenever they feel like it.'

'There will be a memorial in the end. I don't know where it will be,' says Michael Mucci.

It is unclear at the moment whether the decision rests ultimately with the politicians or with the Sanitation Department. But Mucci privately feels that moving the Ground Zero debris now, after it has settled into the fill and become part of the mountain, would be logistically difficult. At some point, one has to draw a halt in the effort to hold onto every quarter inch of dirt.

Back at Ground Zero, the necessary limits of excavation are all too clear. The diggers hit bedrock in May 2002 and there is no more debris to salvage or earth to sieve. When I go to look at it in September 2003, I see what must be the emptiest, cleanest and most analysed sixteen-acre section of the city. There is no additional dirt, no debris unaccounted for. Instead Ground Zero has become a vast seventy-foot deep chasm and also a building site. The new subway station is being hurriedly constructed and I can see already the rails running down to a white roofed building.

But the Governor and Mayor of New York have realised the power, not of literal dust, but of symbolic gesture. Although there is now nothing to 'see' at Ground Zero, there is plenty to attract the pilgrim. The mayor and governor have set up a 'viewing wall' around the perimeter, so that 'the world community can reflect upon and remember the events that took place here'. The 'wall', a steel grid, allows visitors to peer through at the building construction taking place inside (Plate 12). But it has also become a focus for mourning what has been lost. Noticeboards on the wall carry pictures of the towers and the history of the buildings in South Manhattan. A cross has been made from the girders of skyscrapers. A banner is draped over the building at 90 West Street overlooking Ground Zero, containing the message that 'the human spirit is not measured by the size of the act but by the size of the heart'.

I spend a day at the site. It's a cloudless blue-sky day, a typical perfect New York September day, just as it was almost exactly two years before. I peer through at the chasm from every angle, trying to remember the exact position of the towers. I took an elevator to the roof of the south tower with a loyal friend who suffers from vertigo four years ago, so I retrace in my memory my route to the tower with him. I walk over to Battery Park to see the sculpture of the world, which I can vividly recall in the plaza, beside the towers, and which was recovered, battered and broken, by the firefighters. It has now been reinstalled in the Park, its crushed metal telling the story of its devastation.

But what I find most impressive and moving all day is the official lists of the names of the dead attached to the viewing wall and the unofficial tributes and graffiti which cover the scaffolding pillars. Six notice boards on the viewing wall list all the 2,752 victims, from Gordon M. Aamoth, Jr.

to Igor Zukelman. Meanwhile, on the steps leading to the World Financial Center, there are pictures of individuals and messages of support from particular families and cities. 'We love you, Jimmy Quinn', says one notice beside his smiling picture; 'God bless Joe Jordan', scrawls another message. These private memorials are echoed elsewhere around the city. A couple of days later, in Union Square subway station, I spot another list of the dead plastered on the underground station walls. It is accompanied by the plea not to write on this memorial. But this request is almost unreadable under a web of personal messages: 'Gone but not forgotten. RIP.'

What both the city's Mayor and the writers in the subway station are doing is to fill the devastating gap left by the complete vaporisation of nearly 2,000 people. With no actual bodies to mourn, they offer, in compensation, names, faces and individual memories. It was a similar desire to find significance in emptiness which prompted the *New York Times*, in the months following the attack, to publish daily a series of brief biographies of each victim, accompanied by a photograph. Titled the 'Portraits of Grief', these became compulsory reading for New Yorkers each day, a means of focusing their mourning. And I read them too, over the internet, desperate to be able to feel the appropriate response in the numbing aftermath of a national tragedy. According to the New York novelist Paul Auster, 'one felt, looking at those pages every day, that real lives were jumping out at you. We weren't mourning an anonymous mass of people, we were mourning thousands of individuals. And the more we knew about them, the more we could wrestle with our own grief.'

These memorials, in the newspaper, in the subway station and at Ground Zero itself, attempt to bring a human dimension to an inhuman disaster. Instead of empty statistics, they give individual details. Instead of a gaping hole, in which not even quarter-inch pieces of the victims can be found, they offer pictures of smiling faces and poignant bodies of text. In doing this, they could be said to participate in the great tradition of canonical tragedy which responds urgently to bleakness and suffering in the world. Tragedy, in its aesthetic sense, has a vital ethical role to play in our lives, in re-asserting a pattern and a human form upon what seems bewildering and chaotic. So Hamlet tries restlessly to understand the disintegrating world around him, and so New Yorkers leave flowers and tributes at the viewing wall of Ground Zero.

But in all tragedies, there is always a terrible gulf between the human need to question, understand and grieve and the sheer inhuman weight of the world with its inert and unjust matter which refuses an answer. Archaeological excavation highlights this gulf all too vividly. It measures it literally, comparing the dirt with the desire, comparing the absence of evidence with the pressing compulsion to find it. So it was at Ground Zero, with the dwindling piles of earth and the number of body parts still to identify, with the 'sorrowful gap', as the firefighter Keith Dillon called it, between the 'certain amount of dirt that's left' and 'the great number of people that you want to find'.

In his design for the new building to stand on the World Trade Center site, the architect Daniel Libeskind has taken into account the importance of retaining a sense of that tragic 'gap'. Ground Zero is, as he put it in his winning presentation to the Lower Manhattan Development Corporation (LMDC)'s advisory council, 'sacred ground'. But that sacredness is located as much in what is tragically missing as in whatever can be rebuilt between Church and West Street. The relatives of the victims of the September 11 attacks demanded a new building at Ground Zero which was spiritual rather than purely commercial, which suggested what had been lost there rather than simply erasing the history under a mass of skyscrapers. One anonymous comment, sent into the LMDC in the period before Libeskind was finally chosen as architect, summed up the general feeling:

> The site should allow us to forgive but not forget; it should reach for the future without denying the past; it should allow us to remain silent, but not isolated; it should go for renewal while rooted in the event; it should draw us to the edge but no further; it should stand as a symbol of humanity's smallest and tallest.

Libeskind's answer to that demand is to design a series of buildings and memorial park which retain, at their centre, the excavated chasm of Ground Zero. While he plans a tower, which will reach symbolically up to 1,776 feet, he will also allow people to descend seventy feet below ground level to the bedrock, to observe the slurry walls. The slurry walls, built under the foundations of the twin towers to hold the waters of the Hudson River at bay, are all that survive the collapse of the buildings. They represent, according to Libeskind, the 'strength and endurance of American democracy'.

The final technical details of the design for Ground Zero have not yet been decided. Libeskind now finds himself caught up in various commercial pressures to alter the plans, to move the location of the buildings and to allow for more profit-making commercial space. Larry Silverstein, lease-holder of the site, wants to be sure that the World Trade Center will make money in a practical and tangible way. Libeskind's plan, according to one critic, Herbert Muschamp at the *New York Times*, is 'driven more by rhetoric than by urban form'.

But the 'rhetoric' of the slurry walls and the bedrock will be retained. For the rock bottom of Ground Zero, excavated by the firefighters, represents both what was lost and what was found that day, what was inhuman and what was human, what led to despair and what to hope. The firefighters found too little dirt, too few human remains. But they found the slurry

150

wall, the foundations of the building, the basis for something new. Archaeologically the bedrock encapsulates the tragedy and allows the 'rest', as Hamlet would say, to remain as 'silence'.

Holy Ground:
Archaeology and the Sacred

The Swiss lawyer, Jürgen Federer, arrives in Jerusalem on a package tour, after a week spent with the group visiting ancient sites in Greece. It's a dream holiday, a present from his parents to celebrate his recent qualification as a solicitor. He settles into the hotel in the Old City, inside the medieval walls, wandering up for an early drink on the hotel's roof terrace as the red sun sinks slowly behind the Jaffa Gate.

'Sitting on hotel roof in sunset', he writes on a postcard to his mother. 'Can see the gleaming gold and blue of the "Dome of the Rock", now lit by the piercing red beams of the sun. Just make out, over the labyrinth of roofs and alleyways, the grey lead rotunda built over Christ's Holy Sepulchre.'

Sounds of muezzin and church bells filter up to him; shouts of street vendors, the rattle of barrow wheels as they rumble through the souks, the steps and songs of pilgrims single-mindedly threading their way to the next shrine.

It is an idyllic scene, but that night Federer sleeps badly. He tosses and turns, his mind churning while rivulets of anxiety course through his limbs. Next morning, he announces to the others that he wishes to wander around the city alone, away from the group. Freed from the strict timetable of the package tour, Federer takes a long bath, scrubbing away the night's sweat. Grabbing a map from the hotel lobby, he makes his way past various Christian seminaries to the Church of the Holy Sepulchre, the complex of church buildings erected over the site of Christ's crucifixion, death, burial and resurrection. As he stands in the passage between the supposed cross and the tomb, transfixed by the scene, a group of orthodox nuns elbow him out of the way, chanting as they head for the Holy Sepulchre. No sooner has he recovered from this interruption than he is sent reeling by a crowd of American evangelical tourists, Bibles in one hand and cameras in the other, determined to catch their appointed time at the tomb. His moment of meditation is shattered, bustled out by the crowds who have travelled far to capture their moment too.

Jürgen Federer heads swiftly back to the hotel. He needs to shower again, to shampoo his hair and cut his fingernails. His clothes are dusty and not, he feels, suitable for this city. White is the only appropriate colour. Finally clean after the shower, he strips his crisp white sheet from the bed and winds it round himself, a latter-day Jesus or John the Baptist. Now he will show these blasphemous pilgrims and tourists. Venturing out a second time along St Francis Street and the end of the Via Dolorosa, he finds himself singing the hymns and psalms dragged up from earliest memory.

'Who shall ascend the hill of the Lord? And who shall stand in his holy place? Those who have clean hands and pure hearts, who do not lift up their souls to what is false,' he sings as he walks through old Jerusalem towards the Holy Sepulchre. 'Sing praises to the Lord, who dwells in Zion. Declare his deeds among the peoples.'

Now he will testify his faith as he stands between cross and tomb and not be meekly bundled out of the way by tourists. Now he will preach the simple doctrine of Christ and prophesy its imminent corruption at the hands of erroneous pilgrims.

He is still shouting about the New Jerusalem, Zion's holy hill and the True Cross, as the church guards close in on him. Another victim, the guards sigh. A man in his hotel's bed linen, raving about goodness and truth, wringing his hands, disturbing the peace or rather the customary buzzing noise of Christendom's most holy church.

Jürgen Federer has fallen victim to Jerusalem Syndrome. A typical case, he has exhibited all the classic symptoms, the compulsive washing, dressing in white, the impersonation of a Christian figure. Jerusalem Syndrome was first noticed in 1980 and officially identified in 1991 by the Israeli psychiatrist Yair Bar-El, after eleven years of study. Around a hundred people a year fall prey to the syndrome and are seen by psychiatrists. About forty of those are admitted to hospital. Many – the ones in which Bar-El is most interested – have no previous history of mental illness. They exhibit what Bar-El describes as the 'pure' or 'unconfounded' form of the syndrome, where there are no complicating factors, such as previous psychiatric problems or pre-existing religious obsessions, that might explain their strange experience in the holy city. Most, like Federer, recover as soon as they have left the city, reluctant to talk about their 'episode'. While psychotic breakdowns are a recognised hazard of travel – one psychiatrist has identified fits of madness brought on by long-distance trains and another has highlighted a form of airport syndrome – Jerusalem Syndrome is unique in its emphasis upon the wearing of white, the identification with a divine figure and the unusual state of consciousness of the victim during the experience. The conclusion of Yair Bar-El is that there is something specific to Jerusalem which causes this phenomenon, something in the atmosphere of the place which brings about the dramatic change in people's mental state. 'The discrete form of the Jerusalem Syndrome,' he maintains, 'is related to religious excitement induced by proximity to the holy places of Jerusalem.'

But what makes a place holy? So powerful are the effects of Jerusalem Syndrome that it seems self-evident that holiness must exist, must linger around certain spots of ground. And yet that holiness is intangible and inexplicable in physical terms. So what is the relationship between stones and sanctity? What is the connection between the material reality and God, a connection which theologians might describe in terms of the 'sacramental'? How, in our imaginations, are we to link archaeology and the sacred?

On the face of it, Christians might argue that their religion has nothing to do with physical places and that archaeology therefore has no bearing on the subject. Christ, after all, repeatedly suggested that whereas the Old Testament sanctified the land, he was interested in the person. When the priests accused him of breaking the traditional law and doing wonders normally only permitted in the holy temple, Jesus replied cryptically that 'something greater than the temple is here' (Matthew 12:6). Indeed Jesus repeatedly replaced the literal sense of the temple in Jerusalem, built on Herod's platform which is now covered by the Dome of the Rock, with the metaphorical temple of his body. 'I am able to destroy the temple of God and to build it in three days', he famously said, referring to his death and resurrection three days later but apparently, as far as the priests were concerned, blasphemously threatening the stone temple in Jerusalem. St Paul also emphasised the fact that Christianity was a new type of religion where holy buildings were replaced by holy people. He told the Athenians on the acropolis, who were used to worshipping Athene in one of the most beautiful buildings, the Parthenon, that 'God that made the world and all things therein, seeing that he is Lord of heaven and earth, dwelleth not in temples made with hands' (Acts 17:21). And to the newly converted Christians in Ephesus, he explained that Christianity appealed not just to the chosen people living in the land of Israel but to every nation, regardless of place or custom or law. 'You are built upon the foundation of the apostles and prophets, Jesus Christ himself being the chief corner stone. In whom all the building fitly framed together groweth into an holy temple in the Lord' (Ephesians 2:20-1). By replacing the importance of the holy place – the temple, the holy of holies – with the holy person, the body of Christ, everyone could be included just by an act of faith rather than by practising religion in the right place at the right time.

Christianity is also based fundamentally upon the idea of the empty tomb, the fact not that Jesus died and was buried, but crucially that he rose again and is now elsewhere, in heaven. It is, according to the French theological writer Michel de Certeau, a faith based upon absence, a missing god. At the very dawn of Christianity, Mary Magdalene stood before the empty tomb, asking where Jesus' body had been taken. At that precise, historical moment, the religion of Christianity was inaugurated. So Christianity was bound up with a particular place and a particular time, or what de Certeau calls the 'Jesus Christ event'. But that particular 'event' was paradoxically significant because the divinity had disappeared. 'There is a close bond between the absence of Jesus (dead and not present) and the birth of the Christian language', he writes. 'The empty tomb is the condition of possibility for a spiritual knowledge.' And therefore he maintains that 'our relation to the origin is in the function of its increasing absence'.

Yet equally important for the Christian faith is the belief that God became man, and was incarnate in the figure of Jesus Christ. God entered the world at a specific place and at a specific time. History and geography are part of the significance of Christ. He was born in Bethlehem, at an identifiable time, the first census taken during the reign of Augustus while Quirinius was governor of Syria; he grew up in Nazareth; he gathered his disciples and worked miracles on the shores of Lake Galilee; he was crucified in Jerusalem, at 'a place called Golgotha', and laid to rest in the tomb of Joseph of Arimathea, which had recently been hewn out of the rock. The fact that Jesus was a man and lived among us at a particular place and time meant that he was able to sympathise with and share our suffering. Amid all the more doctrinal or theological comments he made while on the cross – 'Today you will be with me in Paradise', 'It is finished' – he also announced that he was 'thirsty', his simple bodily suffering exceeding the divine purpose, the teleological narrative. Christianity is a religion grounded in such crises of the human condition, in the minutiae of everyday practice, in daily joys and sorrows.

Because Jesus tramped the hills around Galilee, he could appreciate the experiences of people living there. The Christian theological world encompassed the most trivial details and petty concerns. It listed individual people and particular towns within its redemptive or punitive vision. 'If anyone will not welcome you or listen to your words', Jesus advised his disciples, 'shake off the dust from your feet as you leave that house or town. Truly I tell you, it will be more tolerable for the land of Sodom and Gomorrah on the day of judgement than for that town' (Matthew 10:14-15). Jesus measured each place or group of people by the literal soil beneath them, to be shaken off, in this case, by the rejected disciples. Every city and every person seems to be numbered and potentially made sacred to God, to be redeemed or punished by him. If this is the case, then archaeology – the study, recording and interpretation of stones and earth – becomes crucial for theological belief. All religions probably have their

156

own archaeology, and certainly the tensions of Jerusalem are partly caused by the fact that the same rocks are contested by three different religions. But while nearly all books about what is called 'biblical archaeology' actually confine the discussion to Old Testament sites, when I was in Israel I found myself, because I am Christian, inevitably thinking about Jesus' footsteps.

*

Archaeology and the sacred have long been connected. Indeed, it could be argued that the world's very first archaeological excavation – the excavation of Jesus' cross – was undertaken for zealous religious reasons. Picture the scene. The Roman emperor, the Emperor Constantine, has just announced the conversion of the Roman empire from paganism to Christianity. Suddenly everywhere, from the cold northern land of Britain, through the milder regions of Spain, Italy and France, right over to the hot, dry regions of Turkey, Syria, Egypt and Palestine, must become Christian. After centuries during which Christians have been persecuted and martyred in public arenas for mass entertainment, now, virtually overnight, the compulsion is to be Christian and to lean heavily upon anyone who retains any inkling of the pagan faith.

In these turbulent and confusing times, Helena, the emperor's mother, decides to make a pilgrimage to the Holy Land in AD 327. Her motivation is mysterious and continues to provoke debate. She may have wanted, as other pilgrims in late antiquity, to experience the historical places described in the Bible. Evelyn Waugh suggested in his novel about her that she was motivated explicitly by the desire to find the cross, in order to show that, at a time when 'everyone is forgetting' fundamental facts about Christian belief, 'there's a solid chunk of wood waiting for them to have their silly heads knocked against'. Or she may have gone as part of an imperial mission to shore up Constantine's rather vulnerable and beleaguered programme of imperial Christian conversion, to win over his enemies and ensure that Christians got the upper hand in the area. One theory, popular among scholars at the moment, is that Helena's was a calculated, political venture, which was only subsequently presented by myth-makers as a pilgrimage.

Or she may have been sent by Constantine to supervise his intensive programme of church building over holy sites. Now that Christianity was the official state religion and no longer the victim of persecution, sacred places which featured in the Bible did not need to remain hidden. Indeed Constantine ensured that they were made publicly manifest, with a series of massive basilicas which dominated the physical landscape and outdid, in size and magnificence, the earlier pagan temples. Chief site to be cleared and transformed was the cave in the centre of Jerusalem, the supposed site of the Holy Sepulchre. According to Eusebius, Constantine's first biographer, he 'gave instructions that the site should be excavated to a great depth and the pavement should be carried away with the rubble a long distance outside, because it was stained with demonic bloodshed'. The site had previously been covered by a temple dedicated to Aphrodite, erected by Hadrian supposedly with the express intention of erasing the memory of Christ and filled daily with the smell of animal sacrifices to the goddess. Once the physical traces of the false religion had been cleared away, the true one could be revealed. 'As stage by stage the underground site was exposed', explained Eusebius, 'at last against all expectation the revered and all-hallowed Testimony of the Saviour's resurrection was itself revealed, and the cave, the holy of holies, took on the appearance of a representation of the Saviour's return to life.'

In this atmosphere of bearing witness to the key moments in Jesus' life by digging away all the later piles of stones and earth, Helena arrives, buoyed up by her recent conversion to the new religion. She visits the building site, which will soon become the Church of the Holy Sepulchre, and she visits the grotto in Bethlehem, site of Christ's birth, and the Mount of Olives, site of his ascension to heaven. These will also have churches built over them, 'beautifying', according to Eusebius, these moments of divine arrival into and departure from this world with 'lofty buildings'. But then Helena's attention turns back to Jerusalem. What happens next has become the stuff of legend, a story which may or may not have any historical foundation.

According to St Ambrose, Helena is inspired by the Holy Spirit to search for the wood of Jesus' cross.

'How can I believe that I have been redeemed if the redemption itself is not seen?' she asks herself. 'I shall search for His cross. I shall give proof that He rose from the dead.'

She instructs men to dig at a spot traditionally thought to be the site of Golgotha. Sure enough, in time, they come across 'three fork-shaped gibbets'. But which is the true cross, and which the inferior ones on which the thieves were hanged? While myth and wishful thinking have governed the first part of the excavation, when it comes to the interpretation of the findings, a more diagnostic type of archaeology is needed. Instead of automatically assuming that Jesus' cross must be the one lying in the middle, since he was crucified between the two thieves, Helena realises that the archaeological fill might have affected the position of the deposits over time. 'It could have happened that the debris had mixed the crosses one with another', Ambrose explained soberly, 'and that chance had interchanged them.'

What happens next depends upon which version of the story you trust.

7. Holy Ground: Archaeology and the Sacred

According to Ambrose, Helena identifies the true cross because the inscription which Pontius Pilate had written to be displayed above Jesus – 'Jesus, King of the Jews' – is still usefully attached to one of the stakes. This, then, is archaeological identification through accompanying artefacts; the stake becomes significant because an inscription is attached. As Ambrose says, a 'sequence of sound reasoning was established'. But according to Gelasius of Caesarea, whose (now lost) version was in turn translated by Rufinius into Latin, the identification of the true cross is achieved by a miracle. Rejecting the 'uncertain' proof of Pilate's inscription, Helena consults Macarius, the bishop of Jerusalem. He tells her to bring all three crosses to the house of a sick woman, who is about to die. Macarius takes each cross and lays it on the body of the woman. The first two crosses provoke no reaction. But when the third is brought near her, the woman opens her eyes and jumps up from her bed, back to her full strength. It is, according to Rufinius, a 'clear sign'. From now on, archaeological identification in the Holy Land is not to be made in conventional ways, by positioning or accompanying artefacts, but by the divine or sacred powers of the object itself.

*

The excavation of the true cross divided the public in terms of credulity even when it first happened, in the fourth century. Some believed that Constantine had found it; others believed that Helena had done so. Still others preferred rather to hush the whole event up. Eusebius ignored the event, when describing Constantine's church of the Holy Sepulchre. He was determined that the church, over the tomb, was to be a monument to Christ's resurrection, and did not even mention the cross, though it was just beside the tomb and eventually housed in the same complex of buildings. But a pilgrim from Bordeaux visiting the half-finished church in AD 333 noted the site of the crucifixion – the 'hillock Golgotha where the Lord was crucified' – as well as 'the vault where they laid his body', giving the archaeological location of the cross as much attention as the tomb. And Constantine himself appeared to refer to the discovery of the cross in a letter to Macarius, the bishop who supposedly worked the cross miracle. Constantine asked Macarius to build a basilica to commemorate the 'token of that holiest passion, long hidden in the earth'.

It seems that Eusebius wanted to divert attention away from the discovery of the cross because he was wary of its implications for a possible sacred archaeology in the future. Holiness, for Eusebius, was to be apprehended not in material objects but in their traces. Divinity was a phenomenon which vanished away, which slipped the grasp, which transcended the earthly world. So, as De Certeau mentioned earlier, he emphasised Christ's tomb, which was of course empty, and which had only housed Jesus' body for three days before the resurrection. But those who were interested in the cross sought holiness in physical things. They believed that divinity somehow infused the wood it had once been in contact with, and that that wood could now work miracles. The way appeared to be potentially open for an industry of excavation, relic collection and pilgrimage, and Eusebius was keen to establish a very different kind of Christianity.

But the alternative strand of the religion, under which devotees believed in the divinity of place which could be exposed by prayer and the spade, could not be utterly repressed. Nearly sixty years after the excavation at Golgotha, Egeria, a nun probably from France or northern Spain, arrived in Jerusalem on a pilgrimage. She was also to visit important sacred sites in the Holy Land, including Mount Sinai, Galilee, the Dead Sea and Jordan. Her chief object was to connect particular locations with the account of them in the Bible, partly to be able to 'picture what happened in these places' when reading the book later and partly apparently to draw nearer to God. In each sacred place, she read the appropriate passage from the Bible and said a prayer. So on Mount Sinai, she saw where Aaron stood while Moses received the ten commandments – it was 'an enormous round rock with a flat place on top' – and she supposedly saw the original burning bush. It was apparently 'still alive and sprouting', miraculously rejuvenated following the holy flames and growing in a 'very pretty garden which has plenty of excellent water'. In the desert in Jordan, she visited the tomb of Job, which had been excavated under the orders of a monk.

'As they dug they at first discovered a cave', she wrote to her fellow nuns back at home. 'Then following it in for about a hundred yards they suddenly came upon a stone. When they had thoroughly uncovered it, they found carved on its cover the name JOB.'

It was a happy discovery with the inscription conveniently preserved for the excavators, but apparently the monk's men decided not to investigate further but to leave the body still buried beneath the stone. Further south, at Mount Nebo in Jordan, Egeria looked down upon the Dead Sea and the site of Sodom, where Lot's wife had been turned into a pillar of salt.

'What we saw, reverend Ladies, was not the actual pillar, but only the place where it had once been', Egeria confessed. 'The pillar itself, they say, has been submerged in the Dead Sea. In fact it was the Bishop there who told us that it was now a good many years since the pillar had been visible.'

Unlike Eusebius, Egeria had no fear of the possible idolatrous consequences of her type of archaeological pilgrimage. For her, divine narrative and divine topography were wonderfully intertwined. It did not worry her whether the pillar of salt was still visible or how Moses' bush had avoided conflagration; what mattered was that it was at these spots that the stories cohered and where they appeared to make most vivid sense. This connection appeared most dramatically at the Easter ritual conducted in Jerusalem, around the site of Golgotha. Pilgrims recreated the last hours of Jesus' life by walking on the same stones at approximately the same hour of the day as he did. Egeria went with them. They began at the garden of Gethsemane, where Jesus was betrayed, walked up to the Lions' Gate and through the city, along what has now been designated the Via Dolorosa, and ended up before the Cross. A few detoured off to Mount Zion, to 'pray at the column at which the Lord was scourged'. Back at Golgotha, the bishop united what until now had been a symbolic sense of place and time with a literal relic of place and time. For he sat behind the richly ornamental symbolic cross, erected over the supposed site of Christ's crucifixion, and opened a box containing a fragmentary piece of the original real cross, the product of Helena's or Constantine's excavation. The congregation proceeded to pay homage to the wood.

'They stoop down over it, kiss the Wood, and move on', Egeria recalled. 'But on one occasion (I don't know why) one of them bit off a piece of the holy Wood and stole it away, and for this reason the deacons stand around and keep watch in case anyone dares to do the same again.'

Biting bits off the cross was going too far. Egeria was bewildered by such frenzy. But what she thought was moving was the fact that these rituals were what she repeatedly called most 'appropriate' because they brought together narrative and material evidence in a way that intensified belief and became arguably a form of sacrament.

*

The significance of sacrament and its place in Christianity are questions which trouble theologians and provoke heated debate even today. Sacrament means a thing which has become holy. It marks a mystical joining together of a material object and the divine spirit. The bread and wine of the eucharist are classic examples. But how does the mystical joining come about and what makes something holy? Is it human prayer and arguably the projection of subjective imagination which hallows a place or an object? Or is it God who invests the world with his redeeming vision until everything within it becomes effectively part of his creation, potentially sacred? According to John Habgood, the former Archbishop of York, everything in the world can be said to be holy because it is 'given', as he puts it, by Christ. Jesus made the world 'meaningful' by his presence within it and his simultaneous divinity. Touching sacramental places or holy relics is not only to project our desires for spirituality upon them, through prayer and meditation, but to touch 'in actuality' a piece of God.

But the Archbishop of Canterbury, Rowan Williams, is more wary of turning everything, without scruple, into something holy. He worries about 'the rather bland appeal to the natural sacredness of things that occasionally underpins sacramental theology'. Instead, he maintains that the material world only becomes divine through an act of 'self-effacement' by God. Holy things mark their sacredness by revealing divine death or disappearance or reduction or loss. Just as Jesus offered himself for crucifixion, and symbolically became bread and wine to be consumed, so holy places and things are 'dead matter', part of a divine transaction in which God has already disappeared or been transformed. Williams explains: 'The divine presence is apprehended by seeing in all things their difference, their particularity, their "not-God-ness", since we have learned what the divine action is in the renunciation of Christ, his giving himself into inanimate form.'

So too Michel de Certeau thinks that fundamental to sacredness is the act of 'disappearance'. The places of Christianity and the borders around sacred spaces are only defined and made holy by the fact that they are 'perpetually transgressed'. As the original 'event' – Christ's death – was characterised by the departure of divinity from us, so Christian practice repeatedly witnesses points of departure and disappearance. The ideal kind of pilgrimage, consequently, is one that never rests and never reaches its destination. It journeys to 'the longed-for land' which 'dissolves on approach'.

The debate about sacrament goes to the heart of the disagreement between Eusebius and Egeria over the importance of the excavated cross. Egeria regards the Holy Land as gifted by God, and every object within it as sacred and significant within the Biblical narrative. The cross at Golgotha, unearthed sixty years earlier, is just the most miraculous example of that divine revelation. Eusebius, by contrast, like Rowan Williams, shies away from the possibly idolatrous implications of regarding things as holy, and prefers rather to think about holiness as a process, a continual arrival and departure of the godhead rather than anything that can be held, possessed and worshipped. Biblical archaeology is the most literal and problematic example of sacrament and it is therefore hardly surprising that the world's first excavation should raise pressing questions about the value of material objects and the location of holiness, questions which have dogged Christian believers ever since.

*

These were the questions which were at the back of my mind as I walked the fourteen 'stations of the cross' along the Via Dolorosa in Jerusalem four years ago. I began, as all good pilgrims must, at the Lions' Gate, which leads out to the Mount of Olives and Arab East Jerusalem, now heavily guarded by khaki soldiers with guns. It was here that Pontius Pilate condemned Jesus to death and from here that Jesus carried his cross through the streets and out to Calvary.

'You want a guide?' a little, check-shirted kid grabbed my hand at the second station, where Jesus was flagellated. 'My name is Amit. You can take photographs.'

The road now is pockmarked with archaeological traces, divots and prints which supposedly were originally created by the divine foot or hand. You can stop at the place where Jesus was tried and condemned and where Pontius Pilate showed him to the jeering crowd, with the words 'Ecce homo'. Amit showed me the place where Jesus' mother Mary had stood to watch her son stagger past. I duly scoured the mosaic floor, unsuccessfully trying to see the supposed outline of her holy sandals. Round the corner, Amit by this stage having lost interest, I paused at the fifth station, the point where the exhausted Jesus fell under the weight of the cross and Simon the Cyrenian was forced by the soldiers to carry the cross instead. On the wall at this corner were five clearly discernible dimples, the reputed traces of the divine handprint made as Jesus lurched out to the wall to seek some support as he fell. I placed my fingers in the holes and must confess that I felt a thrill. If I suspended enough disbelief, I might be pressing the same stone that Jesus once had reached for and which miraculously had preserved the preciousness of that moment ever since, its rocky solidity melting in ecstatic delight. But even if I could not enter into that fantasy world (and, being far from cynical, I find it all too easy to do so), I was physically in touch, through the tips of my fingers and these hallowed divots, with the fingers of thousands of pilgrims over the centuries who had lapped up the same story and devotedly pressed the same bit of wall.

The thrill which I felt in the Via Dolorosa, I discovered, is characteristic of a particularly Catholic or Orthodox attitude to sacred archaeology. Orthodox pilgrims are not interested in the literal, historical facts about Jesus' life and do not concern themselves with unearthing places as they might have been in Jesus' time. Theirs is not a pedantic obsession with preserving the past. But rather they believe that God broke through time in the form of Jesus, and that divinity is something eternal and transcendent. So holy places shine with a timeless aura of sanctity and become sacred because so many other worshippers have met there and responded to the reputed glory. They think, therefore, that every spot in the Holy Land must not be excavated and stripped back to the supposedly authentic conditions two millennia ago, but be marked with churches and shrines in order to make manifest the timeless, divine significance of the place.

Protestants, on the other hand, view archaeological sites in the Holy

Land very differently. Traditionally kept out as an institution from Jerusalem, where Christian sites are divided among the guardianship of the Catholic, Orthodox and Armenian churches, the Protestants aim to strip away the accretions of the ages and to get back to the original landscapes or the original buildings as they might have been in Jesus' time. Just as the Protestant faith is derived straight from the Bible or the Word of God, not transmitted down through the saints and the church fathers, so their contact with God in the Holy Land is to be gained, not through wonder at church buildings, but directly from the same earth and stones trodden once by the feet of God.

This certainly was the argument put forward by various Victorian travelling clergymen. The American evangelical writer, J.M.P. Otts, visiting from Greensboro, Alabama in 1892, described the land of Palestine as the 'fifth gospel', making a direct comparison between reading the Bible and reading archaeological traces: 'To the observant traveller in the land where Jesus lived the written Gospels become in form, and hence in substance to some extent, a new and enlarged revelation.' Over thirty years earlier, Protestant travellers were advised by the Scottish Presbyterian minister, Rev. William Tweedie to 'sit down' at various key places in Palestine 'with the Bible open before us, as it should be habitually in the Holy Land' and to 'try to drink in the lessons which the scene may help to deepen'. At times, the land was to appear a simple metaphor for the word and the ability to learn from viewing particular scenes was the metaphorical equivalent of Bible-study. In that case, as Tweedie pointed out, buildings and shrines on top of biblical archaeological sites were the metaphorical equivalent of critics and distorting church tradition: 'Places not a few appear here as sacred as aught that material can ever be; and that represents the inspired text. But interspersed with these are endless human additions, by which the native attractions of the place are marred; and these represent the vain glosses of many a darkling critic and gloomy chronicler.'

What was most important was the idea of the non-negotiable truth about the archaeological remains in the Bible lands. As the Dean of Westminster, the venerable Arthur Penrhyn Stanley, put it in his book *Sinai and Palestine*, there is, in ancient landscape, 'an element of fact which no theory or interpretation can dissolve'. A great exponent of the logical truth of Christianity, Stanley – who had written books such as *Do We Form Our Opinions From External Authority?* and *The Study of Greatness*, and who actually visited the Holy Land together with the Prince of Wales, the future Edward VII – thought that there was no greater argument for Christian revelation, no greater proof, than a visit to the ancient sites in Israel. While different stories might be subject to different versions, the stones and earth which formed the bedrock of

Palestine were not affected by historical change but remained the same, touched originally with the divine presence of Christ and available for meditation and study. 'If ruins cannot tell the whole truth, at any rate they tell nothing but the truth', insisted Stanley. 'They still remain to be examined again and again by each succeeding traveller, correcting, elucidating, developing the successive depositions which they have made from age to age.' As such, reading books such as Ott's evangelical *The Fifth Gospel*, or better still visiting the Holy Land oneself and viewing the divine truth manifested in the soil, warded off the scepticism about Christianity which was growing in influence in the period. Archaeological accounts of the Holy Land constituted some of the chief ways of defending the Christian faith against a new secular historicism. The historical 'truth' about Jesus, still embedded in the rocks, could conquer historical relativism and evolutionary theory. One need only see the streets of Jerusalem or the shores of Galilee and one would believe; 'mere glimpses of what took place in that remarkable city', wrote Tweedie, 'invest the place with the sacredness that belongs to the abode of a present God.'

*

But how could belief arise so unequivocally from rocks? Repeatedly, in the attempt to explain this conundrum, nineteenth-century archaeologists and travel writers made comparisons between Palestine and Greece, between the Holy Land and the country which was venerated by all classically-educated gentlemen. The ruins of Greece were better known than those in the Holy Land, through artists' records, the exhibition of the Elgin Marbles in London and excavations in Athens conducted by the Greek Archaeological Association. As a result of poets like Byron, who had inspired the philhellenic movement with his long travel poem *Childe Harold* in 1812, the connection between archaeological sites and a quasi-spiritual sense was already well established. 'Where'er we tread 'tis haunted, holy ground', Byron wrote of the Greek landscape in *Childe Harold*: 'Delphi's side' was 'sacred'; Marathon's soil was 'hallowed'; the whole country was a 'land of lost gods and godlike men'. Byron was unashamed in acknowledging that in order to recognise the 'sacredness' of Greece, one had to be in the right state of mind: 'He that is lonely hither let him roam/ And gaze complacent on congenial earth.' The spirit of Greece was created by a perfect mingling of the subjective and the objective, the imaginative desire of the traveller and the mouldering ruins which became the site of meditation. Byron's own melancholy mood tinged the broken columns with a special elegiac kind of sadness: 'Cold is the heart, fair Greece! that looks on thee, Nor feels as lovers o'er the dust they loved.' In this process of blurring the distinction between the imagination and archaeological remains, the earth became anthropomorphised – its dust like the lover's dust to be mourned – while the head became reified into another temple:

> Remove yon skull from out the scatter'd heaps:
> Is that a temple where a God may dwell?
> Why ev'n the worm at last disdains her shatter'd cell.

Yet there are moments of doubt in Byron's poem, when the rocks resist the imagination's attempt to make something meaningful from them. 'Fancy's eye' cannot 'restore what Time hath labour'd to deface', Byron observes wistfully. Indeed his poem oscillates between vision and despair, between episodes when it seems that he can communicate with the divine spirits of the past and episodes when he is debarred and alone in a stony, forbidding landscape. In a line which elegiacally recalls Wordsworth's optimistic poems, 'Lines Written A Few Miles Above Tintern Abbey' and 'Daffodils', and which also foreshadows Keats' 'Ode to a Nightingale', Byron suggests the limits of the imaginative endeavour in the holy land of Greece:

> But one vast realm of wonder spreads around,
> And all the Muse's tales seem truly told,
> Till the sense aches with gazing to behold
> The scenes our earliest dreams have dwelt upon.

Wordsworth's 'gazing' in 'Daffodils' brings imaginative joy and vision later when on his 'pensive couch'. Keats' heart 'aches' in 'Ode to a Nightingale' before he is charioted away on the 'viewless wings of poesy' to 'fairy lands forlorn'. But Byron's 'gazing' and 'aching' garner ambiguous rewards, which mark the faultlines between present and past, imagination and reality, that disturb his poem.

Nearly a century after Byron, Sigmund Freud made his first visit to Greece and found himself confronting the same faultlines. Standing on the acropolis in August 1904, he looked around at the Parthenon, the theatre of Dionysus and the ancient agora spread out on the plain below, and 'a surprising thought suddenly entered my mind: "So all this really *does* exist, just as we learnt at school."' Analysing the experience some thirty years later, he attempted to explain his initial incredulity and strange sense of faith being restored. It was all a matter of the trip seeming too good to be true, Freud decides. When one really desires something, one attempts to repudiate it in order to guard against disappointment or to avoid the guilt of actually having one's desires fulfilled. The trip to Athens is really then the fulfilment of a long held desire, which Freud never allowed himself to believe would happen. 'In an undistorted form this should have been: "I could really not have imagined it possible that I should ever be granted the sight of Athens with my own eyes – as is now indubitably the case!"' Freud explains. But there is a double distortion. The doubt is displaced from his uncertainty about his own worthiness to an uncertainty about the existence of the ancient ruins. And the lack of belief now – 'am I really seeing Athens?' – becomes displaced onto the inability to believe in his childhood – 'We are learning about these ruins at school but do they really exist?' Ultimately Freud decides that this doubt or 'derealisation' is wrapped up with his relationship with his father. His father had never been to Athens and had been deprived of secondary education so that he would not have appreciated the significance of Athens anyway. Freud's guilt at having his desires fulfilled is exacerbated by the guilt of exceeding his father. 'The very theme of Athens and the Acropolis in itself contained evidence of the son's superiority', he argues. 'It seems as though the essence of success was to have got further than one's father, and as though to excel one's father was still something forbidden.'

Freud's account of the story pinpoints the crisis of belief at the meeting point of internal speculation and external stony reality. Rather like Byron's 'fancy' when confronting 'what Time hath labour'd to deface', Freud attempts to project his internal anxieties and feelings of guilt onto the external phenomenon which is Athens. The ruins of Athens themselves become sites of credulity or incredulity and divert attention from Freud's own disavowal and filial shortcomings. But what Freud fails to do in his self-analysis is answer the question: what made the acropolis special in the first place? By turning the episode into an account of the fear of success, of outdoing the father, of the guilt origins of derealisation, Freud effectively denies the particular archaeological and ideological provenance of the story. The point of the anecdote is that the acropolis was really special, so special indeed that it became the focus of almost unmanageable desire for Freud. Certainly the focus for a desire which dare not speak its name. And it was represented as special by the school-teachers because nineteenth-century educators in Germany were caught up in a historically-specific period of philhellenism. In the 1860s and 1870s, when Freud was at school, the old Gymnasium system was flourishing, an education system based upon Friedrich August Wolf's and Wilhelm von Humboldt's admiration for ancient Greece, in which the study of classical languages took up 46 per cent of the syllabus. Freud suggests, in his analysis, that the acropolis is unchanging and objectively always valuable while it is only he who changes from childhood to adulthood, from veneration to doubt and back to veneration again. But in fact the acropolis, as an archaeological site, is as subject to change as he is, as bound up with ideological values and beliefs, traceable to the early nineteenth century when Wolf was developing his theories about Germany's debt to Greece.

*

But Byron and Freud were reflecting on the 'sacredness' of Greece, a 'sacredness' related to ideals of culture, art and poetry rather than strictly to religion. If these were the excitements to be experienced in Greece, how much more could they be felt by the Christian in Israel. 'What has Athens to do with Jerusalem?' the early Christian thinker Tertullian famously remarked in his tract on heresy and its debt to ancient philosophy. 'What has the academy to do with the church? What have heretics to do with Christians?' These thoughts were echoed by the nineteenth-century clergymen who, while impressed by the classical remains of the Greece they had learnt about at school, believed that there was no comparison between these and the holy relics to be witnessed in Palestine. 'Greece and Italy have geographical charms of a high order', wrote Arthur Penrhyn Stanley. 'But they have never provoked a Crusade; and, however bitter may have been the disputes of antiquaries about the Acropolis of Athens or the Forum of Rome, they have never, as at Bethlehem and Jerusalem, become matters of religious controversy.'

Nineteenth-century travellers to Palestine aimed to discover places independent of ideology and history. They wanted to get back to what they imagined were the original sites, to what was 'true' and 'unchanging'. They complained repeatedly about the clutter of shrines which obscured the holy spaces and the corrupting superstitious rituals which were held there. William Tweedie repeated many a Christian pilgrim's experience in the Church of the Holy Sepulchre when he commented that 'amid the legends of the place, the crowding decorations, and frequently the outrageous scenes which are witnessed among the rival worshippers, one is rarely disposed to exercise any faith at all'. Instead, gardens and empty landscapes, which had once been the location of an event in the gospels, were what they found most moving. 'Where can faith more nearly pass into sight?' wrote Tweedie of Gethsemane. William Bartlett advised his readers to stand on the wall by the Lions' Gate and look out over the valley to the Mount of Olives, where one was not 'repelled by the palpable inventions of pious fraud' but could be 'alone with nature, and in a silence unbroken but by the wind sweeping over the city walls'. And Stanley was similarly struck by the contrast between the peopled so-called holy city and the unpeopled space outside it: 'It is useless to seek for traces of His presence in the streets of the since ten times captured city. It is impossible not to find them in the free space of the Mount of Olives.' The urge to find God in gardens outside the Catholic-dominated city led some of the Protestant archaeological writers to locate an alternative 'empty tomb'. Instead of the tomb covered by the Church of the Holy Sepulchre, the

Garden Tomb, located just outside the Damascus Gate over the grotto of Jeremiah and suitably rural and silent, was promoted as a site of adoration. This was supposedly where Jesus was buried.

Go to the outskirts of the Damascus Gate now, of course, and you will find buses, lorries and the only market in Old Jerusalem that stays open on a Saturday, selling some of the best felafel. Go, indeed, to the Mount of Olives and you have to run the gauntlet of armed soldiers, stray dogs, massive coaches turning tight corners and – if you are a lone woman venturing up there at sunrise, as I was – suspicious-looking men lurking under the gnarled olive trees. Hardly the tranquil and meditative experience, guaranteed, as Stanley suggests, to offer you 'traces of His presence'. But to stand near the Sea of Galilee, on the hill where the Sermon on the Mount was supposedly delivered, is to have some inkling of what Stanley, Tweedie and their other Victorian colleagues were seeking. Little, one fondly imagines, has changed. The view down to the blue lake, with the hills of the Golan rising up behind, was what Jesus would have seen as he numbered those who were to be considered blessed. And the warm wind, which blew from behind me and rippled through the cornfields on the shores of the lake, might have carried his voice to the crowds below: 'Blessed are the meek; for they shall inherit the earth.' No place in Israel, it seemed to me that golden evening in August 2000, could be more moving. Here landscape had survived the vicissitudes of time and given me direct communication with God. As Byron commented on the spirituality of the ancient Greek landscape which transcended time:

> Each hill and dale, each deepening glen and wold
> Defies the power which crush'd thy temples gone:
> Age shakes Athena's tower, but spares gray Marathon.

But the archaeological imagination questions the idea of landscape which can be independent of history and concentrates instead on appreciating the disparity between then and now. After all, if I had thought about it, the hills of the Golan, for a start, are not as they would have been in Jesus' time, being now studded with landmines. Indeed, one of the crucial triggering factors for the Jerusalem Syndrome victims identified by Yair Bar-El is anxiety caused by the disparity between the Jerusalem of their imaginations and the modern, bustling Jerusalem they encounter in person. 'A gap appears between their subconscious idealistic image of Jerusalem and the city as it appears in reality', Bar-El comments. 'One might view their psychotic state and, in particular, the need to preach their universal message as an attempt to bridge the gap between these two representations of Jerusalem.' The impossible attempt to deny the passage of time and to seek a place, frozen as it might have been in AD 31, as the only source of 'truth', is to lay oneself open to delusion and ultimately madness. Even Freud, who sought on the acropolis not fundamentally to 'bridge the gap' but tentatively to displace the problem onto personal guilt and problems of credulity, acknowledged this process as one of 'disturbance'. Freud evades the question of the archaeological status of Athens – its changes through history, its state of preservation, the ideological account of its excavation in nineteenth-century Germany – when explaining his strange response to the city and in that way undergoes a further, unrecognised distortion or episode of mild psychosis.

*

Unlike these victims who search romantically for a pure city or landscape which corresponds with their mental image, healthily grounded archaeologists realise that recognising the processes of history in material form is crucial for understanding the past. And even the sacred past is subject to the accretion and decay common to all historical sites. In the nineteenth century, archaeologists in Jerusalem started to recognise that the cross and the tomb could only be identified, not by miracles nor obviously by digging up a buried body, but by finding the walls of Jerusalem as they were in Jesus' time. Jesus was crucified outside the city, but the Church of the Holy Sepulchre, supposedly built over Golgotha, is well inside the old city walls. The only explanation for this, if the Golgotha location is authentic, is that the position of the walls has changed. It is known that by the time Titus besieged Jerusalem in AD 70, there were three city walls (see map). The third wall, the most recent built by Herod Agrippa in about AD 41-44, followed roughly the line of the present Crusader wall, linking the Damascus and Jaffa Gates and including the Church of the Holy Sepulchre within its bounds. The first wall, built around 143-135 BC, ran roughly from the temple to the Jaffa Gate, along David Street, defending the original old city south of its border and with the site of Golgotha clearly outside it. But the crucial question is: where was the second wall, which was built probably by Herod the Great sometime after 31 BC, and which would have been the city wall in Jesus' time? There is no clear written evidence for the route of the wall, yet its location becomes vital for determining the authenticity of the sites of Golgotha and the tomb. If they lie outside that second wall, then they might indeed be the 'true' location of Jesus' death and resurrection.

As there is no written evidence, nineteenth-century archaeological writers and cartographers decided to seek material evidence. Edward Robinson set out from New England in 1841 with surveyor's compass, thermometer, telescopes and measuring tapes, determined, as he put it, to 'avoid as far as possible all contact with the convents and the authority of

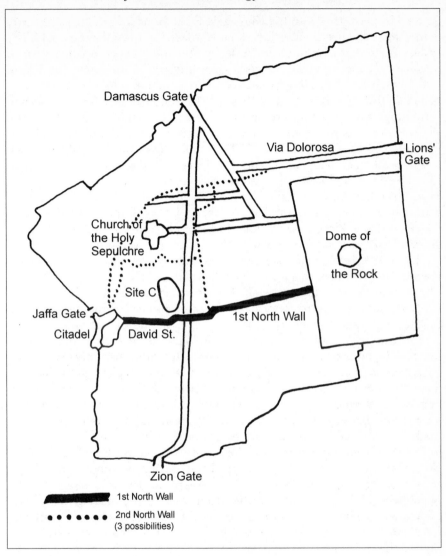

Damascus Gate

Via Dolorosa

Lions'
Gate

Church of
the Holy
Sepulchre

Dome of

the Rock

Site C

Jaffa Gate

1st North Wall

Citadel

David St.

Zion Gate

1st North Wall

2nd North Wall
(3 possibilities)

the monks' and to 'examine everywhere for ourselves with the Scriptures in our hands'. He measured the distance between the temple wall and the Church of the Holy Sepulchre – less than a quarter of a mile – and concluded that the second wall must have curved quite far north to include the site of the Holy Sepulchre within its boundaries if the city in Jesus' time were not to be ridiculously small. The Holy Sepulchre site in the present church was therefore 'untenable and impossible'.

Four years later, Rev. George Williams leapt to the defence of the tomb.

As he admitted, the 'credit of the whole Church for fifteen hundred years is in some measure involved in the question'. Fighting for the credibility of Jesus' sepulchre against the 'unbelievers' like Edward Robinson was a modern crusade, re-enacting metaphorically the battles over the literal tomb which had been fought between Christians and Muslims centuries before. Williams suggests that the Gate of Gennath, at which the second wall supposedly started, might be located not by the Jaffa Gate in the Western wall, as Robinson argued, but halfway along the north wall that ran between the Jaffa Gate and the temple. This would mean that the second wall would run east of the site of the Holy Sepulchre, which would then be crucially outside the city walls. To substantiate his topographical case, Williams claims to have found archaeological evidence of the second wall and Gate Gennath: 'Immediately without the bazaar, on the west, is a sudden rise to Zion, near the top of which is to be seen the head of an old gateway, so much choked up with rubbish that the keystone is nearly on a level with the street .... It appears to have formed a round arch and probably might be excavated with success, if permission could be obtained.'

Two years after Williams' book, *The Holy City; or Historical and Topographical Notices of Jerusalem*, was published, James Fergusson joined the debate. Not deterred by the fact that he had never actually been to Jerusalem, he was keen to pour scorn on Williams' theory, which was, he felt, too dependent on 'miracles and monkish traditions'. Instead he presented himself as the scientific and objective topographer. A 'theological dispute' had wrongly been 'introduced into what should have been a question of pure topography', and a cool head, like his, was required. But having put forward this case for scientific reasons, Fergusson proceeded inadvertently to demolish it in most dramatic fashion. For he argued that in fact the 'mosque of Omar' (the Dome of the Rock) was the Church of the Holy Sepulchre and that Jesus had been buried within the area now known as the Temple Mount. This bizarre theory was supported by hypothesis and speculation, rather than calculated measurement and excavated evidence: Pilate's residence was just beside the temple platform; Golgotha must have been just north of it if Christ had not awkwardly carried the cross right through the city; and the tomb must have been close by Golgotha.

Remarkably, James Fergusson's thesis about the site of the Holy Sepulchre enjoyed immense influence, and when, in 1865, the Palestine Exploration Fund was established in Britain, he was appointed to be a member of the Executive Committee of the Fund, swaying its policies and shaping its decisions. But that influence was to be soon contested since the first archaeological expedition to Jerusalem which the P.E.F. sponsored was led in 1867 by Captain Charles Warren, who was determined to disprove Fergusson's thesis. Possibly because of the rivalry between Fergusson and Warren, Warren's excavations were dogged with difficulties, lack of communication and shortage of funds, so much so that Warren quipped that the 'Fund' should be renamed the 'Debt'. But despite working against phenomenal odds – intimidation from Turkish authorities, no wood scaffolding to support mine shafts, no money for months on end – Warren made, over a period of three years, some serious and important archaeological discoveries. His digging focused upon the site of the temple, but because it was under Muslim authority and no non-Muslim could enter the site, he was compelled to approach it via shafts and tunnels started some 90 feet or so away, outside the walls. One shaft dropped 80 feet below the ground, tunnelled in towards the temple 400 feet, and still found there, deep underground, the large stones which had formed the walls of Herod's temple platform. The immediate implication of Warren's excavation was to challenge Fergusson's theory, for Warren was able to find, through digging down, the four walls of the temple platform and so to locate the temple which existed in Herod's day. The more general consequence of Warren's expedition was to reveal the huge layers of rubble which covered the city and which meant that any stones surviving from Jesus' time were now tens of feet below ground. Warren proved, for example, that the Kidron valley, which separated the old city and the Temple Mount from the Mount of Olives, had silted up with rubbish and that the bottom was some 150 feet below. 'After this', he said, 'I was prepared to find all modern Jerusalem a sham and a delusion, covering unknown valleys and hills.'

Warren proved that charting the holy city meant exploring under-ground Jerusalem as well as the surface topography of streets and visible remains. It involved developing a sense of the tunnelling and silting which had gone on over the centuries and an understanding of the layer upon layer, going down 100 feet in places, of periods of construction. Other excavators followed: Henry Maudsly, Frederick J. Bliss, J.W. Crowfoot. But it was Kathleen Kenyon in the 1960s who finally used sophisticated excavation techniques to solve the problem of the location of the Holy Sepulchre, or, in other words, to combine successfully archaeological investigation with religious motivation.

Digging in Jerusalem is difficult, because the city is so densely popu-lated and every area of ground is owned and venerated by somebody. But Kathleen Kenyon managed to find a patch of ground, between David Street and the Church of the Holy Sepulchre, belonging to the Order of St John, which was lying vacant. This became known as Site C. For two seasons the excavators dug through over 8 metres of 'fill' or archaeological rubbish, containing a mixture of seventh-century BC and first-century AD pottery. Finally they hit bedrock 14.75 metres down, after digging through various cuts and ledges which proved this site had once been a stone quarry. While this excavation does not sound very dramatic in that it found nothing tangible and it was operating in a tiny shaft eventually only 4 metres square, yet for Kenyon it revealed a huge amount of information which really clinched the Holy Sepulchre question. The fact that a quarry had existed there proves that it lay outside the city walls; people don't quarry within their city. This quarry continued until the time that the 'fill' was deposited, which must have been after the first century AD, since the 'fill' included first-century pottery shards. The site must have been filled in at the time when the area was about to be included within the city boundaries and the area would be built on. Therefore, Kenyon concluded, Site C was only incorporated into the city at the time of Hadrian's Roman city in AD 135. As Site C is only slightly south of the Holy Sepulchre, it is reasonable to argue that the Holy Sepulchre remained outside the city until the same time and that consequently the Holy Sepulchre is very likely to be authentic.

Archaeology, in the last few decades, has come paradoxically to give more credence to the legends of the cross and the tomb than existed previously, in the years of speculation. Charles Warren complained that the obstacle to the credibility of his researches was the fact that Jerusalem was not allowed to be 'anything but a shadowy myth'. The Byronic French writer, Alphonse de Lamartine, who admittedly visited Jerusalem during a raging plague in 1832, also confessed his disappointment. He notes mournfully in his diary:

> Jerusalem, where one would visit only one sepulchre, is itself the tomb of a whole people. But it is a tomb without cypresses, without inscriptions, without monuments, whose stones have been broken up, and whose ashes seem to have covered the earth around it with mourning, with silence, and with sterility.

But Kathleen Kenyon proved that the curious combination of factual rubble and missing construction in Site C substantiated the holy centre of the holy city. The lack of 'inscription' or 'monument', as Lamartine would have it, in Site C paradoxically proved that the Holy Sepulchre might well have briefly, for three days, housed a divine body. If, for Rowan Williams, it is the sacrament of disappearance which ensures God's grace, then it is appropriate that the sophisticated techniques of archaeology, which look not for objects but material processes in order to gain insight, have brought us closer to appreciating what might be holy ground.

*

Needless to say, the ground does not feel very sacred or holy or even valuable as I crouch down and hack away at it with my trowel and pick in

El-Ahwat, a hilltop site somewhere between Jerusalem and Haifa (Plate 13). Carefully loosening the earth caught in the crannies between rocks, I sweep up the debris into a bucket, haul it to a growing mountain of earth nearby and tip it out. Occasionally, I empty the contents of the bucket into a huge sieve and pick out what I hope is a bit of pottery and not just a stone. Every twenty minutes I take another swig from my water bottle. It is thirsty, back-breaking work. The earth changes colour from the clay-red of the Roman level, to the dark black of the earlier fill, to the ash-white of the Iron Age floor level, and it smells dusty, like opening old books. I chisel away, brush up the results, chisel some more. By the end of the morning I feel as if I am standing beside the best cleaned set of rocks in Israel.

But at the end of the morning's six-hour session, the leader of the excavation, Adam Zertal, comes round to inspect my progress. Crippled by a devastating attack suffered in the Sinai desert in 1973 and pulling himself over the rough ground on a pair of crutches, Zertal is warm, charismatic, driven by his enthusiasm. For five minutes, while he is with me, I can sense the significance of my efforts with the trowel. It is not just a pile of earth and rocks, apparently, but the foundations of an important early iron-age town (1200 BC). The structures of the outer walls – massive fortifications with curious dead-end corridors within them – bear no resemblance to any other site in Israel but do, Zertal believes, share similarities with that of various ancient towns (or 'nuraghe') in Sardinia. From this, he deduces that El-Ahwat might have been a settlement of the Shardana, a northern Sea Peoples tribe originating in Sardinia. But Zertal has also linked El-Ahwat to the Bible. El-Ahwat, he maintains, must be Harosheth Hagoyim, the headquarters of Sisera, who fought the Israelite leader, Barak, in Judges 4. If the connection with Sardinia is to be believed, then this gives us new information about the identity of Sisera. Known before only to be one of the Gentiles defeated by the Israelites in their fight to establish their nation in Canaan, it now seems that he might have been one of the lost Sea Peoples settled as mercenaries by the Egyptians under Ramesses III but known previously only through vague documentary accounts, not through concrete archaeological evidence.

Adam Zertal is Israel's foremost proponent of the notion that the Bible should be treated as history not myth and he conducts a regular survey of the Manasseh hills, west of the Jordan, looking for sites mentioned in the Old Testament. At stake is the origin of the nation of Israel. According to the book of Joshua, the Israelites were led over the Jordan, conquered various Canaanite towns, like Jericho and Ai, and took 'possession of the land that the Lord your God gives you to possess'. There Joshua divided the land between the twelve tribes, which had followed Moses out of Egypt, and built new settlements. 'These were the cities designated for all the Israelites', states the book of Joshua, 'and for the aliens residing among them.' But according to some archaeologists, there is little material evidence for an arrival of a new culture in 1200 BC, and little evidence for a distinction between 'Israelite' and 'alien'. Excavations at Megiddo show that Canaanite sacrificial practice was not very different from Israelite practice. Archaeological investigation at Hazor has revealed traces of the destruction of one city but not a flourishing new civilisation to replace it. So what was unique about the Israelites? Did they conquer the land of Israel, with God at their side? Did they gradually infiltrate the area, living peacefully in the hill country and only later descending to the plains and facing sporadic conflict with the Canaanites, as Albrecht Alt would have it? Or was the great age of Israelite settlement much later than 1200 BC, a long time after Joshua and Solomon, after a lengthy period of Canaanite dominance?

Zertal is convinced of the uniqueness of the Israelites and the truth behind the Bible's narrative of their unquestioning loyalty to God and the prophets Moses and Joshua. His survey, which, like the Australian Aboriginal songlines, lists the rocks, the soil, springs and rivers supposedly in his land, aims to prove the distinctiveness of the archaeological remains there. It came to a dramatic climax in the 1980s when for six years his attention was focused upon a ridge on the slopes of Mount Ebal, a mountain in the occupied territories near Tel Balata. According to the Bible, after the slaughter of the inhabitants of Jericho and Ai, Joshua built an altar to God on Mount Ebal and gathered all the Israelites there and wrote the law of Moses on stone. 'All Israel, alien as well as citizen, with their elders and officers and their judges, stood on opposite sides of the ark in front of the levitical priests who carried the ark of the covenant of the Lord' (Joshua 8:33). As Zertal and his team dug into the ridge, they became certain that they were uncovering the altar built by Joshua. There were ramps instead of steps, enclosing walls which served no functional purpose, remnants of sacrifices. What is more, the remains seemed to have virtually no archaeological parallel and therefore, as Zertal explained, 'a possible solution should be sought in the rich literature on the subject'. In other words, the Bible. Everything appeared to 'correlate' with the biblical tradition:

> The Lord said to Moses: You need make for me only an altar of earth and sacrifice on it your burnt-offerings and your offerings of well-being, your sheep and your oxen; in every place where I cause my name to be remembered I will come to you and bless you. But if you make for me an altar of stone, do not build it of hewn stones; for if you use a chisel upon it you profane it. You shall not go up by steps to my altar, so that your nakedness may not be exposed upon it (Exodus 20:24-6).

7. Holy Ground: Archaeology and the Sacred

Unhewn stones, ramps, large quantities of animal bones: Ebal, for Zertal, bears all the hallmarks of a site built in accordance with Moses' instructions from God. It was distinct from the local Canaanite settlements. And it was similar, he believes, to the altars in the first and second temples in Jerusalem. The builders of Ebal were, therefore, clearly Israelites. They were the early pioneers of their people, forging a new civilisation, giving thanks to the God who they thought had given them the land. Forget the claim of Canaan, is the message of Ebal. These stones, says Zertal, prove the Israelites' 'will to be different'. Now he seeks other early Israelite settlements to substantiate his claims and investigates the remains of Canaanite towns to learn more about them and to prove their difference.

Each evening during the El Ahwat season, as we sit outside our house in the kibbutz clutching our beers and batting away the summer bugs, somebody gives a lecture on some aspect of the work we are doing. One night, it is the turn of Amit Romano, a young lecturer at Haifa University who is supervising my area of the dig. He begins to tell us the methods for recording an excavation. It is, apparently, a question of organising the data and deciding how to present it.

'How do you decide which of your findings is important and which is not?' Romano asks the impromptu seminar rhetorically. 'How do you decide which level of the excavation is the one which you will cover most fully in your report?'

There is silence. A few murmurs about scientific criteria. As I am not a student on the excavation but only a volunteer I have kept quiet in these teaching discussions up until now but I decide to bite the bullet, or something, at this point.

'Well, surely politics comes into it.'

Uproar follows. This is, after all, only one month after the failure of the Clinton peace negotiations at Camp David, during which Palestinian excavation activity on the Temple Mount became a crucial sticking point. Clearing space for an underground mosque and exit tunnel 36 feet deep under the Temple Mount, the Waqf, the Palestinian antiquities authority, has been tipping the rubble into vast dumps in the Kidron Valley, indifferent to the fact that it is full of artefacts from the period of the first temple. According to Mark Ami-El, at the Jewish Center for Public Affairs, they are 'erasing every sign, remnant and memory of its Jewish past, including the destruction of archaeological findings that are proof of this past'.

But the Palestinians say that their recent provocative digging and discarding of remains should be viewed in the light of a long history of Jewish disregard for Palestinian antiquities. Look, they say, at what the Israelis did in 1996, when they excavated the Western Wall, in order to reveal walls from the time of the second temple, without consulting the Waqf and possibly destabilising the foundations of the al-Aqsa mosque.

177

Look at the number of excavations which they have carried out in the Gaza Strip (fifty-five) and the West Bank (estimated in the hundreds) against the United Nations charter which forbids excavation without authority in occupied territory. Look, too, at the Israeli lack of interest in the pre-Israelite or post-Israelite remains – the layer above or the layer below the all-important one – in ancient sites all over the country. In Tel Sofer on the outskirts of Nablus, for example, Jalal Kazzouh and his team have recently found traces of Canaanite homes, dating back to 3000 BC, ignored by previous archaeological investigations there. Kazzouh points out wryly that 'Israeli research stopped whenever they reached anything dating to the Israelite era in this region'.

In El Ahwat, the group, which is made up of Jews and Arabs and new Russian and Yemeni immigrants and which has been perfectly harmonious until now, has broken up into heated argument following my hapless observation. The Israeli Arabs try to draw me in.

'Yes,' they say. 'Politics has everything to do with archaeology. People don't usually talk about it, but it motivates eveything.'

Amit Romano weighs in. He thumps the arm of his chair with his fist.

'We were given this land in the Bible. We won it again in '67. It is ours. It is our right.'

The argument threatens to become nasty. Students and young lecturers who have spent the summer contentedly studying the Iron Age stones side by side without a thought of politics or religion are suddenly at each other's throats. But then the mildly spoken and always cheerful Avi, an Israeli Arab, intervenes. 'Places should not matter,' he maintains. 'They should not worry about finding places in the Bible. Holiness should be in the heart, not in stones.'

For an archaeologist whose life is devoted to stones and their significance, this is a huge concession. For religious believers and even tourists, who continue to make pilgrimages to special sites, it is, perhaps, a difficult philosophy to accept. But, in the terrible few years in Israel since that warm August night and since Ariel Sharon's provocative visit to the Temple Mount the following month, these are words which I have found it hard to forget. And probably these are words – 'holiness should be in the heart, not in stones' – which archaeologists, politicians, believers and non-believers alike, would be wise to ponder.

8

Postmodern Archaeology:
Trashing our Future

In a memorable episode in Don DeLillo's great postmodern novel, *Underworld*, one character, Brian Glassic, visits the Fresh Kills landfill site on Staten Island while it is still open and busy. It is vast, a mountain of staggering statistics. One hundred million tons of rubbish. Three thousand acres. One hundred and fifty-five feet high. A stench that spreads for miles around. Trucks arriving to dump garbage twenty four hours a day. Hundreds of workers. The highest hill on the 1,500 mile coastline from Florida to Maine.

But what is most striking is that, in DeLillo's description, the landfill becomes an archaeological monument. Brian Glassic imagines he is 'watching the construction of the Great Pyramid at Giza – only this was twenty-five times bigger'. The gigantic mound is stratified into layers, each level representing another week or month of rubbish deposit. Like the sediments uncovered in excavation, these layers can be read as history for 'it all ends up here, newsprint, emery boards, sexy underwear, coaxed into high relief by the rumbling dozers'. The waste managers can be considered the new archaeologists, 'the adepts and seers, crafting the future ... the landscapers who would build hanging gardens here, make a park one day out of every kind of used and lost and eroded object of desire'. But the waste managers have speeded up time, simultaneously constructing the pyramid like ancient Egyptian slaves and deconstructing it as excavators, studying the decomposition of the layers for its environmental impact in the future. As time is compressed in the garbage mound, the rubbish appears ancient even as it arrives fresh from the lorries , a curious hybrid of old and new, 'science fiction and prehistory'.

According to William Rathje, a Harvard-trained archaeologist who pioneered what is known as 'garbology', archaeology has always basically been 'the discipline that tries to understand old garbage'. For him it therefore makes sense to study contemporary garbage and, in this way, to imagine how our present society might appear to the archaeologists of the future. Setting up the Garbage Project at the University of Arizona in

1973, Rathje proceeded first to investigate local refuse disposal in Arizona and later to excavate nine landfills around America, including the one at Fresh Kills. The methods the garbologists use are similar to those used by conventional archaeologists. A long metal rod is sunk into the mound and an augur used to take samples at different depths. The temperature of the unearthed sludge is taken to assess the degree of decomposition. And the objects contained in the augur, or 'findings' in archaeological terms, are sorted and labelled by type. All the deposits are stored and examined in extra-cold laboratories, as frozen waste does not stink so much. Rathje has even developed a special stratigraphy of the rubbish dump, determined not by pottery as in conventional excavations, but by the pull tabs of soda cans. Apparently the manufacturers alter the design of their tabs over the years, and so these can be used to date reliably any layer of refuse.

But despite this surreal type of stratigraphy, it is fair to say that the archaeology of rubbish collapses the distinctions between past, present and future. 'If our garbage, in the eyes of the future, is destined to hold a key to the past', Rathje writes, 'then surely it already holds a key to the present.' Instead of waiting for the due passage of time when future generations will investigate our age, Rathje looks at our own age with an archaeologist's eye, as a collection of material remains to be interpreted. It is an anarchic vision, which decomposes and trashes the objects which surround us in order to make that leap from present to future. And it pays more attention to the little things, the throwaway items, than to the grand monuments of the day. The Garbage Project researcher, Rathje argues, looks upon 'the streaming detritus of daily existence with the same quiet excitement displayed by Howard Carter and Lord George Edward Carnarvon at the unpillaged, unopened tomb of Tutankhamun'. No longer the monumental pyramids and gleaming gold statues which excited the archaeologists of the past, today it is the number of disposable diapers and rotting newspapers found in tips which stirs the archaeological imagination.

In its refusal to accept the traditional course of history and its lack of distinction between past and present, the archaeology of rubbish exemplifies in concrete form the practice of postmodern theory. The culture of postmodernity also compresses time, resulting in a confused collage of past, present and future. It celebrates rubble without organising narratives. It trashes our world, exhibiting disintegrating 'found objects' without aura or identity in its museums and sampling fragments of old tunes as new in the pop charts. So archaeology and postmodern theory are closely connected. Indeed it could be argued that contemporary archaeology is the quintessential postmodern cultural form. But if understood and practised differently, archaeology can actually mount an important resistance to postmodernism's slippery, glib logic.

8. Postmodern Archaeology: Trashing our Future

*

According to various modern philosophers, the postmodern age is one which witnesses the end of history. Francis Fukuyama argued in 1992 that American liberal democracy had advanced so far that we had reached the 'end point of mankind's ideological evolution' and therefore effectively 'the end of history'. History, for Fukuyama, means evolutionary progress, the development of institutions, politics, society. Societies in previous centuries experimented with feudalism, totalitarianism, monarchies, communism. But now that America has perfected liberal democracy, with its twin goals of liberty and equality, and its source of power in capitalism, there is no further stage of evolution to undergo. 'There would be no further progress in the development of underlying principles and institutions, because all of the really big questions had been settled.'

In the light of the terrible Balkan wars of nationalist strife and the current War on Terrorism, Fukuyama's claim that 'all the really big questions have been settled' looks increasingly blinkered and complacent. But his basic connection between global capitalism and the end of history as the organic development from past to present to future is one which has its adherents among the leading thinkers on the postmodern condition. In his book *Postmodernism, or the Cultural Logic of Late Capitalism*, Fredric Jameson attributes the postmodern loss of real history indirectly to the overwhelming totality of capitalism. Since the capitalist system prevails globally, it is impossible to understand its enormity or to gain a perspective upon it. There is nothing 'outside' capitalism from which one could judge or criticise, no longer a political alternative in the form of communism or socialism. There is no longer, either, the historical sense, allied to those political alternative ideologies, which can distinguish past from present, what is lost from what has been gained. 'The prodigious new expansion of multinational capital ends up penetrating and colonizing those very precapitalist enclaves which offered extraterritorial and Archimedean footholds for critical effectivity', Jameson writes. According to Hegel and Marx, dialectic is essential to historical progress, to History itself. Progress is measured and instigated by comparison and opposition. But under late capitalism, dialectic is absent in the all-encompassing, homogeneous economic culture, in which there is no dispensation for radical change or alternative. Jameson explains in his book *The Seeds of Time*: 'The "end of history" thesis ... seems to me a symptom of a development in which the dialectic has suffered the fate of all other philosophical or ideological concepts in the postmodern period.'

With linear history gone, time is speeded up, whirled around, disorientated and driven crazy. Anything goes. The world in which distinctions were made between the past, deposited deep in the earth, and the present, located on the earth's surface, has disappeared or seems no longer possible. We are witnessing what Jameson calls 'a new kind of flatness or depthlessness, a new kind of superficiality in the most literal sense'. This can be seen most vividly in the dramatic change which has taken place in our attitude towards the subterranean. The earth, its depths and surfaces, has shifted in significance. When Jules Verne wrote *Journey to the Centre of the Earth* in 1864, the deep tunnels and caverns into which the novel's hero, Professor Lidenbrock, ventures appeared to contain the truth, the answer to the quest. As Lidenbrock and his nephew, Axel, sail towards Iceland, in order to find the gateway to the centre of the earth located in the volcanic crater of Mount Sneffels, Axel imagines Hamlet joining their subterranean quest for 'the solution of your eternal doubts at the centre of the earth'. And Verne quotes Vergil, implicitly comparing Lidenbrock's venture under Iceland with Aeneas' journey to the Underworld to hear the prophecy about his future from his dead father Anchises. Lidenbrock and Axel, with their silent Icelandic guide Hans Bjelke, hike down tunnels in the geological strata, with early electric torches and diminishing supplies of water, until, after various adventures, they reach a vast underground sea. Here they find not only fossils but also living versions of those fossilised remains, an ichthyosaurus, a plesiosaurus, a twelve-foot giant example of Quaternary man. It becomes clear that by going so deep beneath the earth, they have gone back in history and found themselves at an earlier stage of geological time. The unequivocal truth of what they see is guaranteed by the fact that they encounter all these things in situ, below the ground, not excavated and viewed out of context. 'What the boring-machine could not bring to the surface of the inner texture of the globe, we were going to be able to study with our own eyes and touch with our own hands', Axel announces excitedly. And having travelled below the ground and emerged again at the surface, Lidenbrock becomes a famous man, able to overturn erroneous scientific theories with 'the established facts' of geology, archaeology and history discovered during his quest deep in the earth's core. 'Doubt itself would be an insult to science', says Lidenbrock, in his imaginary lecture delivered miles below the earth, after finding the mummified corpse of Quaternary man. 'The body stands before you! I have no reason to cast doubt on the authenticity of his remote origin.'

In contrast to Jules Verne's underground truth, Don DeLillo's underworld is riven with uncertainty and fear. Like Verne's cavern, it is implicitly compared with the classical underworld of Vergil – its chief constituent, plutonium, comes from Pluto, god of the dead and ruler of the underworld – but DeLillo's underworld is found above the earth's surface, in the waste tips and sewers and Aids-infected ghettos. It assumes its most nightmarish, hellish version in the chapter in which two nuns visit the slum in the South Bronx known as The Wall. Pushing past 'years of stratified deposits', garbage, abandoned cars, slashed tyres and used needles, they journey through the passageways of the projects, distributing food to the needy, glimpsing the elusive Dido-like figure of a lost girl and encountering postmodern monsters such as new babies with crack habits, prostitutes with exploded silicone breasts and crazy guys who self-mutilate. Since this scene is DeLillo's hell, the environment of garbage becomes more and more unequivocally disgusting, to include hospital waste, hundreds of laboratory dead white mice, amputated limbs. But elsewhere in the novel, the underworld in the form of dead, cast-off things or waste, takes on a more uncertain, ambivalent significance. The garbage is not positively disgusting but merely the continuing presence of the material things which we consume and can never get rid of entirely. Nothing can come to an end in the novel. Nothing can disappear but may be merely recycled or heaped in another landfill. Postmodernism, after all, marks an age of imaginary recycling. 'There is now a circulation and recirculation possible between the underworld and the overworld of high-rent condos and lofts', announces Fredric Jameson. 'In the postmodern view, you can return from the lower depths.' So the underworld becomes the overworld.

The circulation of rubbish is crucially linked to the prevailing political climate. DeLillo suggests that, in the past, the nuclear threat represented a real possibility of the end of the world. There is, grimly, nothing relativist or open-ended about the bomb. The cold war lent America a nightmarish certainty, with definite alternatives and apocalyptic futures. Now, post-cold war, there is only uncertainty and endless waste, a trashing of the previously simple dichotomous world. 'Waste is the secret history, the underhistory, the way archaeologists dig out the history of other cultures.' The only use for weapons is to destroy that waste in cavernous underground depths. At the end of DeLillo's novel, the main character, Nick Shay, goes to Kazakhstan to witness the nuclear explosion of plutonium waste deep underground. The event is suitably undramatic:

> No ascending cloudmass, of course, or rolling waves of sound. Maybe some dust rises from the site and maybe it is only afternoon haze and several people point and comment briefly and there is a flatness in the group, an unspoken dejection, and after a while we go back inside.

Following the explosion, there is no sense of closure or satisfaction. There is, in fact, no real sense of the literal depth of the blast nor of the weight of its significance but only a 'flatness' felt in the spectators and readers.

When the distinction between the earth's surface and its depths disappears, all kinds of other important distinctions disintegrate too. There is no clear difference between life and death. DeLillo contemplates the phenomenon of space burials, people preserved forever in an orbit around the earth with 'seven hundred other ashes in the same shot'. There are no clear avenues for political opposition, no stable and well-defined establishment which an underground revolutionary movement can disrupt. 'Where everything now submits to the perceptual change of fashion and media image, nothing can change any longer', Jameson argues. 'The only conceivable radical change would consist in putting an end to change itself.' And there is no clear difference between the sacred and the mundane. Nick Shay, in DeLillo's novel, acknowledges that 'we feel a reverence for waste, for the redemptive qualities of the things we use and discard. Look how they come back to us, alight with a kind of brave ageing.' Since nothing can be lost or disappear into past history, nothing acquires a special aura like the conventional archaeological object. Only the 'quotidian' paradoxically acquires the 'depth and reach of the commonplace'.

The postmodern depthless world is disorientating. Lacking any tangible threats or sources of opposition, it can leave its victim filled only with an empty and unnameable sense of fear. According to Don DeLillo, this is countered only by what can be thought of as a new form of antiquarianism, the fanatical collection of objects of curiosity. In *Underworld*, Nick Shay goes to great efforts to track down the baseball which the Giants player Bobby Thomson hit into the stands in 1951 to score a home run and beat the New York Dodgers. In the process, he encounters other collectors of junk, who are motivated by the same obsessions and fears: 'It was some terror working beneath the skin which made him gather up things, amass possessions and effects against the dark shape of some unshoulderable loss. Memorabilia. The state of loss, the fact.' The novel hangs on the unspoken question of the authenticity of the baseball. Is it the unique ball hit into the stands and grabbed by Cotter Martin in the opening chapter? Or is it one of hundreds of balls which are circulating in the memorabilia underworld?

What DeLillo claims is a defence against fear, Jameson describes rather as the object of an unfocused and misplaced desire. Just at the time when we are losing a sense of real history, we are acquiring an intense desire for images of the past, or what Jameson calls 'an omnipresent, omnivorous, and well-nigh libidinal historicism'. There should be no surprise that as budgets for archaeological excavation in this country are slashed, there should be a simultaneous rise in the number of archaeology programmes broadcast on television and a renewed popular interest in archaeology, registered in the marketing of glossy illustrated books. For what replaces history, in the sense of real political and ideological process, according to Jameson, is 'our own pop images and simulacra of that history, which itself remains forever out of reach'. History is merely a theme park, Disneyfied for entertainment but with no substance or depth behind it. What is worse, according to Jean Baudrillard, the key prophet of postmodernism, is that the degree of simulation is disguised and the representation is passed off as the reality. Disneyland celebrates its fantasy; the rest of America disavows its fantastical nature. 'It is no longer a question of a false representation of reality', complains Baudrillard, 'but of concealing the fact that the real is no longer real.'

Ready-made ruins are the natural response to Baudrillard's state of unreality and Jameson's depthless compression of history. The postmodern imagination is closely allied to the archaeological imagination in its retrospective perspective on the present. The postmodern artist or writer offers the ruin of our contemporary world for analysis to a future which has already arrived. It is sometimes 'difficult not to believe that [we are] living in a future that [has] already taken place, and [is] now exhausted', writes the novelist J.G. Ballard. The characters in Ballard's novels, such as *High Rise, Cocaine Nights* and *Super-Cannes*, help to 'exhaust' that speeded-up future by trashing their surroundings and transforming them into pseudo-archaeological ruins. In Ballard's classic 1970s novel, *High Rise*, a tower block, which rises forty storeys above the ground, becomes an inverted archaeological section of a self-enclosed community. The different floors wage war upon one another, rebelliously preventing one section of the building from moving up or down into another by blocking stairways or sabotaging elevators. The inhabitants of the first ten floors, predominantly film technicians and air-hostesses, become cut off from the fresh air, water and electricity, and mentally 'crushed by the pressure of all the people above them, by the thousands of individual lives, each with its pent-up time and space'. The middle floors, occupied mostly by doctors, lawyers and accountants, continue to enjoy some comforts as the building degenerates but are still oppressed by those living above them, on floors 35 to 40. The occupants of those floors, made up of tycoons, television actresses and (bizarrely) careerist academics, worry about the threat from the depths, the lower floor or 'subterranean' residents who vandalise their cars parked at the foot of the building and terrorise them if they venture down.

Like an archaeological site, the high-rise building conveys its system of values to be interpreted through its vertical spatial organisation. Depth and height are the main indicators of meaning. The building, one could say, offers a hermeneutics of stratigraphy. In order for the building supposedly to be accessible to the archaeological imagination, it must be speeded up in time until it has already been destroyed and reduced to rubble. The building's occupants revel in the fragments and rubbish of the tower block's artificial excavation site. Like the waste which can never disappear in DeLillo's novel, the garbage in the high-rise surrounds the inhabitants, a 'visible museum of their leavings', forming the barricades which allow them to demarcate and fragment the 'vertical city'.

Ballard's image of the high-rise as a vertical city is telling, for it situates his novel within a larger postmodern treatment of cities as pseudo-archaeological ruins. Overwhelmed by urban sprawl as much as by the totality of late capitalism, the postmodern city-dweller finds himself disorientated, without the certain co-ordinates of space and time, and therefore prey to a sensibility of instant ruination. So in Ridley Scott's film, *Blade Runner*, the main character, Deckard, knows no world beyond the dilapidated skyscrapers of Los Angeles. He lives in the lower depths of the city, with the looming, ruined towers above him, and only ventures up to the top of the towers and to a fading daylight when he meets the creator of the new slave robots, or replicants, the scientist Eldon Tyrell. The most successful humans have been lured away by the promise of a better life in the new 'off-world colony', while the remainder struggle for survival in the ruins of the previous age, in the LA streets and the crumbling towers. Even the first replicant we see in the film, Kowalski Leon, has adapted quickly to the ruined and trashed nature of this futuristic Los Angeles by re-inventing himself as an 'engineer of waste disposal'.

Beneath the Planet of the Apes also depicts a society living in the recognisable ruins of our own. In a world now dominated by apes, the last successfully surviving humans hide in the decaying tunnels and stations of the New York subway train system. The astronaut, Brent, having crashed into the planet from an earlier time, stumbles down a crevice in the rock to find himself bizarrely in the dusty remains of Queensboro Plaza station. And having ventured along one of the tracks, he finds a society worshipping the last nuclear missile left over from our time. This discovery is, of course, all preceded by the most iconic image of the *Planet of the Apes* series, the Statue of Liberty on the shoreline, buried up to her chest in sand. Humans have blown up the world in a nuclear conflict and this ruined statue is all that remains. 'Oh, my God. I'm back. I'm home!' cries the astronaut Taylor, as he stares at the statue.

If these filmmakers present the world already ruined because of the wasteful or militaristic ambitions of present society, some artists create what might be termed archaeological installations which actually chart the process of ruination itself. Robert Smithson's landscape sculpture of 1970, 'Spiral Jetty', was a heaped-up earthwork set in a salt lake in Utah. As the waters rise, the earthwork will crumble and finally disappear. According to the *Guardian* newspaper, 'American art is young, but Smithson gave it a history that seems ancient.' The British artist Rachel Whiteread takes casts of rooms in houses and occasionally whole buildings which are about to be destroyed. A library from a house in the Jewish quarter of Vienna, for example, was moulded and recast by her, the empty covers of the books on the shelves suggesting the wealth of cultural memory and creativity which was destroyed with the victims of the holocaust. These casts function rather as Fiorelli's casts of the victims of Pompeii, signifying through a negative image a world that has been lost.

Smithson and Whiteread suggest, elegiacally, the course of history which will eventually lay everything to waste. In a sense, their awareness of the linear process of time, embedded in their sculptures, although definitely archaeological, runs counter to the postmodern interest in archaeology, which celebrates the simultaneity of time and the confusion of narrative interpretations. Far more archaeologically postmodern is the work of Mark Dion, whose installation, 'Tate Thames Dig', houses in a great chest every object which was dredged from the section of the Thames which flows past Tate Modern in London. No explanation accompanies each object. Or take the work of the British sculptor, Tony Craggs, who creates archaeological sediments of found objects, artificially crushed by Craggs to give the illusion of the geological passage of time.

*

If writers and artists have been pillaging archaeological images – or at least what they believe is the archaeological imagery – since the early 1970s, philosophers have not been slow to follow suit. Nothing, in the postmodern world of theory, is cool unless it has been 'mapped' and 'surveyed', tracked as 'sediment', submitted to 'ruptures' and 'seismic shifts', and ultimately 'displayed' in the theoretical museum of 'discourse'. Michel Foucault, for example, actually wanted to replace history with archaeology. Rather than a grand narrative which links events together in a causal chain, he argued, the account of the past should be attentive to the underlying structures which made these events possible. 'Archaeology', he wrote in 1969 in a manifesto for his new approach, *The Archaeology of Knowledge*, 'tries to define not the thoughts, representations, images, themes, preoccupations that are concealed or revealed in discourses; but those discourses themselves, those discourses as practices obeying certain rules.'

Theorists of the postmodern are interested particularly in subterranean space and coin terms from archaeologists to describe it. Foucault drew upon the archaeological model of stratigraphy in order to distinguish between surface events and what he called underlying 'autochthonous transformations'. By 'autochthonic' he seems to have meant self-contained levels deep below the ground acting as tectonic plates which determine everything in a given period. They allowed things to be said or thought; they grounded knowledge and marked its boundaries. Deleuze and Guattari, writing more recently, replace Foucault's image of 'deep strata' with the image of the 'plateau'. These 'thousand plateaus' overlap one another, some lying side-by-side, others layered on top or underneath, a confused jumble of different strata. One 'plateau' is supposedly 'a single plane of consistency or exteriority', a particular assemblage that make up an ideology or a politics or a form of culture, but just as the earth seeps from one layer to the next, so one ideological plateau is hard to distinguish from the next.

But in fact Deleuze and Guattari invoke images of archaeological stratigraphy only to resist or undermine them. The division of the world of knowledge into sedimented plateaux turns out to be a necessary illusion. 'Every stratum', they announce, 'is a judgement of God.' It is necessary to believe that the world is organised into self-contained, well-defined planes of ideas, because otherwise we would find it hard to run our lives and crucially to understand anything. Stratigraphy, in other words, enables knowledge, and it is only through knowledge that we can organise political campaigns, establish communities, create a vibrant culture. But these well-defined planes and this knowledge are in fact illusions. The earth – both literally and metaphorically – is far more confused. Deleuze and Guattari write poetically of 'lines of segmentarity, strata and territories' which are just as likely to become 'lines of flight, movements of deterritorialisation and destratification'. The metaphor of the earth, of thought grounded and mapped like an archaeological section, is presented to us only for that metaphor to be dissolved or modified to allow for the plurality and elusiveness of modern thought.

So archaeology is used by these philosophers of the postmodern to suggest the limits of understanding. Celebrating the impossibility of grasping the totality of contemporary life, they seek images of confusion and mystery and find them, as they believe, in archaeology. That something is of 'archaeological interest only', meaning that it is obscure, is a well-worn cliché. However, it has been given new currency in the tough and obscure writing of postmodern philosophers. Foucault writes of the 'opacity' of the past, its transformation into solid 'monuments', its evasion of explanation. He believes that archaeology is best placed to approach this past because 'it does not claim to efface itself in the ambiguous modesty of a reading that would bring back, in all its purity, the distant, precarious, almost effaced light of the origin'. According to Foucault, archaeologists do not explain or interpret but merely describe the stones and bones before them. They deal with the exterior nature of things. Archaeology then is 'nothing more than a rewriting; it is the systematic description of the discourse-object'. For Deleuze and Guattari, the destratification of the earth, which leaves it a confused and unreadable mess of lines and cracks, without origin or pattern, evokes the irrational and uncontrollable nature of postmodern life. The earth's strata do not form a linear narrative, which can be read to understand our historical and political past. Rather they form rather confused 'superficial underground stems in such a way as to form or extend a rhizome' – roots with multiple branches and no origin. They connect different plateaux, honeycombing the earth's crust, but cannot be traced back to a central core, to the earliest bedrock. The sediments are always in the middle, not at the beginning nor the end, and therefore cannot be interpreted and grounded in significance. Erupting, disintegrating, the archaeological sections spill out of our understanding, reducing rational progress to a state of rubble.

*

Given the fact that philosophers of the postmodern condition actually give us an anti-archaeological impression of archaeology, one would expect contemporary archaeologists to keep well clear of postmodern theory. 'Rewriting', 'opacity', 'destratification': these images of confusion and the abrogation of understanding would not, you might think, endear them-selves to professionals whose lives depend upon excavating and reading the earth and its remains. But you would be wrong. For in fact there is a whole group of archaeologists who are enthusiastically responding to the implications of Deleuze, Guattari and others in their work. The archaeolo-gist Michael Shanks, for example, is particularly struck by Deleuze and Guattari's image of the 'rhizome'. According to him, the rhizome – the endless subterranean root with lots of branches and shoots and no origin – offers a new way to approach archaeology:

> The characteristics of rhizomes-thinking are: making connections, anarchic associations rather than hierarchical procedures of thinking, denial of final and definitive identities of things in reconstructions of the object-world, rather than reflections.

According to the rhizomatic approach, archaeology should move away from the hierarchical privileging of depth over surface and examine rather surface sites, delimited areas, nebulous spaces. It should be prepared to leave objects without a definitive explanation. And it should see archaeol-ogy as a form of rhetoric, rather than as a 'reflection' upon this world. Postmodernism, according to Michael Shanks, witnesses 'a failure of the compact between word and world'. As archaeologists excavate the world around us and write about their findings, they should ponder that rupture between 'word and world'.

The excavation sites that stir the popular imagination and cause the most media attention today are precisely the ones which could be de-scribed as rhizomatic or postmodern. Some are above the ground and

189

involve the sprawling detritus of contemporary life. The Garbage Project's excavation of the New York rubbish tip is a fine example. 'Landfills are fitting symbols of many of the developed world's twentieth-century preoccupations,' says garbologist William Rathje, 'and they are the great wellsprings of mythology as well'. Responding to these ventures in excavation, museums are starting to exhibit rubbish. A few years ago the Tate Gallery in London displayed a large blue skip filled with all the items a family might throw out after Christmas. And the worthy and traditional Ashmolean Museum in Oxford now presents a few of its antiquities in the 'Ancient Greece' gallery in what is apparently a metal dustbin. Shards of pots and broken oil lamps and olive stones spill out of this garbage can in the glass case as if they were the overflow of the refuse from a typical ancient Greek family.

In Stratford, Connecticut, the council has decided, rather than bringing rubbish into a conventional archaeological museum, to take the museum to the rubbish. I was so intrigued that I made a special trip from England to see it. The Garbage Museum, Stratford, is located at the South West Connecticut Recycling Center. The entrance hall contains displays of crushed tin cans and artificial, plastic representations of compost. Children are invited to match the people through the ages with their typical garbage and to marvel at a large sculpture of a dinosaur made from recycled rubbish. But upstairs a viewing gallery allows visitors to watch actual rubbish deposited by lorries, bulldozed in mountains onto conveyor belts, sorted by masked and gloved workers in the separation room and crushed into bales (Plate 15). The museum blurs the distinction between labour and the aesthetic, as we watch disconnected, from behind glass, the workers picking out different types of crushed plastic bottle from a conveyor belt, piled high with rotting debris and revolving endlessly.

Other excavation sites straddle the distinction between depth and surface. They could be described as being located both above and below the ground, in a liminal world that corresponds to Deleuze's and Guattari's 'destratification'. And we are drawn to them arguably because of our postmodern sensibilities. In Mesoamerican archaeology, for example, the most exciting new discoveries are being made, not beneath the Belizean or Guatemalan soil, but in the caves deep in the jungle, places neither above nor below the earth. While I spent a relatively sedate time in July 2001 excavating the foundations of a post-classic Mayan domestic house in a humid field near San Ignacio, on the Guatemalan border, other archaeologists staying at our base headed off for the week with ropes, torches and vast water bottles, to spend a week in a cave in the dark.

'We are being sent out this first week to Tarantula cave,' John, a laconic student from University College London tells me, in the archaeologists' drinking hole in San Ignacio. John arrived at the excavation campaign at the same time as I did, so we newcomers have bonded together.

'Why's it called that?' I ask, half naively and half in hope that 'tarantula' means something else in Mayan.

John doesn't bother to raise his head from his beer to reply.

The cavers, as they are known, do not actually do any excavating. There is no need since all the remains in the cave are above the ground, on the cave's floor. There is no covering soil to crush and compact the offerings left by the ancient Mayans, so the remains are often still intact. The archaeologists need only map the remains, measure their location and draw their findings. It is more of an archaeological survey than a dig.

One evening, back at the base, I get talking to Harri Kettunen. He is writing a PhD on the Mayan idea of the underworld. It means reading ancient accounts of the underworld, found in the hieroglyphic texts, but it also involves archaeology and the caves. The ancient Mayans believed that these caves held the entrance to the Underworld and apparently would venture vast distances up the underground tunnels and rivers to make human sacrifices there.

'Do the Mayans seem different now that archaeologists know they spent half their time in caves?' I ask him. 'Is there a sense in which they seem darker? More mysterious?'

'Archaeologists don't think like that,' Harri laughs. 'But you should definitely see one of these caves. You should talk to Jaime.'

Jaime Awe leads the Belize Valley Archaeological project, in which we are all participating. He arranges for me to see the cave, Actun Tunichil Muknal, which he surveyed in the summer of 2000. I am excited and nervous in equal measure. What if Tunichil actually means 'tarantula' in Mayan? After following my machete-wielding guide, Ramon, through the jungle for an hour, killing a deadly fer-de-lance snake which lies sleeping on our path en route, I swim fully clothed, including climbing boots, into the entrance of the cave and half-clamber, half-swim along an underground river bed, lit only by our head torches. After about an hour, we reach a point where the river rushes on in one direction but another, dry, cave system opens up to our left. We remove climbing boots, and set off up a huge underground cavern, as large as a temple or a mosque. It soon becomes clear why it is necessary to tiptoe in socks, rather than hike along in boots. For there are ancient remains everywhere. Whole pots, left standing on stones or piled up against one another. Animal bones. Human skulls, staring blankly up at us. One false step and I might send my foot through a classic Mayan antiquity, a vase perhaps dating back to AD 500.

At the far end of the tunnelling system, we look down at a whole skeleton, now becoming calcified but still clearly a sacrifice victim, apparently just thrown down upon its back without careful arrangement after being garrotted (Plate 14). It is a sobering and also bewildering sight. Is one to feel respect? Scientific interest? Historical continuity? Here is a body, buried and yet also left in the open air, a victim of sacrifice yet possibly also envied for that role. We have violated its privacy by venturing down here with our torches and cameras and, in many ways, the body should have been left undisturbed. And yet its death was already a violation, the body left to rot above ground, surrounded by the litter of other sacrifices, in a liminal place between one world and another.

Postmodern excavation sites are, of course, determined by improvements in technology. It is only with the development of caving techniques and expert knowledge that archaeologists have been able to venture into the most inhospitable caves. It is only with the invention of the Alvin, a deep-sea craft which can descend up to 13,000 feet below the sea, and the Remote Operated Vehicles (ROVs), which can examine objects using cameras and robotic arms, that marine archaeology has become possible. But there is also a sense in which archaeologists have wanted to explore these sites because they appeal to the postmodern imagination. They offer a different perspective upon our world, neither above nor below ground, and they challenge interpretation and understanding. They appeal to the irrational preoccupations of postmodernism. Graham Hancock's underwater search for an Atlantis, a lost civilisation to connect all other civilisations, which has taken him diving off Malta and the Maldives and the coast of Gujurat, is somewhat discredited by other archaeologists. But it is directly in the tradition of a type of postmodern archaeology, Michael Shanks' 'anarchic associations' or Don DeLillo's paranoid conspiracy theories. Fredric Jameson, after all, remarked that 'conspiracy theories are a poor man's cognitive mapping'. It is most appropriate that the false lines of illusory connection, which may be able to map the confusing jumble of contemporary culture, are to be discovered where two worlds overlap, down on the seabed.

The discovery and excavation of the *Titanic* was no Atlantis. But it does offer a classic example of the close connection between marine archaeology and the postmodern sensibility. The exploration of the wreck, sunk 12,000 feet below the icy waters south of Newfoundland, was necessarily conducted remotely, via cameras and robotic arms. Indeed during the expedition when the ship was first located, in 1985, the scientific team never ventured below the sea's surface. They dragged an unmanned submarine, known as *Argo*, loaded with video cameras across the ocean floor, beaming back pictures of the depths to the scientists in the control van on the ship's deck. Robert Ballard, the team leader who first discovered the *Titanic*, appreciated the bizarre experience of watching the television monitors: 'Here I was in a comfortable chair, drinking a Coke

Classic and eating a warm piece of pie, while the submarine landscape rolled by.'

Ballard was not interested in the artefacts that the *Titanic* contained. Even during his second trip to the wreck site in 1986, when he actually dived down to the ocean bottom in the Alvin submarine, he was content simply to send out his ROVs down inside the ship, collecting images of the remains. But since then, expeditions have gone out to salvage the objects. This deep-sea archaeology has been intimately bound up with the remote video technology necessary for work at such depths and the simultaneous potential of this technology for translation into instant film. In 1987, a French expedition which brought up over 1,800 objects from the wreck arranged for special film footage of the salvage operation to be broadcast from Paris. Titled 'Return to the *Titanic* ... Live', it was hosted by Telly Savalas and watched by millions. The 1991 Russian expedition also resulted in an IMAX film, *Titanica*, distributed the following year. And in a final example of archaeological investigation following the moving image rather than preceding it, James Cameron, director of the 1998 blockbuster film *Titanic*, has actually been moved to mount another expedition to the site, diving down to the ocean floor himself in a submarine to see images of the looming wreckage beamed onto the television monitors. This most recent expedition, led by the movie director, will itself become the subject of another film.

The *Titanic* continues to be a site where film and actual experience overlap, where the boundaries between virtual reality and material reality meet and are blurred. Stories about the largest ship in the world were already circulating before it set off on its doomed maiden voyage. And myths quickly formed after the tragic sinking. Now with these archaeological salvage films circulating, not to mention the blockbuster film, it is impossible to read anything about the excavation of the *Titanic* without a certain degree of emotional investment and Celine Dion's song ringing in one's ears. Even Robert Ballard admitted that, back in 1985 before James Cameron's film, when they were searching for the *Titanic*, the expedition team members would relax on deck by watching the videos of the two old Titanic films, *A Night To Remember* and *Raise the Titanic*. It must have been hard sometimes to distinguish their hours on duty watching the television monitors for traces of the ship and their hours off duty, watching the videos.

It was with these thoughts in mind that I decided to visit the *Titanic* exhibition in London's Science Museum last summer. Advertised as the 'Artefact exhibition', an exhibition with 'Real Objects. Real Stories', this seemed to trumpet its decided break with virtual reality and the return to a grounded, material archaeology. Would it, I wondered, restore some politics into the tear-jerking, familiar narrative?

As I enter the dark filmset of the exhibition, one of the museum staff hands me a 'boarding pass' with the name and cabin class of one of the original 1912 travellers.

'Find out at the end whether you survived,' she tells me.

Inside the first room, a film of the salvage of the *Titanic* is playing on a four-minute continuous loop. A vast piece of the hull is levered from the sea again and again, and we turn our heads from the screen briefly to see another huge piece of metal (the same?) hanging and dramatically spotlit beside us. Each of the following three rooms represents a different class of passenger, a different deck on the ship, with mock-cabins recreated to transport us to that other world. Around the walls, boards tell the stories of individual passengers and their fate. Below the boards, glass cases contain some of the possessions of those passengers salvaged from the seabed and positively attributed to particular individuals. I look at the wallet of Marian Oglen Meanwell, a sixty-three-year-old third-class passenger who was emigrating to New York. Beside the wallet, a £3 bank deposit slip, originally in the wallet, is carefully displayed. Marian Meanwell, I read, did not survive the sinking.

The objects are arranged as relics. There is a minute dice, only one centimetre long, which has somehow been retrieved from the deep. There are tiny phials of perfume, which one commercial traveller was taking to America to try his fortune in business there. Maybe it is the mournful background music that plays throughout the exhibition but I can feel my eyes welling up as I gaze at a couple of London East End bus tickets, which must just have been left in somebody's pocket, as he or she boarded at Southampton. These artefacts can tell us nothing that we did not previously know about historical or social trends in 1912, nothing about class division or political activism or business incompetence. Instead they become precious objects simply for the myth now attached to them, for the tragically-lost lives they symbolise.

The night of the sinking is recreated in the exhibition. A 'real' iceberg is dripping at the side of the room and we are invited to touch it.

'Gosh, that's cold!' a woman from Manchester gasps to me, as we stand side-by-side, pressing our fingers into the block until they start to make melted imprints.

'And it says here that it was even colder in the water,' I reply, shivering a little. The exhibition board helpfully tells us that falling into the Arctic waters at midnight in April would cause hypothermia very quickly.

At the end of the exhibition, the names of all the passengers on *Titanic*, both victims and survivors, are listed. For the two hours of my visit, I have been holding the boarding card of Mrs Samuel Abelson, so I look to see whether 'I' was saved. It is with some relief that I discover that I did, although my 'husband', on the second-class deck, was lost. 119 second-class passengers survived, while 166 were lost. But I notice that when it came to the crew, only 214 were saved while 685 died. There have been no 'real objects' in the exhibition belonging to the crew and no information boards about their fate. Were any of the visitors to the exhibition given their identity cards to hold? Did anyone check their statistics?

After stopping briefly to read about Millvina Dean, the ninety-one-year-old *Titanic* survivor who is still alive and now a minor celebrity in Hampshire, with a star and a local street named after her, I reach the final exhibit which is the *pièce de résistance*: a piece of the *Titanic* which we are allowed to touch. I look at it initially mystified, uncertain of what to do.

'You can touch it if you want,' the curator standing beside the case says, pointing to a three-inch hole in the top of the case.

Somewhat sheepishly, I push my fingers through the hole and stretch down to stroke the black metal. It feels soft and worn, after so many other visitors have rubbed it.

'I have touched the Titanic,' one entry in the visitors' book beside the case reads ecstatically.

'The best bits were touching the Titanic and feeling the iceberg,' reads another. 'This is a wonderful tribute to all those who tragically lost their lives.'

Later, as I sit back at home, drinking my tea from the 'authentic reproduction' White Star Line third-class cup purchased at the exhibition shop, I wonder about the whole point of the exhibition. If visitors are most struck by the iceberg, why bother to spend millions of dollars excavating the objects 12,000 feet below sea-level? Yet on the other hand, there is a strong need in the general public to sense the 'reality' of what happened by touching exhibits, rather than relying on visual images and films. Perhaps the answer is for all exhibitions to become touch-and-feel experiences in the future, with all glass cases fitted with little holes to squeeze through. Perhaps only a few 'real objects' are necessary, to focus the longing to touch the piece of history which is built up by the virtual reality simulation which makes up the rest of the exhibition.

What is clear is that, judging by *Titanic*, exhibitions need to be long on emotion and short on historical or political analysis to make an impact. The postmodern sensibility wants individual narratives and lives with which it can identify, rather than broad historical trends and abstract lessons which it can learn. For, according to postmodern theorists, there is no political lesson which we can learn from history; we can only feel sympathetic tugs of the heart for its victims. Nowhere does this become more possible than at the watery site of *Titanic*. Disconnected from our world by 12,000 feet of water, with no earthy lines of continuity, the link with the past becomes one of fantasy, supported by the fetish objects salvaged from the deep: the shoes, the bus tickets and all the other ordinary, meaningless but heart-wrenching detritus of daily life.

*

If the postmodern archaeologist searches for unusual archaeological locations, liminal sites which challenge the conventional distinctions between the surfaces and depths of the earth and do not fit the traditional concept of grounded excavation, then the most unusual site nowadays must surely be the human body. With the identification and study of DNA, the body becomes a repository of its own history, which can be retrieved and mapped. Bio-archaeologists can test the tissue from ancient human remains and develop a picture, based on the genetic information, of the individual's history, background and environment. The scientists working on the Ice Man, for example, have proved that he was a hunter, because his tools – arrows, axe and knife – have traces of blood, but he was reduced to a diet of plants in the months before his death, according to the isotopic evidence in his hair. His genetic fingerprinting is almost identical to the present day inhabitants of the Italian-Austrian Alps, thus proving the stable nature of the human population in the area.

As well as bringing biomolecular methods to apply to the ancient human body, archaeologists investigate contemporary peoples for the information they can give us about the past. They use genetic data from mitochondrial DNA to chart the origins of racial identity and population migration in prehistory. Mitochondrial DNA is the only part of DNA which is solely inherited from the mother and thus not subject to genetic interchange between parent and offspring. As a result, it has become an excellent tool for evolutionary study. In 1990, for example, three groups of Native Americans – the Pima-Papago of Southern Arizona, the Maya from the Yucatan and the Ticuna from Brazil – were screened for genetic mutations previously found in low quantity in some East Asian populations. Since the mutations were found in high quantity in all three geographically-distant native American groups, it could be argued that these native Americans derived from just a few Asian ancestors, who had crossed into the Americas through a genetic 'bottleneck'. But a subsequent study in 1992 presented a far more complicated scenario. Genetic material was taken from 130 Na-Dene people in northern North America, from 500 Amerind people across central America and from a large number of people in Siberia It was found that all three groups shared the same sets of genetic mutations termed A, C and D. But only the Siberian population and the Amerinds shared the set of mutations termed B. The Na-Dene people, who live in the area geographically between Siberia and central America lacked the B mutation. There are many conclusions which can be drawn from this strange genetic discovery and debate is continuing to rage. But the most convincing and interesting hypothesis is that the Americas were populated not by one migration from Asia, as previously thought, but by two. By calculating the time it takes genetic mutations to evolve in mitochondrial DNA, the genetic archaeologists have been able even to date these migrations. The first migration, from Siberia down through north America to the rest of the continent, must have happened between 24,000 and 32,000 BC. The second migration, from Siberia along the coast and by-passing the northern part of the American continent, bringing genetic mutation B, must have taken place between 10,000 and 13,000 BC.

According to these biomolecular developments, the body, moving across continents, becomes its own archaeological site. The genetic code of native Americans today contains the history of events some 30,000 years ago. But what are we to do with this information? At its best, bioarchaeology teaches us the difficulty of isolating racial groups, the fluidity of peoples based upon various waves of global migration and intermingling and the problems inherent in the drafting of maps and boundaries between genetically coherent groups. As the geneticist Cavalli-Sforza puts it, 'gene frequencies are not geographic features like altitude or compass direction which can be measured precisely'. There can be as much genetic variation between inhabitants in one village as between people in different continents.

However, at its worst bio-archaeology threatens to reduce culture to biological determinants and to trace populations back literally to the blood and soil of their roots, in a move which echoes the preoccupation of the Victorians with race, only now with the veneer of even more scientific credibility. Luca Cavalli-Sforza is engaged in the attempt to prove a correlation between genes and language, such that the family tree showing the spread of genetically coherent groups mirrors the family tree of the spread of languages. Language, after all, he believes 'requires a precise anatomical and neurological foundation'. The indirect consequence will be to prove that language, society and the whole of culture is dependent upon one's genetic constitution and that environmental factors play a secondary role. 'Culture resembles the genome in the sense that each one accumulates useful information from generation to generation', Cavalli-Sforza argues. 'The genome increases adaptation to the world by the automatic choice of fitter genetic types under natural selection, while cultural information accumulates in a person's nerve cells, being received from another person and selectively retained.'

*

The archaeology of DNA, if misappropriated, can be used to justify the most reactionary attitudes to the human subject. But the body, if excavated with different priorities and in a different context, can actually be used to mount a crucial site of resistance to postmodern evasion. Up until the last two decades, archaeology played little part in the investigation of human rights abuses and in the work of the international court. The prosecution of those responsible for mass genocide – in Nazi Germany, for example, or in Cambodia – relied upon the testimony of witnesses and documentary evidence. But in 1984, a team of forensic scientists from the United States, led by the forensic anthropologist Clyde Snow, was invited by the Grandmothers of the Plaza de Mayo and a government commission to investigate the fate of those who 'disappeared' during the years of the Argentine military junta (9,000 according to the government; 30,000 according to human rights groups). The team's task was to exhume the bodies found in mass graves and also to train local archaeologists, anthropologists and medical students. While the Argentinian government passed amnesty laws in 1987, which effectively meant that very few of the men responsible for the killings could be brought to justice and that therefore lawyers would not actually use the information gathered from the excavations in court, nevertheless the experience in Argentina proved to be a milestone in the forensic application of archaeology. The notion that people could just 'disappear' and that history could be erased to support the most powerful, tyrannical regimes had been seriously challenged.

Since then, archaeologists have been employed in the former Yugoslavia, in Kosovo, in Rwanda, in Guatemala, Brazil, El Salvador, the Philippines and most recently in Iraq. Indeed twenty-one new democracies have launched truth commissions in the last fifteen years, all drawing upon evidence from forensic archaeologists and anthropologists to understand their recent history of atrocity. In the cases of Yugoslavia and Rwanda, the United Nations has actually appointed international tribunals which have been hearing evidence gathered from the exhumation of mass graves undertaken since 1996 under the auspices of the Physicians for Human Rights. And in June 1999, the Yugoslavian tribunal, known as the ICTY, began in Kosovo the largest investigation of war crimes ever, with more than a dozen forensic teams. Back in Argentina, genetic material gathered by the American forensic anthropologist team will be used as compelling evidence in the case against military junta leader Jorge Videla and other army officers, should they ever finally be extradited and brought to trial.

Forensic archaeology is becoming a recognised and important discipline. Responding to the growing international need for trained forensic archaeologists, the British archaeologist Margaret Cox established in 2001 an international centre of excellence, based at the University of

Bournemouth and known as Inforce, for the investigation of genocide. One of its remits, besides going out to Rwanda and Iraq and other places to assist in the exhumation of mass graves, is to develop a system of guidelines and established working practices for this new discipline. Is the forensic archaeologist digging to establish the truth or digging to prosecute a case? Should the forensic archaeologist identify every corpse or skeleton in the grave or just look out for general trends? Cox explains that, in the past, excavation has been conducted either for forensic or for humanitarian reasons. In Kosovo, the ICTY dug up thousands of bodies to prepare its case for the court but did not identify the victims. 'The mandate was for facts, not for individuals', says Cox with regret. As a result, evidence essential for thousands of families to know the fate of their relatives was destroyed, and an opportunity for closure upon private grief lost. But in Central America, where amnesty laws concerning the leaders of previous totalitarian regimes have been passed, excavations of mass graves have been undertaken for humanitarian reasons only. If the amnesty laws are revoked and cases against the leaders are prepared, the evidence from the mass graves will not be admissible because the excavation was not conducted to forensic standards but only haphazardly to retrieve the bodies of loved ones.

Margaret Cox is campaigning for one standard of operation and a broader mandate allowing archaeologists to look for evidence for both purposes, forensic and humanitarian. 'There should be closure on all levels: legal, political, moral', she says. 'It is important for survivor communities to know their own history and to take control of their own process of justice. It is only by knowing the facts and by having closure that you can facilitate reconciliation.' But while this seems to carry the simple force of moral truth, excavation is actually, as Cox puts it, 'mired in complication and ethical dilemmas'. It has emerged, for example, that, during the war in Bosnia, Milosevic sponsored the digging up of mass graves from the Second World War as 'evidence' to incite ethnic hatred and to encourage revenge killing. There are also controversial cases of teams of western specialists going out to the developing world allegedly to sort out their problems by excavating their past for them and perhaps exacerbating the original trauma.

This is precisely the kind of situation vividly portrayed in Michael Ondaatje's novel, *Anil's Ghost*. Set in Sri Lanka, where there has been no independent truth commission or international tribunal, the novel weighs the vitally important political function of the archaeologist against the delicate and morally complex world in which she intervenes. In the book a forensic pathologist, Anil Tissera, is sent out by a human rights organisation to Sri Lanka to work with a local archaeologist, Sarath Diyasena, in investigating the spate of organised government and rebel murders. They excavate some skeletons in a government-protected archaeological

199

preserve and find that one of the skeletons is not actually prehistoric but recent, dead only in the last five or ten years. The task of the archaeologists, and of the novel as a whole, is to establish the identity of the skeleton and the cause of death. It is, in other words, to reconstruct his last days and the perpetrators of the murder.

Near the beginning of the investigation, Anil tags the skeleton – now code-named Sailor – by cutting a notch on its heel. Unlike an ordinary archaeological project, the Sri Lankan investigation is conducted in an atmosphere of threat and suspicion and she fears that the government might easily force its way into the laboratory and replace Sailor with another skeleton. That would matter greatly for the forensic archaeologists want to explore Sailor's bones in minute detail, in order to build up a picture of his life, his work, the manner of his death. Ondaatje writes that normally Anil 'turned bodies into representatives of race and age and place', looking at general trends for which one body excavated might be much like another. But in this case, it is the specificity of Sailor which is at issue. Forensic archaeologists differ from bio-archaeologists precisely in this respect, that they are interested in the individual rather than in the group or general class.

The team proves, from the ligament stresses on his ankle bones, that Sailor was a miner in a gem mine. Ananda, the eye painter, reconstructs the man's face from his skull and somebody in the village recognises and identifies him. And Anil confirms that the body was moved, after death, from elsewhere to the government-protected archaeological site, clearly to disguise the fact of its murder. From these small, specific details, a compelling picture emerges of the government reign of terror, the disappearances and denials. Sailor's particular name and identity carries these large political implications. 'Who was he?' Anil ponders. 'This representative of all those lost voices. To give him a name would name the rest.'

The body's capacity to retain a physical record of its injuries, etched onto its bones, means that the government cannot erase the history of its regime of torture and murder. The truth is retained in marks on the skeleton and ultimately will be revealed, read and interpreted by the archaeologists. However, the novel does raise a question about the ethics of exposing this kind of uncomfortable truth. In braving government officials and bringing Sailor's story to light, Anil jeopardises the lives of several other men involved in the investigation. Sarath, her main co-worker, seems reluctant at times to press on with the inquiry and is aware of the complexity of the truth in the Sri Lankan political environment. A conversation which takes place between Sarath and Anil towards the end of the novel indicates their different approaches to the situation. Anil, an outsider, can look at archaeological questions dispassionately; Sarath, deeply implicated in the environment which witnessed the death of Sailor and others like him, realises that truth has its consequences and its costs:

> 'Secrets turn powerless in the open air.'
> 'Political secrets are not powerless, in any form,' he said.
> 'But the tension and danger around them, one can make them evaporate. You're an archaeologist. Truth comes finally into the light. It's in the bones and sediment.'
> 'It's in character and nuance and mood.'
> 'That is what governs us in our lives, that's not the truth.'
> 'For the living it is the truth,' he quietly said.

In the end, Sarath takes a great risk and smuggles the skeleton out to Anil under the very noses of the terrifying government officials, so that Anil can publicise the news of their findings to the outside world and bring the Sri Lankan government to account. Shortly afterwards, Sarath is brought into the mortuary, one of seven Friday victims. His brother, a doctor, examines and cleans the body, laying it out as Sailor had been laid out some six weeks before. It is not clear whether his murder is a direct reprisal for his work in the archaeological investigation but that is certainly the implication. Sailor is redeemed as Sarath is lost; one living body is sacrificed to reveal the truth about the dead.

Ondaatje shows the pain of archaeological truth as well as its necessity. The novel exposes the difficulty of bringing powerful forces to account and the extent to which the community is embroiled in a history of love and hatred, betrayal and sacrifice. Truth, according to Ondaatje, is not simple but is shaped by the intractable medium of human lives, the 'sediment', as Adorno said, 'of human misery'. Anil flies back to the West with her evidence and her excoriating tale of government oppression, so that international human rights groups can, in time, bring a case to the international court of justice. But she leaves behind a family blighted by Sarath's sacrifice and a community scarred by the process of finding out the truth.

'People have every right to dig up their past and our duty is to help them,' says Margaret Cox, just back from Iraq and in her office in Bournemouth. Rather than wielding the spade herself in these foreign countries, she is training local archaeologists in each country to excavate their dead to a standard which will stand up in court and bring torturers and killers to account. At present she is training Iraqis so that they themselves can investigate the mass graves which are being uncovered in the post-Saddam era. 'It is important for a survivor community to take control of its own history,' she stresses.

*

The exhumation of the disappeared in Argentina, Bosnia, Iraq and On-daatje's fictional Sri Lanka reminds us of the vital connection between archaeology and public justice, which might otherwise appear to be diminishing in the postmodern climate of virtual reality.

Forensic archaeology depends upon the eloquence of material reality. Bodies dug up from the ground cannot lie, as governments might try to do, and they cannot be misrepresented or sanitised to mean something more palatable. 'The skeleton is its own best witness,' said Clyde Snow, showing slides of the remains of one victim at the trial in Buenos Aires in 1985 of nine generals who had formed the military juntas. The court had already heard dozens of eyewitness accounts but it was visibly shaken as Snow showed the fragments of a skull, shot to pieces by the bullet of the standard gun issued to all police and army security agents.

Forensic archaeology also highlights the recalcitrant nature of history, which resists postmodern or totalitarian attempts to erase it. While subsequent governments might try to deny the past and, in the case of Argentina, even issue amnesties to those responsible for thousands of deaths and acts of torture, still, in many cases thankfully, the evidence of what was done remains below the ground, in mass graves, waiting to be excavated and analysed. Archaeology, in this case, plays a vital political role in revealing what is permanent and lasting and inescapable when the general trend is to evade responsibility and to live only for the moment. The earth, we might say, is a medium of justice. It holds the evidence, records the history, and allows itself to be opened up later in order to bring the guilty to account.

This earth is, of course, dirty. Fredric Jameson has written about the role of what he calls 'dirty realism' in the postmodern consciousness. According to him, the dirty realist simulates the conditions of lowlife reality in order to give the impression of some form of engagement with problematic conditions of social deprivation and injustice without actually participating in political debate or intervening radically in the course of events. The dirty realist must 'merely *replicate* the chaos and turbulences all around' him. For Jameson, dirt represents a replica gritty reality, a commodified suggestion of mess and underprivilege without any of the attendant difficulties and struggles. It can be conjured up and – just as easily – conjured away.

This is the similar kind of simulated reality which Susan Stewart maintains is conjured up by the souvenir. The memento which is bought, she observes, 'must be removed from its context in order to serve as a trace of it'. It becomes a substitute for real understanding, an object of nostalgia and emotion rather than serious, intellectual reflection. Like the objects salvaged from the *Titanic*, which meant something only to those individuals who owned them, the souvenir 'moves history into private time' and disrupts the continuity of past and present with some fantasised, alternative derivation. So the souvenir, in other words, sanitised and carefully selected to satisfy private wistfulness, actually prevents a genuine act of remembering.

But archaeology deals not with 'dirty realism' nor with souvenirs, but with real dirt. It digs through the hard soil to find its material and it must confront the bodies and other archaeological remains through a filter of covering earth. It crucially encounters resistance. Resistance became one of the corner-stones of Freud's theory. It represents our active efforts not to remember by resisting recollection through distortion or evasion or apparent amnesia. Resistance has to be maintained and added to as the years go by, like the layers of the earth laid down each year, burying the original event to be remembered or forgotten. 'An important element in the theory of repression is the view that repression is not an event that occurs once, but that it requires a permanent expenditure of energy', Freud explains. So the analyst, like the archaeologist reading the soil, works on the patient's resistances, trying hard to understand their context and underlying causes, rather than hacking straight through to the original trauma. He 'contents himself with studying whatever is present for the time being on the surface of the patient's mind, and he employs the art of interpretation mainly for the purpose of recognising the resistances which appear there', Freud writes. 'The doctor uncovers the resistances which are unknown to the patient.'

But resistances run deep. Even below the surface determination not to remember, there are other levels of distortion and disavowal which the analyst must combat. Even the unconscious has deep strata of resistance to the act of recollection. And recognising these strata is tough, often painful, something to be 'worked through'. The analyst must wait while the patient becomes more 'conversant with this resistance', struggling to overcome it and defying the temptation to retreat back into other forms of evasion. This 'working through', recognising both the resistances and the original traumatic event in its context, amounts to a healthy act of remembering which is akin to the process of mourning. Gradually 'each single one of the memories and expectations' is 'brought up' and examined and the reasons for the subsequent resistance understood.

This 'working through', this excavation and sieving of dirt, is, of course, tough. It necessarily deals with recalcitrant material, deep below the ground, with layers of rock above. So Ondaatje rightly draws attention to the difficulties and pain of archaeological truth in his novel, the terrible repercussions in the Sri Lankan community of Anil's research and recovery of atrocity. But the very intractability of the matter is important. According to the Marxist critic Terry Eagleton, it is necessary before we endeavour to change our social or political situation that we recognise the 'burden of history under which we stagger'. The postmodern imagination supposes that the world is protean and culturally relative. We can fashion ourselves as we wish and have instant transparent access to information. But Eagleton points out that, in certain respects, we live not in a world of change but one of geological deep time. We are here for the *longue durée*, our history is 'striated' like the earth, and therefore revolutionary or political activity is understandably difficult. To think otherwise would be to underestimate the burden of past oppression and to fail to do justice to the legacy of suffering against which we protest. 'The impulse to freedom from oppression seems as obdurate and implacable as the drive to material survival', writes Eagleton. Revolutionary knowledge should therefore not just be of the ideals in the future but also, as the philosopher Sebastiano Timpanaro writes in *On Materialism*, of 'what distresses, harms and oppresses man'. Only by confronting our constraints and intractable difficulties can we build the foundation of an effective ethics or politics.

Watching the dirt silt up and settle over the past and digging it up again is to confront what is most painful in our history and to give it its due weight. Only by appreciating the intractability and resistances of the earth can due justice be done to past events. 'Through thickened time, as through a viscous element, items descended so slowly as to acquire a patina that seemed to transform their contingencies into the necessities of a meaningful tradition', writes Fredric Jameson in a wistful paean to depth and dirt and 'viscosity', which he imagines prevailing in a pre-postmodern age. But the archaeological imagination allows that 'meaningful tradition' to continue, by celebrating and revealing the 'thickness' of time and the dirty 'patina' of events. The earth it excavates allows us to engage in a collective act of memory and renews our sense of what holds us together. The painful burden of history, which the soil symbolises and preserves, can be shared and transformed, until it becomes what Eagleton sees as an urgent 'communality of meaning'. 'Suffering is a mightily powerful language to share in common, one in which many diverse life-forms may strike up a dialogue', he writes.

So the archaeological imagination, which returns us to the depths, to what is lost or recovered or merely imprinted in the strata as it disappears, reminds us of matter, of the heavy, material significance of the ground beneath our feet. And it reminds us why it matters.

Notes on Reading

1. The Poetics of Depth

Among the many philosophers who have drawn on archaeological metaphors to explain their ideas, these should be of particular interest to the reader: Michel Foucault, *The Archaeology of Knowledge* (1972), Theodor Adorno, *Aesthetic Theory*, translated by Robert Hullot-Kentor (1997), and Paul de Man, who described literary criticism as 'archaeological labour' in *The Rhetoric of Romanticism* (1984). The most archaeological of thinkers is Walter Benjamin. The essay on 'excavation and memory' is published in the 2nd volume of the excellent new Harvard edition of Benjamin's *Selected Writings* (1999). Benjamin discusses 'aura' in his essay 'The Work of Art in the Age of Mechanical Reproduction', published in his *Illuminations*, translated by H. Zohn (1970), and the traces of memory and the storyteller in 'On Some Motifs in Baudelaire', also in *Illuminations*. Readers interested in the way places stir the imagination may also be interested in Bachelard's book, *The Poetics of Space*, translated by M. Jolas (1994).

The post-processual archaeologists I refer to in this chapter *think* most interestingly about the imaginative dimensions of their subject but *write* in a rather technical style. See, in particular, Christopher Tilley, *Metaphor and Material Culture* (1999), Ian Hodder (ed.), *Interpreting Archaeology: Finding Meaning in the Past* (1995) and also his *The Archaeological Process: An Introduction* (1999). If readers want to pursue more traditional archaeological theory, they could consult David Clarke's *Analytical Archaeology* (1968).

Two of the archaeological books that most influenced Shelley, because they emphasised the politically radical implications of ruins, are Count Volney's *The Ruins; or a Survey of the Revolutions of Empires* (1795) and James Parkinson's *Organic Remains of a Former World* (1804-11). Frederick Catherwood's wonderful drawings of ancient Mayan friezes can be found in John Stephens, *Incidents of Travel in Central America, Chiapas, and Yucatan* (1988), originally published in 1841.

2. Romancing Stones:
The Archaeological Landscape

William Stukeley's two main books, *Stonehenge: A Temple Restor'd to the British Druids* (1740) and *Abury: A Temple of the British Druids* (1743), were republished by the Garland Press in 1984 in a single volume. His fieldnotes and jottings were published as *The Commentarys, Diary and Commonplace Book of William Stukeley* by the Doppler Press in 1980. The only biography of Stukeley, written by the archaeologist Stuart Piggott in 1950, contrasts the 'reliable and objective' early years of Stukeley's field-work with the 'speculative and fantastic' later years when he wrote his books. The best book on Avebury today is Joshua Pollard and Andrew Reynolds' *Avebury: The Biography of a Landscape* (2002).

Texts of William Wordsworth's poems read like archaeological sections, since he continually revised them throughout his life. I have quoted from the Routledge edition of the *Lyrical Ballads*, edited by R.L. Brett and A.R. Jones, from the Cornell Wordsworth edition of *The Salisbury Plain Poems*, edited by Stephen Gill, and from the Norton edition of *The Prelude*, edited by Jonathan Wordsworth, M.H. Abrams and Stephen Gill, since these editions wonderfully excavate and preserve the different versions.

Michel de Certeau's essay, 'Walking in the City', is published in his book *The Practice of Everyday Life* (1984). The closest any archaeologist has got to thinking about archaeological poetics is Christopher Tilley in his rather technical book, *Metaphor and Material Culture* (1999). The closest a literary critic has got is Geoffrey Hartman, who once noted that Wordsworth moves 'psychology closer to archaeology' but then back-tracked by saying that he *replaces* 'lapidary inscription' with the 'meditative mind': see his 'Wordsworth, Inscriptions and Romantic Nature Poetry', in F.W. Hilles and H. Bloom (eds), *From Sensibility to Romanticism* (1965). Marjorie Levinson's criticism of Wordsworth's poem, 'Michael', can be found in her book, *Wordsworth's Great Period Poems* (1986).

3. Unearthing Bodies:
The Disruption of History

The story of the Cripplegate parishioners digging up Milton can only be read in the British Library: *A Narrative of the Disinterment of Milton's Coffin, in the Parish Church of St Giles, Cripplegate* (1790).The account of the excavation of Robert Burns can be found in James Hogg's memoir, which was published in the five-volume edition of Burns which he edited jointly with William Motherwell (1834-39). I discovered the story of

Lawrence Sterne in an article by Arthur Sherbo published in *Notes and Queries* (September 1987). As Sterne's biographer, Ian Campbell Ross, describes, Sterne's grave was disturbed again in 1969 and his bones were removed to Coxwold, Yorkshire. Jeremy Bentham's bizarre tract in favour of embalming corpses – 'Auto-Icon; or Farther Uses of the Dead to the Living' – is also difficult to get hold of outside the walls of the British Library, as is Southwood Smith's *A Lecture Delivered Over the Remains of Jeremy Bentham in the Webb Street School of Anatomy and Medicine* (1832). In contrast, the two classic books on preserved ancient bodies – P.V. Glob's *The Bog People* (1969) and Konrad Spindler's *The Man in the Ice* (1994) – can be found in any good bookshop.

Freud's essay on 'The Uncanny' is published in *The Penguin Freud Library*, vol. 14. Nicholas Royle is one of the best theoretical writers on the uncanny at the moment: see his essay 'Déjà-vu' in Martin McQuillan (ed.), *Post-Theory: New Directions in Criticism* (1999). I also found very helpful Terry Castle's book, *The Female Thermometer: Eighteenth Century Culture and the Invention of the Uncanny* (1995), and the article by Ian Duncan, 'The Upright Corpse: Hogg, National Literature and the Uncanny', in *Studies in Hogg and his World* 5 (1994).

Michel Foucault's reflections on history and archaeology can be found in *The Archaeology of Knowledge*, translated by A.M. Sheridan Smith (1972). For his theories about the regulation of bodies, see in particular *Discipline and Punish: The Birth of the Prison* (1977).

4. Fulfilling Desires: Erotic Excavation

William Hamilton published two accounts of his discoveries in Pompeii. *A Letter from Sir William Hamilton. On the Cult of Priapus* (1786) is quite graphic; the earlier *Account of the Discoveries at Pompeii communicated to the Society of Antiquaries of London* (1777) was intended for more sensitive ears. Further Pompeian pornographic fantasies were published in the nineteenth century: see Le Famin, *Musée Royal de Naples, Peintures, Bronzes et Statues Erotiques* (1836); Louis Barre, *Herculaneum et Pompei* (1840) and Dominique Vivant Denon, *L'Oeuvre Priapique de Dominique Vivant* (1850). Hunting down the macabre and erotic poems and books which I describe in this chapter involved much rifling through catalogues and many hours sitting at the 'naughty table' in the British Library. For a more chaste read, see Wolfgang Leppmann, *Pompeii in Fact and Fiction* (1986). There are also, of course, the outwardly genteel and inwardly sleazy Victorian novels set in Pompeii: Edward Bulwer Lytton, *The Last Days of Pompeii*, republished in 1979, and Theophile Gautier,

'Arria Marcella', retitled 'The Tourist' in *My Fantoms*, selected and translated by Richard Holmes (1976).

Freud's observations on the analogy between archaeology and psychoanalysis can be found in The Standard Edition of Freud, published by the Hogarth Press: 'Constructions in Analysis' (vol. 23), the case history of the Rat Man (vol. 10) and the opening of his book, *Civilisation and Its Discontents* (vol. 21). He compared himself to Schliemann in his letter to Fliess on 21 December 1899, published in *The Origins of Psycho-Analysis*, translated by Eric Mosbacher and James Strachey (1954). His analysis of Jensen's *Gradiva* appears in vol. 14 of The Penguin Freud Library. I found Rachel Bowlby's account of Freud's 'Gradiva' essay stimulating, even if ultimately I disagreed with her conclusions: see her essay, 'One Foot in the Grave', in her book, *Still Crazy After All These Years: Women, Writing and Psychoanalysis* (1992). Details of Fiorelli's excavation can be found in M.L.A. Gaston Boissier's *Rome and Pompeii: Archaeological Rambles*, translated by Havelock Fisher (1896) or, for Italian readers, in Giuseppe Fiorelli, *Giornale degli Scavi di Pompei* (1861-79).

5. Fundamentalism:
Digging our Trojan Origins

The 1790s search for Troy is surveyed briefly in A.C. Lascarides, *The Search for Troy 1553-1874* (1977). But, if possible, readers should try to track down the original accounts, complete with maps: Robert Wood's *An Essay on the Original Genius and Writings of Homer* (1775), Chevalier's *A Description of the Plain of Troy* (1791), and Jacob Bryant's *A Dissertation Concerning the War of Troy and the Expedition of the Grecians, as described by Homer: shewing that no such expedition was ever undertaken and that no such city of Phrygia existed* (1796).

Schliemann published two major accounts of his Trojan excavation: *Ilios: The City and the Country of the Trojans* (1880) and *Troja: Results of the Latest Researches and Discoveries on the Site of Homer's Troy* (1884). David Traill (*Schliemann of Troy: Treasure and Deceit*, 1995) and Susan Heuck Allen (*Finding the Walls of Troy*, 1999) have led the attack on Schliemann. Donald Easton and David Turner have defended him: see, for example, Easton's articles in *Studia Troica* 1 (1991) and 4 (1994), and Turner's review of Traill's book in *Journal of Hellenic Studies* 116 (1996).

The rise of racialist interpretations of prehistory and the appropriation of archaeology for anti-Semitic, ideological purposes can be traced in John Lubbock, *The Origin of Civilisation and the Primitive Condition of Man* (1871), Bertram Hartshorne, 'Dr Schliemann's Trojan Collection', *Archaeological Journal* (1877), Emile Burnouf, *The Science of Religions* (1888), Michael Zmigrodski, *Histoire du Swastika* (1891), Count Goblet

D'Alviella, *The Migration of Symbols* (1894), Thomas Wilson, *The Swastika: Earliest Known Symbol and Its Migrations* (1896), Houston Chamberlain, *The Foundations of the Nineteenth Century* (1910) and W. Norman Brown, *The Swastika: A Study of the Nazi Claims of its Aryan Origin* (1933). I found John Atkinson, Iain Banks and Jerry O'Sullivan (eds), *Nationalism and Archaeology* (1996) a useful introduction to the topic.

Samuel Butler's memoir of his visit to Troy in April 1895, when Dörpfeld was excavating, is unpublished but can be read in the manuscripts room of the British Library (*BL Add Mss* 44047).

6. Rock Bottom:
Digging and Despair

The archaeological consequences of Henry VIII's dissolution of the monasteries can be found recorded in *John Leland's Itinerary: Travels in Tudor England*, edited by John Chandler (1993), *William Camden's Britannia, from the edition of 1789, translated from the Latin by Richard Gough*, edited by Gordon Copley (1977) and *The Oglander Memoirs*, edited by W.H. Long (1888). For the poets' reactions to the London plagues, see *The Plague Pamphlets of Thomas Dekker*, edited by F.P. Wilson, *A Journal of the Plague Year* by Daniel Defoe, and *The Sermons of John Donne*, edited by E.M. Simpson and G.R. Potter, vols 6 and 10. Thomas Browne's sceptical and archaeological writings can be found in *Urne Burial* and *Religio Medici*. For more scepticism, see also John Moore's *A Mappe of Man's Mortalitie* (1617) and Francis Bacon's *History of Life and Death*, in *The Works of Francis Bacon*, edited by Spedding, Ellis and Heath, vol. 5. For an excellent survey of attitudes to death in the renaissance period, see Michael Neill, *Issues of Death: Mortality and Identity in English Renaissance Tragedy* (1997). And for details on the plague, I matched topographical facts in F.P. Wilson's *The Plague in Shakespeare's London* (1927) with the modern London *A-Z*.

The essential guide to Victorian barrow-digging remains Barry Marsden's *The Early Barrow-Diggers* (1974). The only copy of Stephen Isaacson's poem, *Barrow-Digging by a Barrow Knight* (1845), apparently now existing is kept in the Thomas Bateman archive in the City Museum, Sheffield. Charles Woolls' satire, *The Barrow Diggers: A Dialogue in Imitation of the Grave Diggers In Hamlet, with numerous explanatory notes* (1839), may be read in the British Library. Among the many barrow-diggers' bleakly tedious accounts of endless barrows opened and flints numbered, which I dutifully trawled through for the reader's benefit, the following can be enjoyed: James Douglas, *Nenia Britannica* (1793); Richard Colt Hoare, *Ancient History of Wiltshire* (1812-19); Bryan Faussett,

Inventorium Sepulchrale (1856); Thomas Bateman, *Ten Years' Diggings in Celtic and Saxon Grave Hills, in the Counties of Derby, Stafford and York* (1861), William Miles, *A Description of the Deverel Barrow, opened AD 1825* (1826) and John Skinner, *Journal of a Somerset Rector 1803-1834*, edited by Howard and Peter Coombs (1984).

7. Holy Ground:
Archaeology and the Sacred

The best account of Helena's 'excavation' is by J.W. Drijvers, *Helena Augusta: The Mother of Constantine the Great and her Finding of the True Cross* (1992), while Evelyn Waugh's fictional treatment of the event, *Helena* (1950), is worth a glance. The most vivid description of the Holy Land in the days of the early church was provided by the Gallician nun, Egeria. See J. Wilkinson's edition of *Egeria's Travels to the Holy Land* (1981), which also includes the impressions of the 'Bordeaux Pilgrim' in AD 333. I also found useful details in Eusebius' *Life of Constantine*, translated by A. Cameron and S.G. Hall (1999) and Ambrose's oration for Theodosius in his *Funeral Orations*, translated by L.P. McCauley (1953).

Among the nineteenth-century clergymen who invoked archaeology to confirm their faith, the following could be consulted: Edward Robinson, *Biblical Researches in Palestine* (1841); William Bartlett, *Walks About the City and Environs of Jerusalem* (1844); Rev. George Williams, *The Holy City, or historical and topographical notices of Jerusalem* (1845); Arthur Penrhyn Stanley, *Sinai and Palestine in Connection with their History* (1856); Rev. W.K. Tweedie, *Jerusalem and its Environs* (1859); J.M.P. Otts, *The Fifth Gospel: The Land Where Jesus Lived* (1894). The two major excavators of Jerusalem who are worth reading are Charles Warren (*Underground Jerusalem*, 1876) and Kathleen Kenyon (*Digging Up Jerusalem*, 1974). Biblical archaeology, which concentrates almost exclusively on Old Testament sites, is a vast subject. A lively recent addition to the literature on the subject is Amy Dockser Marcus, *Rewriting the Bible: How Archaeology is Reshaping History* (2000).

There is a huge literature on sacramental theology and the notion of sacred space. The two most useful introductions to the topic I found were David Brown and Ann Loades (eds), *The Sense of the Sacramental: Movement and Measure in Art and Music, Place and Time* (1995) and Philip Sheldrake, *Spaces for the Sacred* (2001). Michel de Certeau's philosophy is central to the question of the sacredness of material reality but it makes quite hard reading. The best place to begin is with his essay 'How is Christianity Thinkable Today?' in Graham Ward (ed.), *The Postmodern God* (1997). The more adventurous could attempt the journey which is *The Mystic Fable*, translated by Michael Smith (1992).

Freud's alternative, psychoanalytic attempt to explain the particular aura of archaeological sites may be found in his 'A Disturbance of Memory on the Acropolis', The Standard Edition of Freud (vol. 22). Yair Bar-El's psychiatric account was published in the *British Journal of Psychiatry* 176 (2000).

8. Postmodern Archaeology:
Trashing Our Future

The benchmark of postmodern archaeological practice is arguably represented by William Rathje's *Rubbish: The Archaeology of Garbage* (1992). Other interesting examples include Graham Hancock's *Heaven's Mirror: Quest for the Lost Civilisation* (1998), his *Fingerprints of the Gods: The Quest Continues* (2001) and Robert Ballard's *The Discovery of the Titanic* (1998). I found Ian Jack's article on the *Titanic*, 'Leonardo's Grave', published in *Granta* 67 (1999) interesting for its analysis of the blurred distinction between virtual and concrete reality in the *Titanic* phenomenon. For analysis of the postmodern museum experience, see Michael Shanks and Chris Tilley, *Reconstructing Archaeology: Theory and Practice* (1987) and Kevin Walsh, *The Representation of the Past: Museums and Heritage in the Postmodern World* (1992).

Two of the major exponents of postmodern theory are Jean Baudrillard and, perhaps unwittingly, Francis Fukuyama. Try Fukuyama's *The End of History and the Last Man* (1992) and 'Simulacra and Simulations' in *Jean Baudrillard Selected Writings*, edited by Mark Poster (2001). The most important critiques of postmodernism have come from Jean-Francois Lyotard, *The Postmodern Condition: A Report on Knowledge* , translated by G. Bennington and B. Massumi (1984), and Fredric Jameson, *Postmodernism, or the Cultural Logic of Late Capitalism* (1991) and *The Seeds of Time* (1994). Archaeologists find themselves drawn to the writing of Giles Deleuze and Felix Guattari, because of its spatial metaphors. See in particular their book, *A Thousand Plateaus: Capitalism and Schizophrenia* (1988). For a good introduction to postmodern metaphor in archaeology, see Michael Shanks, *Experiencing the Past: On the Character of Archaeology* (1991).

Two good books on the imaginary significance of the subterranean are Wendy Lesser's *The Life Below the Ground* (1987) and Rosalind Williams, *Notes on the Underground* (1990).

Martin Jones' book, *The Molecule Hunt: How Archaeologists are Bringing the Past Back to Life* (2001) is a good introduction to 'bio-archaeology'. Luigi Luca Cavalli-Sforza's controversial theories about the connections between genes and culture can be found in his *Genes, Peoples and Languages* (2000). I found the story of the prehistoric migrations to America as revealed in the genes of Native Americans in an essay by Antonio Torroni, 'Mitochondrial DNA and the Origin of Native Americans', published in Colin Renfrew (ed.), *America Past, America Present: Genes and Languages in the Americas and Beyond* (2000). For more information about forensic archaeology, see Christopher Joyce and Eric Stover, *Witnesses from the Grave: The Stories Bones Tell* (1991) and Victor Buchli, Gavin Lucas and Margaret Cox, *Archaeologies of the Contemporary Past* (2001).

Susan Stewart's reflections on memory are gathered in her book *On Longing: Narratives of the Miniature, the Gigantic, the Souvenir and the Collection* (1984). Freud reflects upon 'resistance' throughout his work, but two of the best essays on memory and resistance are the addenda on 'resistance and anticathexis' to 'Inhibitions, Symptoms and Anxiety', in The Standard Edition of Freud (vol. 20) and 'Remembering, Repeating and Working-Through' (vol. 12). Terry Eagleton contests the glibness of postmodernism and celebrates the intractability of history in *The Illusions of Postmodernism* (1996) and *Sacred Violence: The Idea of the Tragic* (2003).

Acknowledgements

Research for this book has taken me to some far-flung places. I would like to thank Adam Zertal for letting me join the dig at El Ahwat, Israel; Jaime Awe, Carolyn Audet and the BVAR team for the excavation experience in Belize; Manfred Korfmann, of the University of Tübingen, for the days on the plain of Troy; Keith Mellis and Michael Mucci for taking the time to explain everything I wanted to know about the New York Sanitation Department; Chris Thomas at the Museum of London for the Spitalfields tour; and Bernard Nurse and Adrian James at the Society of Antiquaries for showing me the pictures and papers of James Douglas and other barrow diggers.

I must acknowledge various institutions which have helped me produce this book. I am grateful to Gill Woolrich at the City Museum of Sheffield for sending me a photocopy of the extremely rare *Barrow-Digging by a Barrow Knight*; to the Cambridge University Library and to the British Library for their assistance with obtaining illustrations and for permission to quote from manuscripts; and to Peterhouse for money to send me to Naples to look at Pompeian erotica, to Central America to climb up Mayan pyramids and to various other crucial destinations. I am grateful also to the estates of Yeats, Heaney and Pound for permission to quote from their work.

Every archaeologist can benefit from another pair of eyes and I have had some excellent travel companions and secret spies in various sites. In particular, I owe much to Emma Carmichael, Matilda Carmichael, Mari Jones, Alice and Tom Pavey, Sophie Jackson, Annelies Woutjers, Nick Burnoff, Miran Bozovic, Phil Rupprecht and Cathy Shuman. Phil and Cathy were great hosts in New York and long-sufferingly spent several evenings watching key archaeological moments in the *Planet of the Apes* film series with me.

I have been talking archaeology for years and it is hard to remember every important conversation which has shaped my love of stones and bones. But I recollect warmly discussions with Rosemary Joyce, Meg Conkey, Karin Sanders, Cathy Gallagher and Celeste Langan in Berkeley, California; with Norman Hammond, Mary Jacobus, Nigel Leask and

213

Acknowledgements

Cornelius Holtorf in Cambridge; with Jack Green in Israel and London; and with Nick Roe, professor at the University of St Andrews, during a summer conference at the University of Keele. I would like to thank Deborah Blake for being such a friendly and patient editor to work with at Duckworth, and Holger Jacobs for a great jacket design.

The following friends have read all or parts of this book at various stages of its development and I have really appreciated their comments and suggestions: Paul Cartledge, Sian Griffiths, Roddy Houston, Peter Howarth, Jan Schramm, William Taylor, Gillian Wallace and Robert Wallis. In particular, Peter Howarth has lived with this book over numerous coffee breaks in the British Library and virtually dug me out of every hole, chapter by chapter. Robert Wallis only arrived late at the scene but provided much needed reassurance, advice and vodka in the final stages.

As always, I would like to thank my family. My father dispenses encouragement and scepticism in equal measure but is always interested, and Linda has followed the progress of the book with characteristic enthusiasm. But I thank especially my sister, Gillian, the most wonderfully grounded 'life-organiser'. This book is dedicated to her, with much love.

Index

215